WE FOUND
HER HIDDEN

WE FOUND HER HIDDEN

The Remarkable Poetry of
Christina Rossetti

Paul Hullah

PARTRIDGE

To order additional copies of this book, contact
Toll Free 800 101 2657 (Singapore)
Toll Free 1 800 81 7340 (Malaysia)
orders.singapore@partridgepublishing.com

www.partridgepublishing.com/singapore

CONTENTS

Rationale & Acknowledgements vii

Preface xi

1. All That Was But Showed What All Was Not: Beginnings 1

2. The Whole World Stands At 'Why?':
   Romanticism And Christina... 19

3. I Answer Not For Meaning: Dreams And Dreaming............. 38

4. Sugar-Baited Words:
   Modes Of Temptation In *Goblin Market* 76

5. For Minds Such As Mine: *The Prince's Progress*...................... 94

6. Women Are Not Men: Approaching *Monna Innominata* 137

7. Spoken For Herself: Reading *Monna Innominata* 179

8. The Fire Has Died Out: The Earlier Devotional Poetry 241

9. Wearied Of Self, I Turn, My God, To Thee:
   The Later Devotional Poetry 264

Notes 287

Selected Bibliography 309

RATIONALE & ACKNOWLEDGEMENTS

Properly insightful twentieth and twenty-first century critical work on Christina Georgina Rossetti (1830-94) is lacking. Short discussions of her poetry appeared intermittently in journals such as *Victorian Poetry*, or as chapters or parts of chapters in books such as Sir Maurice Bowra's *The Romantic Imagination* (1949), W. W. Robson's *Critical Essays* (1966) and Angela Leighton's *Victorian Women Poets: Writing Against the Heart* (1992). As the lights went out on the last century, Rossetti was at last acknowledged as a poet of true significance: only during the last thirty years, with the publication of works such as David Kent's *The Achievement of Christina Rossetti* (1987), Antony Harrison's *Christina Rossetti in Context* (1988), Katherine Mayberry's *Christina Rossetti and the Poetry of Discovery* (1989), and Kathryn Burlinson's *Christina Rossetti* (1998) has usefully sustained, innovative, and critically original (as opposed to biographically-determined) analysis of this long-neglected poet's work been offered. Critical analysis published this century has been largely disappointing, adding little to what has already been said.

This book seeks to isolate thematic elements in the writings of Christina Rossetti by offering close and detailed textual readings of some of her poems. Past commentators have rightly recognised and applauded the rhythmic and metrical craftsmanship displayed in Rossetti's lyric verse, but this monopoly of attention afforded to the formal felicities of the poetry has often been at the expense of adequately sensitive interpretation of its content. This study aims to show that Rossetti's rigorously controlled use of language and symbolism indicates that there are important levels of meaning implicit

viii   Paul Hullah

in the poetry other than that produced by the biographical decoding
which many critics have hitherto seemed to prefer. My argument will
be that, from her earliest 'secular' (or, we might say, 'non-devotional')
lyrics - which, in fact, display a sustained interaction between inherited
modes of Romantic and Tractarian thought - through longer pieces
such as *Goblin Market* (1862) and *The Prince's Progress* (1866),
Rossetti's verse continually resists complacency of interpretation,
subtly questioning and subverting the traditions of writing – love
lyric, fairy tale, quest myth, sonnet – that it simultaneously extends.
Gradually and persuasively constructing a case for the inability of
poetic tradition to cope with the expression of an active female identity,
Monna Innominata (1881) deconstructs the poetics of lyric tradition,
casting together mediaeval, renaissance and Victorian ideologies. This
remarkable sonnet cycle disturbs the conventions of the love lyric and
forms the most concentrated, sustained demonstration of the struggle
to articulate the self outside patriarchal poetic tradition to be found
in the Rossetti canon, and I will therefore unashamedly linger longest
on that work. The painful sense of irresolution and despair pervading
Monna Innominata sheds important light upon the almost exclusive
production of heavily devotional literature by Christina Rossetti in the
final stages of her career.

Some sections of the text to follow have appeared, in embryonic
form, in various journals, and I thank the editors and all those involved
with said journals for allowing me platforms from which to float my
ideas and test the responsive waters. I am grateful, too, to Meiji Gakuin
University for many things, not least their granting me a funded
sabbatical year's leave during which I was able to travel to Vasto in Italy,
the original Rossetti hometown, and examine Rossetti manuscripts
and materials housed in the USA at Princeton University and at Bryn
Mawr College, both of whose staff were very efficient and very kind.
My students at Meiji Gakuin also deserve to be thanked. Their reviving
curiosity and boundless enthusiasm for the British poetry I read with
them has made me rethink my ideas regarding Rossetti more than
once. I want to thank the brilliant teachers (specifically Anne Carrick,

Richard Horton, and Graham Finch at Ripon Grammar School, and Aidan Day and Paul Edwards at Edinburgh University) who got me going and kept me going on this four-decade long quest to here.

I am forever grateful to my friend, the gentle and talented Martin Metcalfe, not least for the beautiful Christina image he carefully created to adorn the cover of this book. And, finally, I need to thank Etsuko Shimoya, who did her quiet and selfless best to keep me afloat during some dark times of doubt and despair. I owe her a debt I can never properly repay.

PREFACE

The facts of Christina Rossetti's life are fairly well known. Though it is decidedly not the purpose of this study to overplay or be the slave of biographical details, it is pertinent to preface it with a brief summary of the poet's own history. Past criticism of this misunderstood poet's work has been so plagued and polluted by biographically determined decoding that, before proceeding to offer my own reading of her work, it is helpful to be aware of what Rossetti's poetry has too often been taken to represent: its maker's autobiography.

Christina Rossetti was born on 5 December 1830, at No. 38 Charlotte Street, Portland Place, London. Her father, Gabriele Rossetti, had sought political refuge in England in 1824 after fleeing his native Naples where he had found fame as an operatic librettist and also worked as a museum curator. In 1826, he married Frances Lavinia Polidori (whose brother John William later became Byron's infamous travelling physician and author of *The Vampyre* (1819)) and they settled together in London. Gabriele taught Italian, eventually becoming Professor of English at King's College, London, publishing volumes of poetry in his native language and prose works in which he undertook detailed studies of what he identified as the philosophical subtext of Dante's writings. Christina was the youngest of the four children born into this intellectual but financially unsound family atmosphere. Her eldest sister, Maria Francesca, was to become a nun. Her eldest male sibling, Gabriel Charles Dante, better known as Dante Gabriel, was himself a poet of ravished beauty and engaging style. He was also a co-founder of the Pre-Raphaelite Brotherhood of painters. (Christina would long be linked with this movement, though it is not my intention to emphasise that connection in this study.) The younger brother, William Michael Rossetti, became a diarist, editor, and reminiscer, always keen to promote and preserve his youngest sister's reputation as a writer, as we shall see.

Christina Georgina Rossetti herself became a poet. Overcoming chronic, crippling illness from the age of fifteen onwards, she wrote verses which, in her lifetime, were amongst the most popular of the day. At the height of her popularity, she rivalled the Poet Laureate of the period, Alfred Lord Tennyson. One contemporary reviewer insisted that 'her place among the highest English poets is secure', whilst another enthused over her verses as 'perfectly rendered, so fragile and yet so flawless'.[1] Seventeen years after her death in 1894, Rossetti's reputation was still unquestioned: Ford Madox Ford, in an essay in *The Critical Attitude*, went further than most with his recommendations, all the while reflecting the esteem in which his subject's work was held. His opinion was unqualified and emphatic: 'Christina Rossetti seems to us to be the most valuable poet that the Victorian age produced'.[2]

Though Rossetti's dexterity and ingenuity with rhyme and metre, coupled to her use of plain, direct language, is as highly regarded today as it was when her work first appeared, time and critical opinion have not been so kind in their analysis of content of her verse and the philosophy of deferral, self-denial, and abnegation which it has been understood to express. For various reasons, twentieth-century criticism of Rossetti tended to overlook the subtle, symbolic nuances of her poetry (and prose) in favour of a largely dismissive overview which saw her life as more interesting than the poems which, it is proposed, form a simple diary of disappointment and patient, sad existence. This search for the author behind the writing has plagued Rossetti scholarship, and one of the aims of this study is to locate levels of meaning in the poems which, for whatever reason, beg more than a reductive biographical decoding. The time for exploring these elements is long overdue, though some recent studies have started to scratch the surface, and is the way forward to properly resurrecting the literary reputation of an undervalued and understudied Victorian poet.

The biographical bias that has unduly impinged upon critical appraisals of this poet's body of work has been unfortunate, but is perhaps understandable. The definitive biography of Christina Rossetti is yet to be written and perhaps never will be, most certainly not by me. Of the studies in existence, Lona Mosk Packer's *Christina Rossetti* (1963) is notable for being detailed, but is rendered largely worthless owing to its author's repeated insistence upon a lifelong, secret love affair between Christina and the artist William Bell Scott, which is both improbable and unsupported by concrete evidence.[3] Georgina Battiscombe's *Christina Rossetti: A Divided Life* is too sentimental and overly reliant upon the 'Memoir' of William Michael Rossetti (*Works*, xlv-lxxi) to shed any useful new light upon its subject. Kathleen Jones' *Learning Not to Be First: The Life of Christina Rossetti* (1992) shines a little new light and is refreshingly unsentimental. *Christina Rossetti: A Biography* (1994) by Frances Thomas is somewhat fragmentary and mostly retreads old ground, but Jan Marsh's *Christina Rossetti: A Literary Biography* (1995) is praiseworthy for its comprehensiveness and lively tone.[4]

Christina Rossetti wrote poetry communicating a wistful, resigned worldview which, on one level, might be held (and has been held) as accurately reflecting her own experience of a consciously repressed, sad, and disappointed life. It is a life that seems easy to summarise. An attractive and lively child, Christina became withdrawn in her teens as a series of debilitating illnesses drained her health and, at times, her spirit. Though she moved in a lively London social set of scholars, painters and literary figures, Christina never married. James Collinson, a lesser painter of the Pre-Raphaelite Brotherhood, was her first suitor; differences in religious leanings (Christina was always a High Anglican, Collinson was not) led to Collinson's proposal of 1848 being graciously declined, accepted over the next two years as Collinson feigned a reversion to Protestantism, then ultimately re-declined. The scholar, Charles Bagot Cayley, was the second admirer; he knew Christina for thirty-six years. Fastidious in every point bar religion - where he exhibited the shifting inclinations of a dilettante - he was adored by her but never became her lover. His proposal of marriage, in 1866, was also turned down, again for religious reasons. It is suggested (by Violet Hunt and by Christina's brother William Michael) that Christina had received a further proposal, also declined, from the painter John Brett during the 1850s, an episode inspiring her poem 'No Thank You John'.[5]

Matters of love aside, Christina Rossetti had an enigmatic personality. Subdued, reserved and well known for her shyness, she never lived an outwardly active life; it might be said that she lived expressively through her poetry. Her earliest extant poem is a dedicatory octet (*Poems*, III, 76-7), dated by William Michael Rossetti as written on 27 April 1842 (*Works*, 82, 464) - the work of an eleven year old girl. In 1847, when Christina Rossetti was only sixteen, her maternal grandfather, Gaetano Polidori privately printed and bound a collection of her juvenilia. The printing took place in Polidori's garden shed above Regent's Park Canal and the unofficial collection, titled *Verses by Christina G. Rossetti* (1847), became Christina's first published poetry. Officially, her first volume of poetry appeared in 1862. *Goblin Market, and Other Poems* was the first Pre-Raphaelite verse to attract public attention and met with universal acclaim. Four years later, *The Prince's Progress, and Other Poems*, featuring, as had its predecessor, designs by Dante Gabriel Rossetti, consolidated Christina Rossetti's strong reputation as a writer to whom clarity of expression and lyrical fluency were as second nature. *Sing-Song, a Nursery Rhyme Book* contained 120 plates by the illustrator Arthur Hughes and appeared in 1872, two years after *Commonplace and Other Short Stories*, an excursion into prose which, as much as anything else, confirmed that it was in the area of poetry that the author's major talent lay. The children's book *Speaking Likenesses*, again illustrated by Hughes, was published in 1874. The same year saw the appearance of *Annus Domini: A Prayer for each Day of the Year, Founded on a Text of Holy Scripture*, a collection of 366 short prose prayers prefaced by the single untitled devotional poem 'Alas my Lord' (*Poems*, III, 44-5). *Annus Domini* is the first of six exclusively 'devotional' tracts which indicated the direction in which Christina Rossetti's work was latterly to progress: *Seek and Find: A Double Series of Short Studies of the Benedicite* (1879), *Called to be Saints: The Minor Festivals Devotionally Studied* (1881), *Letter and Spirit: Notes on the Commandments* (1883), *Time Flies: A Reading Diary* (1885), and *The Face of the Deep: A Devotional Commentary on the Apocalypse* (1892) complete the sequence of final devotional prose works published during Christina Rossetti's lifetime. *A Pageant, and Other Poems* (1881), a new and enlarged edition of *Poems* (1890), and, in 1893, a volume of *Verses* comprising poems reprinted from *Called to be Saints*, *Time Flies*, and *The Face of the Deep*, complete the poetry published during the author's lifetime. The semi-autobiographical novella *Maude: A Story for Girls*, written in 1850 and containing half a dozen original verses, was posthumously published in 1897. In 1904, William Michael Rossetti edited *The Poetical Works of Christina Georgina Rossetti*, with a 'Memoir' and 'Notes' composed by himself. Until recently, this work, notorious for its inconsistencies, annoying lapses in chronology and lack of editorial objectivity, was the standard text of Christina Rossetti's poetry. A boon for Rossetti scholars came in 1990, however, with the publication of the third and final volume of Rebecca Crump's variorum edition of *The Complete Poems of Christina Rossetti*, the date for the appearance of such a work being long overdue. This is the standard scholarly edition of Christina Rossetti's poetry, and will be used as such in this study.

Christina became extremely ill in the later years of her stifled life. She was brave and steadfast, but cancer overcame her gradually and in 1894, on the morning of 29 December, she gave up the struggle. She is buried in Highgate Cemetery, in the same grave as her mother, to whom she dedicated much of her work. She is not read as much as Tennyson now. When read nowadays, or included in anthologies, Christina Rossetti is frequently seen as alien to the broader Victorian tradition, an anomaly interesting for her marginality, her awkward simplicity of tone in an age of sculpted ornateness and aesthetically-oriented verbosity. This study aims to show that her marginality to tradition was consciously sought and utilised by Rossetti in her best work as a clever subversion of the patriarchally established poetic canon. It is my belief that Christina Rossetti needs to be looked at again in the light of certain twentieth century poetics and the radical criticism running after (though without the two, I would make the same case).

Any poet who writes contrary to a substantial tradition merits consideration on that ground at least. Rossetti was a woman ensnared in a period when to be a woman was to be expected to be silent. She tried to give woman an original voice. Some of the radical shifts in sensibility and bias that her poetry dramatises have been overlooked (or actively ignored) by commentators who have mistaken her quiet, resigned tone for one of passive submission. This study seeks to redress the balance a little. Knowing that ideology masquerades as truth in the central tradition of poetry inherited by poets such as herself, Rossetti seeks to illuminate the traps set by a male tradition of writing which a woman wanting to express her true self must negotiate, avoid, re-set. Poem by poem, the idea of the stability of 'truth' is reassessed in one way or another. The ways were chosen carefully because of the age. In Christina Rossetti's finest poetry, the notion of absolutism is addressed and deftly rejected in favour of relativism.

Christina Rossetti's poetry is above all else aware of its own limitations. It consistently refutes the authority of the patriarchal, male determined tradition within which it superficially operates, and yet can only exist within that age and that tradition. Religious faith is to be recontextualised and painfully doubted, and only offered unambiguously as the route to salvation in the later writing. This unwillingness to embrace certainty (finally relinquished in the face of divine instruction) is the cause of many contradictions within the poetry of Christina Rossetti, and it is the presence of these contradictions, the sense of unease the reader experiences, the sense that much of the poetry simply *does not add up*, which makes Rossetti's best work enigmatic, compelling, and singularly attractive.

1

ALL THAT WAS BUT SHOWED WHAT ALL WAS NOT: BEGINNINGS

For all that was but showed what all was not...
Christina Rossetti, 'An Old-World Thicket'

I

In 1842 Christina Rossetti produced a short poem called 'The Chinaman' (*Poems*, III, 341).[1] She was eleven. 'The Chinaman' was later pronounced by her elder brother, William Michael, to be 'quite, or very nearly, the first thing that Christina wrote in verse' (*Works*, 464). Her precocious effort was prompted by an assignment that William had been given at school.

> The year 1842 was the year of the Anglo-Chinese Opium War. I was told by one of my school masters to make an original composition on the subject of China, and I think the composition had to be in verse. What I wrote I have totally forgotten. Christina saw me at work, and chose to enter the poetic lists. She produced the present lines.   (*Works*, 464)

William Michael recalls discussing 'The Chinaman' with his sister three months before her death in 1894, making the following entry in his diary on 9 October 1894: 'Saw Christina, who is surprisingly cheerful, considering. She recited to me her old verses about a Chinaman's pigtail...'[2] Elsewhere, William Michael concludes that

1

the poem is 'not of high importance to the literary world' (*Works*, 465).
Whether or not this is so, 'The Chinaman' is my starting point here.

THE CHINAMAN.

'Centre of Earth!' a Chinaman he said,
And bent over a map his pig-tailed head, -
That map in which, portrayed in colours bright,
China, all dazzling, burst upon the sight:
'Centre of Earth!' repeatedly he cries,
'Land of the brave, the beautiful, the wise!'
Thus he exclaimed; when lo his words arrested
Showed what sharp agony his head had tested.
He feels another tug - another, and another -
And quick exclaims, 'Hallo! what's now the bother?'
But soon alas perceives. And, 'Why, false night,
Why not from men shut out the hateful sight?
The faithless English have cut off my tail,
And left me my sad fortunes to bewail.
Now in the streets I can no more appear,
For all the other men a pig-tail wear.'
He said, and furious cast into the fire
His tail: those flames became its funeral-pyre.

This thoughtfully constructed piece, with its flexible (mostly)
pentameter couplets, already manifests the poetic control for which
Christina Rossetti's verse has always been praised: the rhyming is
lively, caesurae intelligently employed and neatly balanced, and the
symbolism suggestive and mature. The poem also exhibits a sensitive
appreciation of the predicament of the Chinese in the political
atmosphere of the day - their refusal to trade in opium being met, in
the justificatory words of Thomas Carlyle, by England's decision '...
to argue with them, in cannon-shot at last, and convince them that
they ought to trade!'[3]

'The Chinaman' may be read at (at least) two distinct levels. A historical reading might focus on the poem's ironic presentation of British imperialism and its effects. An investigation of the poem at a different level, however, may produce a less historically specific reading. The text constructs a vignette that, concisely and effectively, introduces and analyses the concept of identity. The Chinaman is involved in an identity quest, dramatised by the use of very basic, easily interpreted symbols, which, in a deceptively nonchalant manner, question notions of representation and signification. Complete with the pigtail which signifies his (national) identity, the Chinaman is first introduced in the poem staring at a map. In doing so, he presents the image of one attempting to locate himself with regard to a fixed system, the frame of reference before him. He is, so to speak, placing himself, identifying himself. '"Centre of Earth!" repeatedly he cries', as he perceives the point, China, from which he is signified as having origin, 'The Chinaman'. From the basis of this certainty, the text intimates desire to establish a 'Centre', a principle of intelligibility from which stability may proceed. China is projected as not just the central defining factor of the Chinaman's identity, his home and origin, but as a centering principle in general. Within the fiction of the poem, the Chinaman's identity becomes not an absolute, but a destabilised, relative concept.

Lexically, the poem reflects this destabilisation; the writing, too, desires an ordering centre, around which its signifiers may close in blissful certainty. But this is not to be so, for the oriental nor for the poem. '(W)ords arrested', a 'sharp agony' is felt in the next as its complacency is dislodged, its self-justifying pattern of signification abruptly underwritten by the intrusion of an opposing ideology and system of value - 'The faithless English have cut off my tail'. The Chinaman is no longer whole; unity of reference has been violently demolished in the metaphorical terms established by the poem. Reduced (or is it promoted?) to this recognition of the relativity involved in the sphere of signification, the text itself loses singularity of import - 'For all the other men a pig-tail wear' - as the sarcastic rejoinders displace the initial value of the 'pig-tail' signifier, re-allocating its meaning now to a different metaphorical status. The poem closes with the distressed speaker wielding a tone of (active) indignation at the (passive) self-gratifying observations with which it opened. It forms a denial of the premises initially offered as reliable reference points.

The radical final act described – 'He said, and furious cast into the fire / His tail: those flames became its funeral-pyre' - symbolises a rejection of the system of signification, marker of identity, alluded to at the start of the text. The protagonist sacrifices that which guaranteed the stability of his identity as a 'Chinaman', he cremates his pigtail. In doing so, no new fixed identity is established in the text: its purpose is to negate the possibility of such a fixed position. In this important respect, 'The Chinaman' may be termed an open-ended text.

The (admittedly ambitious but undeniably possible) reading of 'The Chinaman' I have given reveals an extra dimension to the text by which (over and above the fact of the date of its conception) it may be regarded as an apposite poem with which to preface a study of the writing of Christina Rossetti. It prefigures, I think, the type of subtle semantic strategy operational in the majority of Christina Rossetti's poems. This poetry enacts a conscious interrogation of the system of values from which it might initially seem to derive its energies. The text engages itself in discourse that refuses any one fixed position of authority. In doing so, a destabilisation of complacent notions of fixity is effected, disrupting all manner of certitude, wilfully exchanging such fixity of reference and closure for plurality of meaning and open-endedness. It is a poetry aware of its own form and limitations. All these functions are carried out within a poetics rooted in symbol and begging for intertextual, rather than a biographical reading.

II
The publication, in 1979, of the first volume of Rebecca Crump's now complete variorum edition of *The Complete Poems of Christina Rossetti* generated fresh critical interest in a poet hitherto neglected for over half a century by the academic world.[4] Two subsequent book-length

studies - *The Achievement of Christina Rossetti* (1987), a collection of essays edited by David Kent, and Antony H. Harrison's *Christina Rossetti in Context* (1988) - are important works: they marked the long overdue application of analytical techniques belonging to the period after New Criticism to Christina Rossetti's poetry and prose.[5] Before those books, and since the early 1930s, the single sustained piece of critical work presented in this field was Lona Mosk Packer's *Christina Rossetti*, a grossly speculative, biographical- historical study, grounded in the supposition of Christina Rossetti's secret adoration of and clandestine love affair with the artist William Bell Scott, a hypothesis swiftly and notoriously thereafter dismissed as entirely lacking in evidence by William E. Fredeman.[6]

Packer's imperceptions do perhaps serve to illustrate one thing: the fact that, in the words of another critic, Betty S. Flowers, Christina Rossetti's 'poems deserve more than a biographically reductive reading'.[7] Antony Harrison is in accord with this evaluation of the fundamental nature of Rossetti's work. He clarifies further the critical position best adopted in an endeavour to extract a more sophisticated reading of the poetry.

> One typical thematic mode of [Christina Rossetti's] poetry, then, is intertextual directing her reader away from the apparently simple surface meanings of her poems and toward historically layered literary statements and traditions, consideration of which complicates, amplifies, and redefines the meanings of her own verse.[8]

Empirically founded, biographical detective work, as Packer's speculative study illustrates, is all to reductive and risky a method of interpretation to apply to poetry such as Rossetti's which, rather than offering specific documentation of events from history, more often turns its attention toward the specific literary, artistic, theological and philosophical traditions it functions to extend and rewrite. William

Michael's picture of his sister as a 'casual and spontaneous' poet (*Works*, lxviii) rightly finds itself more often quoted as a mistaken surmise than an authoritative opinion, especially so since Professor Crump's research began to appear, or if one examines Rossetti's manuscripts properly. Harrison has concisely summed up the general feeling on this matter among modern critics of Christina Rossetti.

> In his memoir William Michael is... in part transmitting an image of his sister - as a pious and ascetic woman unconcerned with worldly achievements - that she herself had been at some pains to cultivate... This image suppresses half of the truth of Christina Rossetti's values and aspirations.[9]

Form available manuscripts, such as those I have recently examined at Princeton and Bryn Mawr, we know Christina Rossetti to have been a scrupulous, detailed reviser of her work. Moreover, her poetry is highly conscious of its status as such, aware of its place in the tradition of which it is a part. Rossetti's writing, as we aim to show, knowingly inhabits that position which T. S. Eliot recognised in 'Tradition and the Individual Talent':

> I [have] tried to point out the importance of the relation of the poem to other poems by other authors, and suggested the conception of poetry as a living whole of all the poetry that has ever been written.[10]

Like all genuine poetry, Rossetti's verse functions in and around the knowledge of literary tradition (whether it embraces, challenges, parodies, subverts or honours that tradition) and is wrought out of a language it does not itself invent, but inherits along with all its value laden terms. Unlike much poetry, the Rossetti text shows itself *conscious* of the implications of this function and of the weight of this inheritance. Just how acutely aware is Rossetti of the weight of tradition will become clear when I turn to specific analysis of pieces such as *Monna Innominata* (*Poems*, II, 86-93) later in this study. But even her earliest lyrics exhibit a considered assimilation of certain aspects of Christina Rossetti's thought - though the doctrine is by no means wholly embraced even at this formative stage of her development as a poet. Even William Michael is at pains to convey the attentiveness to literary legacy displayed by his 'spontaneous' and 'least bookish' sister.

> ... indeed she was from first to last much the best of the four [Rossetti children] at all matters of acquired knowledge... plunging with great ardour, before reaching the age of twelve or eleven, into such themes as the career of Napoleon, the Iliad, Grecian mythology, etc... (*Works*, xlvii)

As she matured, it seems that Christina Rossetti certainly acquainted herself with the notion of a received literary tradition. William Michael again:

> In poetry she was (need I say it?) capable of appreciating whatever is really good; and yet her affections, if not her perceptions, in poetry, were severely restricted. The one poet whom she really gloried in was Dante: next to him perhaps Homer, so far as she could estimate him in one or two English translations... Among very great authors, none (making allowance for Dante) seemed to appeal to her more than Plato: she read his Dialogues over and over again, with ever renewed or augmented zest. For Shakespeare her intellectual reverence was of course very deep... (*Works*, lxix-lxx)

William Michael (himself a writer) shows in his reverentially qualifying (and, it might be said, somewhat patronising) tone, 'really good... very great authors... of course', the entrenched position the predetermined literary canon occupies in the formation of any new artistic position. Tradition, whether it be accepted as worthy or not, cannot be ignored.

> Another great thing that she disliked was Milton's Paradise Lost: the only poems of his which she seems to me to have seriously loved were the sonnets. Among modern English poets, I should say that Shelley, or perhaps Coleridge, stood highest in her esteem; certainly not Wordsworth, whom she read scantily. As to Shelley, she can have known little beyond his lyrics; most of the long poems, as being 'impious', remained unscanned. Tennyson she heartily enjoyed and admired, and Mrs. Browning; and Browning she honoured without eager sympathy. The poems of William Morris were mostly unread by her - not unvalued. Of Swinburne she knew Atalanta in Calydon, and some few other things, including (I suppose) Erechtheus; and she regarded Atalanta as - what it is - a stupendous masterpiece.   (*Works*, lxx)

The contradictory citations of Shelley in this list of influences are troubling: a poet who 'stood highest in her esteem' is, in the same breath, said to have largely 'remained unscanned'. I would suggest (without a scrap of supporting evidence) that the whole observation becomes more coherent if the first 'Shelley' is, in fact, a slip of William Michael's pen for 'Keats' - who, though a clear influence on Christina Rossetti's writing (and to whom she dedicated one of her earliest pieces (*Poems*, III, 168) - is oddly absent from this catalogue of poets supposedly 'in her esteem', while Shelley appears, contradictorily, twice. Whatever the case, I do not include this listing as firm evidence of Christina Rossetti's taste and allegiance in matters of literature. This is not her argument, but her brother's and, anyway, William Michael's 'facts' are notoriously speculative and ought to be regarded with a healthy degree of scepticism, certainly not trusted as dependable biographical data. But what his loaded presentation of a literary history does illustrate is the burden of tradition, imbued with predetermined opinion and value, inevitably involved in the construction of any fresh literature. 'The poems of William Morris were mostly unread by her - not unvalued': this is an odd statement. The overreaching implication is that reputation precedes acquaintance with the text - tradition potentially outweighs evaluation. In a letter sent to William Aytoun, then editor of *Blackwood's* magazine, in 1854, Christina Rossetti acknowledges this importance, clarifying her own position and demonstrating a considered selectivity in her own assimilation of poetic influence.

> I hope that I shall not be misunderstood as guilty of egotism or foolish vanity, when I say that my love for what is good in the works of others teaches me that there is something above the despicable in mine; that poetry is with me, not a mechanism, but an impulse and a reality, and that I know my aims in writing to be pure, and directed to that which is true and right.[11]

This is an important pronouncement. It forms an admission on the part of the poet that while her creations are to be read in terms of 'the works of others', in other words that poetry is a self-referential mode of discourse, at the same time, creative energies outside patterns of articulation already predetermined - 'poetry is with me... an impulse' - are recognised as equally fundamental to the generation of poetic discourse by the artist. Tradition is acknowledged as such, but simultaneously identified as something that can be tempered by 'impulse[s]' outside its jurisdiction. As we shall see in chapters to follow, this willingness to recognise, but not idly to follow poetic conventions (or any received ideological system relied upon for the transmission of those conventions) forms a significant part of Christina Rossetti's strategy as a radically original female poet.

In this fashion, even Christina Rossetti's earliest poems may be read as calculated attempts actively to explore her own assimilation of certain specific literary traditions. Complacent acceptance of tradition is avoided through the objective, but self-conscious scrutiny of poetic nuance and convention. As I have said, this feature of Rossetti's work is characterised by an intellectual energy manifest in a retreat from action toward a life constructed around speculative investigations of religious and artistic discourse. Christina Rossetti's poetry is necessarily the work of a female poet inheriting and writing within a tradition of verse defined by male values, a tradition which has held woman to be the 'other' in a version of experience orientated from the perspective of a dominant male-ordered subjectivity. This fact alone places her work as already at odds with the broad tradition from which her poetry sprang. This sense of exile, being outside poetry looking in, and exclusion - overtly addressed in longer, later works such as *The Prince's Progress* (*Poems*, I, 95-110) - is already present in Christina Rossetti's early lyrics. Notably, however, at this stage, it is framed in terms which show a concern to embrace certain aspects of Romanticism and pre-Victorian address, rather than defiantly to abnegate the import of male-ordered poetry *per se*, as *Monna Innominata* would attempt to do later in Rossetti's career. Her early writing shows that Rossetti felt a warm affinity with particular areas of experience as related in the poetry, particularly that of the Romantics, with which she had been in contact since a child.

On St. Agnes' Eve 1849, the then eighteen-year-old Christina wrote a eulogistic sonnet to Romantic principles entitled 'On Keats' (*Poems*, III, 168). Though far from mere pastiche, the poem immediately shows itself as one with the typically Romantic idiom:

> A garden in a garden: a green spot
> Where all is green: most fitting slumber-place
> For the strong man grown weary of a race
> Soon over. Unto him a goodly lot
> Hath fallen in fertile ground; there thorns are not,
> But his own daisies: silence, full of grace,

Surely hath shed a quiet on his face:
His earth is but sweet leaves that fall and rot.
What was his record of himself, ere he
Went from us? Here lies one whose name was writ
In water: while the chilly shadows flit
Of sweet Saint Agnes' Eve; while basil springs,
His name, in every humble heart that sings,
Shall be a fountain of love, verily.

Superficially an elegy to the dead poet, whose perennial appeal is imaged (in true Romantic fashion) in terms of the fecund, evergreen setting of his grave, 'On Keats' casts together with earthly mutability the notion of artistic (and pious, admitted in the pseudo-sermonising tone) permanence. For this reason alone - the juxtaposition of Romantic and Christian transcendent values - 'On Keats' assumes an energy, and a puzzling denouement, which takes effect beyond the surface literal level. The 'His' of the penultimate line could arguably invoke the divinity, or Keats, or both. The poem also marks the first recorded appearance in Rossetti's verse of the oft-to-be-repeated 'garden' image (narrowly beating its inclusion in the second part of 'Three Stages' (*Poems*, III, 232-4), written four months later, where the speaker wants to 'Dig up the pleasure-gardens of my soul'). The image is a commonplace, but Rossetti's particular placing of it with regard to Keats and the notion of earthly mutability, and her repeated use of the idea in her early lyrics, is a clue to her initial attempts to locate herself in poetic tradition. Here the image appears again:

The door was shut, I looked between
Its iron bars; and saw it lie,
My garden, mine, beneath the sky,
Pied with all flowers bedewed and green.

From bough to bough the song-birds crossed,
From flower to flower the moths and bees;

> With all its nests and stately trees
> It had been mine, and it was lost.

These are the opening two stanzas of the 1856 poem, the tellingly titled 'Shut Out' (*Poems*, I, 56-7), which maintains the 'garden' image and again frames it in terms familiar from Romantic writing. To be 'Shut Out' implies a division, a separation, forcing a partial sphere from that which previously was whole. The speaker occupies a point of exile from that which she considers to be her right and natural domain. There are direct echoes here of Wordsworth and Coleridge's reinstatement of a tradition going back to Milton's sonnet 'How Soon Hath Time' - one of a group of poems Christina was said to have 'seriously loved' (*Works*, lxx). Milton's poem expresses distress at his seeming poetic sterility in language coincident with that we see employed by Rossetti in 'Shut Out' and, indeed, repeated in many of her early poems. 'But my late spring no bud nor blossom showeth', admits Milton's disillusioned speaker,[12] and Rossetti's poem echoes 'Let me have / Some buds to cheer my outcast state' (the same image is offered in *Later Life* - 'Still here a bud and there a blossom seem / Hopeful' - see below). Christina Rossetti makes use of similar symbolism in a piece of the same period, the (once more) appropriately titled 1857 poem 'Introspective' (*Poems*, III, 264-5), which again offers a lapsed-pastoral vision of the seemingly spent creative self:

> On my boughs neither leaf nor fruit,
> No sap in my uttermost root,
> Brooding in an anguish dumb
> On the short past and the long to come.

Often in Rossetti, regret over this lack of natural fecundity is explicitly linked with a lost Edenic ideal (another literary convention) as in the 1855 lyric 'An Afterthought' (*Poems*, III, 242-3): 'Oh lost garden Paradise: - / Were the roses redder there / Than they blossom otherwise?' Here, directly Miltonic (though we are informed that

Christina 'disliked... Milton's *Paradise Lost*' (*Works*, lxx), possibly for its anti-female implications?) and scriptural imagery are preferred as a means of conveying the speaker's strain at her exile from a once innocent state. But just as often the natural world is cast as an absent goal in non-pious terms - a luxuriant metaphorical conceit against which the speaker's oppositional sense of harnessed, inner torment may be measured.

Linked to the 'garden' device, this image of the imprisoned spirit is pervasive in Rossetti's poetry of the 1850s, epitomised in the almost nihilistic 'Reflection' (*Poems*, III, 266-8) where the speaker is so conscious of her incarcerated, exhausted soul that she attempts by measures to remove herself from its stultifyingly 'Deaf' influence. In 'Shut Out', the archetypal lost 'garden' from which the spirit of the poet is excluded self-consciously replays the Wordsworthian tradition of alienated youth. In 'Ode: Intimations of Immortality', the standard is artfully set by Wordsworth with the speaker's wistful admission that the 'things that I have seen I now can see no more' and the ensuing relation of those 'things' in images from Nature. Midway through the 'Ode' comes the beautifully poignant, ominous observation, 'Heaven lies about us in our infancy! / Shades of the prison-house begin to close / Upon the growing Boy'.[13]

'Shut Out' is clearly a similar expression of the sense of powerful impulses frustrated, which relies, in part, for its impact upon a resurrection of pre-Romantic and Romantic notions of the fractured self and its transfiguration into natural images. So, beyond the surface level of dramatic relation of suffering, Rossetti's symbols also function on a literal-historically intertextual plane. Rossetti's speaker identifies herself with Romantic notions of relinquished creativity, using images and symbols directly inherited from Romanticism to do so. This place of Romantic 'song-birds', hence of poetic articulation, is an Eden-like environment, innocent and free, from which the speaker, through no fault of her own, is now banished. The poem exerts a desire to reinhabit this unspoiled territory (in doing so, inhabiting a poetic territory decidedly traditional in form), but is prevented from doing so by a deathly figure, imposing and prosaically described.

A shadowless spirit kept the gate,
Blank and unchanging like the grave.
I, peering thro', said: "Let me have
Some buds to cheer my outcast state."

He answered not. "Or give me, then,
But one small twig from shrub or tree;
And bid my home remember me
Until I come to it again."

The spirit was silent; but he took
Mortar and stone to build a wall;
He left no loophole great or small
Through which my straining eyes might look...

'Shades of the prison-house' are closing on the growing poetic girl -
not just by reasons of encroaching age, but by reason of her sex and
the socially enforced repression of woman in the nineteenth century;
notably, the original title of 'Shut Out' was to be the personalised,
appropriative 'What Happened to Me' (see *Poems*, I, 252), rightly
regarded as 'too significant' by William Michael (*Works*, 480). At
this point in her development as a female poet, Rossetti turns gladly
to the Romantic poets she enjoyed reading and borrows their lexical
and symbolic structures to use as an expressive means of ordering her
own feelings and youthful identity. In the Romantic tones of disquiet
at one's place in the world, and uncertainty as to one's (artistic) future,
Rossetti recognises a sympathetic voice and, understandably, adopts it
as her own. The wistful, questioning discourse of Romantics, such as
Coleridge and Wordsworth, latterly unsure as to the permanence they
had sought to establish in their verse becomes the platform from which
Christina Rossetti begins her own quest for the construction of female
identity. Conventional Romantic idiom is inhabited in a seemingly
comfortable manner, and is found appropriate to convey, ironically, a
sense of dissatisfaction with one's current means towards self-definition.

My trees are not in flower,
I have no bower,
And gusty creaks my tower,
And lonesome, very lonesome, is my strand.
(*Poems*, I, 145)

This concluding quatrain from the 1858 poem, 'Autumn' (*Poems*, I, 143-5), at once shows itself, like 'Shut Out', content to re-verbalise Romantic notions of alienation but, again, compresses the images together so that they themselves appear to stifle and imprison the desire for true expression. At this stage in her poetic career, Christina Rossetti uses Romantic poetics in a positive manner to make statements, themselves made by Romantic poets, hinting at the dissatisfaction with the channels of expression open to a female poet which would be more fully and radically explored in her later poetry. Utilising the same unusual verse form as Tennyson's *In Memoriam* (1850), thereby marking empathy for Tennyson's own articulations of loss and doubt, 'Shut Out' (1856) ends with its speaker's despair at being unable to achieve free expression, acutely aware of the partial nature of the song's import, of the sense of isolation from a unified, idyllic principle.

So now I sit here quite alone
Blinded with tears; nor grieve for that,
For nought is left worth looking at
Since my delightful land is gone.

A violet bed is budding near,
Wherein a lark has made her nest:
And good they are, but not the best;
And dear they are, but not so dear. (*Poems*, I, 57)

This despair is nothing new, and neither is the language in which it is framed. 'And good they are, but not the best...' echoes another of Rossetti's favourite poets, Coleridge, and his sentiments in the 'Dejection Ode':

> I see them all so excellently fair,
> I see, not feel, how beautiful they are.
> My genial spirits fail;
> And what can these avail
> To lift the smothering weight from off my breast? [14]

The carefully ordered sentiments of Rossetti's lyric simultaneously recall Shakespeare's 'Sonnet LXXIII' and its image of 'Bare ruined choirs, where late the sweet birds sang', [15] and, perhaps, the whole narrative of 'Shut Out' has some foundation in Blake's mournful lyric 'The Garden of Love'. Without doubt, Christina Rossetti would have read this through Dante Gabriel's ownership of what is now known as the *Rossetti Manuscript* - a Notebook of Blake's writing between 1791-2, now priceless, purchased from the British Museum in April 1847 for ten shillings (which Gabriel borrowed from William Michael), which was still in his possession when he died on 9 April 1882. In the 1860s, Dante Gabriel was in the process of publishing an edition of the poems contained in the Notebook, but this project never came to fruition.[16] 'The Garden of Love' is the fifth poem in the *Rossetti Manuscript*:

> I went to the Garden of Love,
> And saw what I never had seen:
> A Chapel was built in the midst,
> Where I used to play upon the green.
>
> And the gates of this chapel were shut,
> And "Thou shalt not" writ over the door;
> So I turn'd to the Garden of Love,
> That so many sweet flowers bore,
>
> And I saw that it was filled with graves,
> And tomb-stones where the flowers should be;
> And Priests in black gowns were walking their rounds,
> And binding with briars my joys and desires. [17]

Blake's Garden becomes 'filled with graves' attended by the sinister 'Priests'; Rossetti's sinister 'shadowless spirit' attends her 'garden' and is 'unchanging like the grave'. In Blake's poem 'the gates... were shut'; in Rossetti's lyric 'The door was shut'. Though Rossetti's work eschews the direct tone of anti-clericism prominent in 'The Garden of Love', the dramatic narrative of 'Shut Out' firmly recalls that of Blake's poem, and the quatrain patterning is also coincident. Far from rejecting the 'male' tradition of poetry (as we shall witness Rossetti at pains to do in her later work) here, Christina Rossetti actively and finely exploits it, so acknowledging the continuity of her song - a position we shall see revised considerably by the time of *Monna Innominata*.

There are two points to be taken from a reading of 'Shut Out' and the many similar pieces among Christina Rossetti's early poetic productions that display the conscious assimilation of these predominantly Romantic formative inputs. The first is that, at this stage, Christina Rossetti's reading has led her into a kind of poetry which draws considerably upon her acknowledged admiration for poetic tradition as bequeathed by male writers. This position would later be modified in varying degrees through *Goblin Market* to *Monna Innominata*, as Rossetti's subsequent poetic development brought with it revisions in her attitude to literary tradition. What begins as an adopted, soon becomes an adapted influence. The second point to be stressed is that Rossetti openly invokes the male Romantic poets at this juncture in her career to re-articulate their confessions of alienation, she finding her own artistic articulation stifled and inspiration lacking. Christina Rossetti reinvests the Romantic agony with the drama of her own particular predicament as a woman writer in a man's world, currently content to inhabit a masculine poetic form but soon to become infused with the desire to overcome formal constraints. 'Shut Out' is given an additional, particularised poignancy by fact of its author's sex, and at the level of personal distress the images of relinquished flowers and buds - 'good they are, but not the best' - are expressive of a sense of sterility and repression linked to Victorian womanhood. Victorian novels - particularly those of the

Brontës and, in Dickens, through figures like Esther Summerson and Little Dorrit - had articulated this image of the patient but distressed, repressed female self. Male poets had also been free to handle the topic of female eroticism and its expression, notably in Keats' 'Eve of St. Agnes', Coleridge's *Christabel* and Blake's 'Vision of the Daughters of Albion' - but not female poets. 'Shut Out' ventures into this area, as, later, *Goblin Market* would.

At this stage of her general development as a poet, Rossetti is prepared to embrace the male poetic tradition at a level of her own womanly desires, pain, and stress. Where the male poet has been sensitive and perceptive, his vision will be thus far assimilated into Rossetti's own, though the crasser elements of male (im)perception are seen as open to rejection or drastic revision. In this sense, Christina Rossetti's earliest poetry may be seen to anticipate her later work, but can in no sense be viewed as a radical reworking of a male tradition of writing. That directive would arrive explicitly in *Monna Innominata*, by way of *Goblin Market* and *The Prince's Progress*, in which poems, as we shall see, Rossetti progressively grows to realise has position as a woman-poet, both sharing and not sharing with her male poetic predecessors.

2

THE WHOLE WORLD STANDS AT 'WHY?': ROMANTICISM AND CHRISTINA

Stammering Oracles have ceased,
And the whole world stands at "why?"
Christina Rossetti, 'Maiden May'

One discourse that substantially informs the intertextual amalgam that constitutes Rossetti's poetry is that arising from her inheritance of certain poetic doctrines purveyed by the Romantics. I will attempt here to clarify Rossetti's position in this regard. As to the revision of Romantic ideology undertaken in Rossetti's writing, the devotional aspect of her verse, coincident with her Anglo-Christian beliefs, is highly relevant.

Christina Rossetti's religious background relied upon a specifically nineteenth-century coupling of Low Church Evangelism (in which tradition her mother had tutored her) and a warmly embraced High Church Tractarianism. During her teenage years, Christina found the Anglo-Catholicism of Pusey, Keble and Newman immensely affecting as a system of belief and, when the female members of the Rossetti family became regulars of the congregation at Christ Church, Albany Street, her conversion to Tractarianism became complete.[1]

As Mayberry points out, whilst Rossetti's religious beliefs were firmly moulded around the central tenets of Tractarianism, her poetry is also conditioned by some 'central aesthetic assumptions' of

Newman and Keble in particular, and of the Oxford Movement in general. Literal biblical typology does not predominate in Rossetti's most appealing (I would argue, earliest, though others may disagree) devotional poems but baptismal motifs and those of holy communion and marriage are frequently employed as metaphors: the desirability of discipline, submission to divine instruction, asceticism, prayer-like meditation and notions of guilt and penitence increasingly pervade the writings of Rossetti through time which deal explicitly with matters of piety. Whilst Chapman frames a persuasive case for regarding Rossetti as directly a product of the Oxford Movement,[2] Mayberry's qualifying conditions must be recognized as pertinent here. Rossetti's finest art is an intertextual synthesis of multiple perspectives, and not simply the unilateral regurgitation of one dominant philosophy which her final devotional productions became. In summary, Mayberry's conditions are these: 'it is at a broad, general level that [Rossetti's] religious sensibility is most valuable as a gloss to her poetry ... In Rossetti's case, the aesthetic implications of the [Tractarian] movement had a far greater and long-lived influence than did its theological subtleties'.[3]

It would be difficult to dispute G. B. Tennyson's statement that Rossetti is a 'far finer poet than her Tractarian predecessors',[4] but the reasons I would offer in support of this claim - those over and above her precise use of diction, metrical ingenuity and innovative employment of Tractarian conventions and motifs mentioned above - are those which need careful attention. Again, the fundamental Tractarian values are plainly evident in Rossetti's verse. These have been classified as 'typology, nature, art, liturgical forms, and above all, the yearning for oneness with God'.[5] More than anything else, the Tractarians invoked a vision of the world as a system of symbols: nature becomes, in this system, a symbolic register through which mouthpiece the divinity - via the processes known as Analogy and Reserve - communicates clues to us of a better, hidden world beyond our own temporal dimension. This sacramental world-view was attractive to the Pre-Raphaelites, who adopted pregnant natural images in their art, both visual and written, offering beauty itself as a work's subject matter in a post-Romantic quest for spiritual permanence. In Keble's 'Tract 89', where both Analogy and Reserve are explicitly defined, the fundamental Tractarian position is formulated: 'In like manner, the Mystical, or Christian, or Theological use of (the material world) is the reducing to a particular set of symbols and associations, which we have reason to believe has, more or less, the authority of the GREAT CREATOR Himself'.[6]

The belief, adopted in some of Rossetti's earliest lyrics, is that material instances in the natural world are types of elements unseen in the next world (Analogy), this condition being a divine truth that God, being ultimately incomprehensible, could only gradually, indirectly (by Reserve) allow us hints of in this life. 'Thou Sleepest where the Lilies Fade' (*Poems*, III, 221), a two stanza lyric composed before 1853, illustrates Rossetti's early acceptance of the notion that the natural works of God on earth are but fleeting types of the eternal, joyous truths to be experienced in the afterlife:

> Thou sleepest where the lilies fade,
> Thou dwellest where the lilies fade not;
> Sweet, when thine earthly part decayed
> Thy heavenly part decayed not.
>
> Thou dwellest where the roses blow,
> The crimson roses bud and blossom;
> While on thine eyes is heaped the snow,
> The snow upon thy bosom.

This poem works by simple antithetical juxtapositions - 'sleepest ... dwellest ... decayed ... decayed not'. A winter landscape encloses the dead party's tomb and yet perennial spring is simultaneously enjoyed in heaven. Heavenly correlatives of the natural instances on earth (the Analogical process) are seen as permanent universal essences - knowable only through the Reserve exercised by the divinity (Who does not appear in the poem, but remains the unquestioned centre of intelligibility behind it, guaranteeing its conditions, the controller of the whole scheme of things), where death must precede higher knowledge. 'Shadows today, while shadows show God's Will' (*Poems*, II, 331), Rossetti affirms of the Analogical mode elsewhere and, in a late piece form the 'Songs for Strangers and Pilgrims' series published in the 1893 *Verses*, the Tractarian philosophy is unambiguously expressed:

> The twig teacheth,
> The moth preacheth,
> The plant vaunteth,
> The bird chanteth,
> God's mercy overflowing... (*Poems*, II, 332)

Rossetti's inheritance of the Tractarian position is clear, and yet it is only one element of the full equation that her most effective poetry attempts to solve. In her latest, heavily exegetical texts (all but one published by the Society for Promoting Christian Knowledge, between the mid-1870s and her death in 1894), Rossetti consistently offers a specifically Tractarian adherence to unity with the Christian deity through unquestioning repetition of devotion. In these later pieces, the fervent artistic quest for personal, individual expression which characterizes Rossetti's best work is finally overtaken by what G. B. Tennyson refers to as 'Keble's bedrock principle that poetry is the expression of intense religious longing'.[7] In this manner, through a self-imposed exile from questioning and doubt, Rossetti was ultimately to achieve that centred pose of stability and coherence which is constantly denied as an available option in her earlier poems.

But it is my purpose here to outline the formative influence that religious belief exercised upon Rossetti's earlier work, and how this brought about tension through a repeated interplay with other values inherited from romantic thought. G. B. Tennyson urges us to read Rossetti's 'yearnings' as wholly 'religious' rather than 'psychological',[8] but the two cannot be regarded as mutually exclusive where Rossetti is concerned. In fact, it is the intensely doubtful, ever-renewable debate between post-Romantic, proto-feminist and ascetic Tractarian ideological positions which frequently complicates the already complex intertextual strategies at work in Rossetti's finest work. In a post-Romantic sense (Wordsworth and Coleridge were enormous influences upon Keble in particular) the poetic faculty was the element which allowed us potentially to reconstruct a stable sense of identity from the mutable but sacramentally loaded natural world around us.[9] 'Images' and 'similes', said Keble, 'guide us by gentle hints and no uncertain signs, to the very utterances of Nature, or we may more truly say, of the Author of Nature'.[10]

Poetry thus becomes a form of religious experience and this is, as we shall see, one distinct energy informing Rossetti's earliest, so-called 'secular' lyrics as well as her many devotional poems. Yet the correspondence in Rossetti's poetry between this divinely allocated role for the artist and the many other ideologies operating upon her as a Victorian woman writer lends her work a lively sense of distrust and self-doubt that is highly appealing in its consequent resistance of complacency, until this tension becomes progressively checked into monotonous exegetical repetition in the devotional poetry and prose with which Rossetti self-consciously chose to conclude her career.

A collision of ideologies then - between the essential quality allocated to nature and the human imagination by Romanticism, and the subjugation of both of these to divine omnipotence demanded by Christian dogma - may be witnessed in Rossetti's work. This markedly conditions many responses within the poetry and carries implications concerning first the redirecting of Romantic ideals and, second, the simultaneous commentary on religious iconography and doctrine enacted by the text. The Romantics aspired towards communion with nature as the ultimate goal with which human imaginative capabilities could be rewarded. Coordination with nature on a successful, reciprocal basis for the individual and, organically, for society is seen as a necessary prerequisite by the Romantics in their endeavours to sustain faith in the primacy of human constructiveness.

Wordsworth himself began by elevating this position but, in *The Excursion*, moved towards a form of Christian orthodoxy. Devotional codes, such as those inherited by Rossetti from her vigorous biblical studies, also promote the human imagination, but as a gift from a god who is a greater universal essence of those particular instances which He has bestowed upon earth for us to construe. Similarly, from a Tractarian standpoint nature is significant not as an infinite end, but as a revelation, a concrete manifestation of a divine, ethereal presence. Cantalupo, distinguishing between this Romantic 'immanence' and Christian 'transcendence', remarks upon Rossetti's perception of the ambiguity: 'Believing that [a] single flower was a type ... of God's love, Rossetti could not accept the implication of some Romantic poetry that God was, for example, in the tree rather than the tree's maker'.[11]

The pre-eminence afforded to human imagination and the world of nature by conventionally expounded ideology is challenged, as it had been by elements of late Romantic thought, as an absolute ideal in the poetry of Christina Rossetti. The sequence (date of composition unknown) of twenty-eight sonnets titled *Later Life* (*Poems*, II, 138-50) may be read as illustrative of Rossetti's ambivalent opinion in this area.[12] The cycle begins with a direct, unambiguous declaration of divine permanence and omnipotence:

> Before the mountains were brought forth, before
> Earth and the world were made, then God was God:
> And God will still be God when flames shall roar
> Round earth and heaven dissolving at His nod...
> (I, 1-4)

God is conceived of as the origin of all else in the ontological system the poem begins to construct. God made the 'mountains', symbolizing nature, and so nature is seen not as an absolute but as a sacramental reflection of divine power. God is given as the principle of intelligibility, the centre, the guarantee of meaning. 'God was God' and 'God will still be God' - the system of signification generated within this devotional sonnet is one with certainty of reference. But, typically for Rossetti, this complacency is rapidly analyzed and questioned in terms of its implications. This stable devotional frame of reference established, the text immediately steps outside its jurisdiction and offers criticism of the certitudes it implies, presenting religious security as a wholly ambiguous prospect. The absolute certainty promoted by the first sonnet implies a closed system. That the sequence continues at all (for another twenty seven stanzas) represents rejection of that closure. Anxiety is felt in the text as activity, which begins to set itself against the devotional dogma:

> Let us today, while it is called today
> Set out, if utmost speed may yet avail -
> The shadows lengthen and the light grows pale:
> For who through darkness and the shadow of death,
> Darkness that may be felt, shall find a way,
> Blind-eyed, deaf-eared,
>   and choked with failing breath?   (II, 9-14)

Again, somewhat in the spirit of the poems of faith and doubt in Tennyson's *In Memoriam*, this disturbing and compelling image proceeds from a desire to circumvent or escape the stifling clutches of a closed system. The text desires, with 'utmost speed', to set itself apart from an atmosphere of self-satisfying ('today while it is called today') reference. Such a system, in its dogmatic certitude, stifles all possibility of articulation, leaving the text 'Blind-eyed, deaf-eared, and choked with failing breath'. The cycle continues its deconstruction of the devotional epistemological framework it initially promoted, in places - 'If making makes us Thine then Thine we are' - adopting sarcasm as a manner of reproach toward the closed referential process from which it is moving (literally as the poem continues, and philosophically) away. By the mid-point of the sequence, its own formal centre, the very notion of a 'centre' has been soundly rejected. Unity is shown to be a *relative*, not an absolute idea:

> Our teachers teach that one and one make two:
> Later, Love rules that one and one make one:
> Abstruse the problems! neither need we shun,
> But skilfully to each should yield its due…
> Both provable by me, and both by you. (XVI, 1-8)

There is a tone of *jouissance* pervasive here, *le plaisir du texte* no less, as the poem celebrates its achievement of an exchange. Those redundant certitudes, the notion of closure inherent in the dialectics of the opening sonnet, have given way to open-ended semantic activity:

> Befogged and witless, in a wordy maze
> A groping stroll perhaps may do us good;
> If cloyed we are with much we have understood…
> (XVI, 9-11)

This emphatic desire to dislodge the mechanics of a significatory system built upon certitude and closure must be accompanied by a total decentring process, a rejection of traditional principles of reference:

> I am sick of where I am and where I am not,
> I am sick of foresight and of memory,
> I am sick of all I have and all I see,
> I am sick of self, and there is nothing new;
> O weary impatient patience of my lot! (XVIII, 9-12)

This anaphoric passage (characteristic of Rossetti's poetry), repeated rejections of potential stability, marks something of a turning point in the *Later Life* sequence. The antithetical juxtaposition 'impatient patience' - two oppositional signifiers made to relate directly to one other - marks a complete usurpation of the closed, self-congratulatory system of signification offered earlier in the sonnet cycle from a conventional devotional position. Stability has been demolished by the text, and reconstruction is now attempted, heralded by a turning towards a new frame of reference. With God displaced as a principle of intelligibility, the text looks now to nature.

A *manner* of reconstruction begins. For the poem to continue, it must. The natural world may offer potential escape from the centreless 'wordy maze' the text has come to represent. A 'Winter' landscape is envisaged 'not so drear as was my boding dream', to ensure that the text itself does not become frozen by its own lack of centring principle.

> Still here a bud and there a blossom seem
> Hopeful, and robin still is musical.
> Leaves, flowers and fruit and one delightful song
> Remain... (XIX, 7-10)

The isolation of '[R]emain', achieved by caesural stopping and the accumulation of qualifying subjects in the preceding line, makes emphatic the aspect of endurance and permanence that the text has now allocated to nature, as the quest for a new mode of articulation begins. It is surely not coincidental that the natural images are closely associated here with 'musical' notions of 'delightful song' as the cycle seeks a new voice. Neither is it by chance that the text turns attention directly away from the 'robin', traditionally the bird of endurance, and the 'hundred solitary birds [which] salute the day' to rest emphasis upon another particular bird from nature - the nightingale:

> One solitary bird salutes the night:
> Its mellow grieving wiles our grief away,
> And tunes our weary watches to delight;
> It seems to think the thoughts we cannot say,
> To know and sing them, and to set them right;
> Until we feel once more that May is May,
> And hope some buds may bloom without a blight.
> (XX, 2-8)

This new mode of articulation is conceived in terms of the song of the nightingale, an important image in Romantic poetry, conveying not firm belief and confidence in Romanticism unqualified but a strong note of scepticism, the Romantic agony. In his *Defence of Poetry*, Shelley had likened the poet to this bird: 'A Poet is a nightingale who sits in darkness and sings to cheer its own solitude with sweet sounds'.[13] Shelley's haunting image carries the sense of loss which infuses some Romantic texts, a step down from high Romantic dogma, springing from doubts that the imagination may not be, as Wordsworth terms it in *The Prelude*, an 'absolute strength', guaranteeing communion with what Shelley calls 'the eternal, the infinite, and the one.[14]

The nightingale, immortalised as a symbol in Keats' 'Ode' (and ingeniously remanaged in Yeats' 'Sailing to Byzantium'), presents an ambivalent image of potentially distressing isolation. In restating this image, Rossetti shows herself allied to the scepticism already urged by some Romantic texts towards the Romantic belief in the existence of a vital relationship between the individual poetic imagination and a broader realm of existence in the world of exteriors. In *Later Life*, Rossetti's use of the nightingale also implies scepticism towards this relationship. The text goes on to study this relationship, making this study a direct response to its own recent destabilising process. The basis of the search for a principle of intelligibility becomes the realisation that a *stable* principle will not be forthcoming. The sequence begins to borrow familiar Romantic codes:

> A host of things I take on trust: I take
> The nightingales on trust, for few and far
> Between those actual summer moments are
> When I have heard that melody they make. (XXI, 1-4)

Conveying scepticism towards what many Victorian commentators dogmatically regarded as Romantic unities, this nightingale image prefaces a direct commentary upon a high Romantic notion - that of Wordsworth's often ambiguously presented 'spots of time'. A sceptical stance is adopted by the text 'on trust' towards the Wordsworthian 'summer moments' of intensity and communion with the natural world. The sonnet continues, simultaneously inhabiting and deconstructing Wordsworthian discourse. In doing so, Rossetti shows herself aware of the pitfalls in the reading of Wordsworth as prophet and sage, which ignores what we now see as areas of questioning. The 'boy and boat' episode of Wordsworth's *Prelude* is addressed: its inherent uncertainties, overlooked by many nineteenth-century champions of Romanticism, are emphasised in Rossetti's re-reading.

> So chanced it once at Como on the lake:
> But all things, then, waxed musical; each star
> Sang on its course, each breeze sang on its car,
> All harmonies sang to senses wide awake.
> All things in tune, myself not out of tune… (XXI, 5-9)

The poetry here is informed with what appears to be a standard expression of that conjunction achieved in archetypal modes of Romanticism between the innermost self and the natural world of exteriors. But the lines that follow are more of a sceptical commentary upon this platitude than an affirmation. The ultimate Romantic attachment of self and surroundings is suffixed by a tone of calculated detachment:

> Those nightingales were nightingales indeed:
> Yet truly an owl had satisfied my need,
> And wrought a rapture underneath that moon,
> Or simple sparrow chirping from a reed;
> For June that night glowed like a doubled June.
> (XXI, 10-4)

Later Life here reminds one of Wordsworth's own doubts as to Romantic stability and certitude as to subjectivity, recasting that objection in a reminder of the redundant nature of closed signifying systems - the nightingales 'were nightingales indeed' and June similarly justifies itself as 'like a doubled June'. Aware of the stagnation (illustrated in the sequence's opening sonnet) that such a manner of conjunction can imply, Rossetti here gently mocks post-Romantic, popular Victorian enthusiasm concerning the stable subject. If the object world has been assimilated into the subject sphere, the problem of the object is not solved, but simply placed within a different frame of reference. Representationalism is exchanged for idealism, but the subject/object relation still pertains. having established stable subjectivity and absolute communion with the natural world, assimilating subject and object, Rossetti immediately attacks this complacent pose by ridiculing its implications. If the problem of the object is no more, then what does it matter which object we settle upon? Anything will signify - 'truly an owl had satisfied my need … Or simple sparrow' - given Rossetti's desire to inhabit the margins of a Romantically inspired position which once regarded stability as an attainable end.

Later Life makes provocative judgements about systems of signification and, notably, by insinuating an ambivalent interplay between Christian and Romantic ideologies, rejects any notion of a stable subjectivity. By considering signification and articulation as topics, the poem becomes self-referential, its own subject. The rejection of dogmatic readings of Romanticism is emphasised in sonnet XXII, which again adopts a Wordsworthian register only to collapse its arguments from within. The famous Alpine scenes of 'Book Six' of *The Prelude* are invoked:

> 1 he mountains in their overwhelming might
> Moved me to sadness when I saw them first,
> And afterwards they moved me to delight;
> Struck harmonies from silent chords which burst
> Out into song, a song by memory nursed… (XXII, 1-5)

The contradiction within the image arrives in a manner similar to that effected in the preceding sonnet, simultaneously recalling

Wordsworth's own ambivalence in *The Prelude*: Tumult and peace, the darkness and the light / Were all like workings of one mind, the features / Of the same face'.[15] In Rossetti's sonnet, the 'pleasure and ... wonder' of this spiritual communion are reduced and crystallised into one obvious object-image, the 'forget-me-not' flower. But what power of reference can this image have if the subject-object gap is closed in blissful concordance? If signification closes in certainty of reference what place is left for a 'crown'-ing metaphoric enhancement? 'Yet why should such a flower choose such a spot? / Could we forget that way which we once went / Tho' not one flower had bloomed to weave its crown?' (XXII, 12-4)

Through establishing affinity in her earliest lyrics with those areas of scepticism and fear of mutability present in Wordsworth and Coleridge, Rossetti has come, by this point, to confront complacent readings of Romanticism with their inherent formative inconsistencies. The poetry actively deconstructs the premises from which it appears to proceed. Notions of stability are dislodged and replaced by a regard for fragmentation, disunity and, finally, relativity. The Romantic assertion of stable subjectivity is upsetting to Rossetti as a woman writer and is this cancelled in favour of the later ambivalent presentation of selfhood, resulting in a formulation of the self as divided, unstable. Duality abounds - 'we consider what this life we lead / Is not, and is' (XXV, 1-2) - and the irrational is promoted to a level coincident with the rational. The unconscious is recognized as a site of meaning, and this identification colours further the rewriting of Romantic values one finds in Rossetti's poetry. Belsey points out the implications of this attention when she speaks of 'the notion of a unitary and autonomous subject, ultimate origin of its own choices', noting that the 'existence of the unconscious puts this notion into question'.[16]

Indeed, acute consciousness of self is a pervasive theme in Rossetti's work: 'All my walls are lost in mirrors, whereupon I trace / Self to right hand, self to left hand, self in every place, / Self-same solitary figure, self-same seeking face' (*Poems*, I, 149). The idea of the self as irreconcilably divided is present in 'Reflection' (*Poems*, III, 266-8) with its image of the imprisoned autonomous 'soul':

> Gazing thro' her chamber window
> Sits my soul's dear soul;
> Looking northward, looking southward,
> Looking to the goal,
> Looking back without control…

The speaker's unconscious, 'my soul's dear soul', is envisaged as 'without control', a site of production of meaning formed around no fixed centre, a measure of the irrational. again, this offers a modification to the Romantic ideals inherited by Rossetti. Imagination itself is thus revalued in Rossetti's poetry.

In a prose work of 1883, *Letter and Spirit*, one can detect, from the creative artist's standpoint, some dissatisfaction with the degree of primacy allocated to imagination, albeit coupled with admission of the imagination's importance: 'To modify by a boundless license of imagination the Voice of Revelation, or of tradition, or our own perceptions, concerning the universe, its Ruler, features, origin, destinies, falls within the range of human faculties'.[17] Imagination is conceived of here, in Coleridgean fashion, as a power with 'boundless license' and yet, in the same breath, is allocated boundaries. It is reliant upon 'our own perceptions', which, in turn, are drawn from a 'universe' with a controlling 'Ruler'. Perception is vouched for as 'other' to imagination and these two exist exterior to a 'Ruler' beyond. But the admission that imagination can 'modify by a boundless license' the data received by means of these other epistemological sites does in fact guarantee imagination the primary status, which the devotional aspect of Rossetti's argument is elsewhere at pains to revoke: 'For if (as I have seen pointed out) God is not to be called like His creature, whose grace is simply typical, but that creature is like him because expressive of His archetypal Attribute, it suggests itself that for every aspect of creation there must exist the corresponding Divine attribute'.[18]

There is an awkward tone of hollow self-justification about these statements - 'as I have seen pointed out ... it suggests itself' - which functions to undermine their apparent resolution. The speaker is involved in a blinkered attempt at convincing herself of the validity of the pious dogma she regurgitates. The semi-pantheistic conception of nature and the Platonic view of 'the inadequacy of ought temporal to shadow forth that which is eternal' are clearly at odds with the aesthetic of Romanticism, but this thesis sits uncomfortably with the reverence for human imagination as essentially 'boundless'. An ontological system of existence is generated, and the element which deconstructs this system, necessary to its formation yet simultaneously outside its parameters, is imagination. Rossetti negates the stable concept of subjectivity offered by insensitive interpretations of Romanticism and heralds a re-reading of nature and imagination, thus a re-reading of the nature or reading (perception) itself. Cantalupo is right to declare that Rossetti is 'ambivalent about the Romantic view of nature':

> Clearly she inherits the Romantic concern with epistemology; she wonders: 'How do subject and object meet in a meaningful relationship? By what means do we have a significant awareness of the world?' Consequently, Rossetti sometimes records the process of reading nature as well as the content of that reading, valuing the flux of her experience of nature, with its misrepresentations as well as its insights.[19]

This is a crucial point. Rossetti's poetry extends inherent Romantic ambivalence and forms an intertextual investigation of the premises upon which 'certitudes' are founded. It shuns absolutes in favour of relative concepts, aware, as a stanza from 'An Old World Thicket' (*Poems*, II, 123-8) neatly summarizes, that to posit one system of 'truth' is to acknowledge all opposing alternative 'other' possible truths.

> For all that was but showed what all was not,
> But gave clear proof of what might never be;
> Making more destitute my poverty,
> And yet more blank my lot,
> And me much gladder by its jubilee.

Presence denotes absence: with Rossetti, it is through absence that presence is often conveyed. The sadness left behind by a departed love, memories, the past, echoes, thoughts of one now dead; Rossetti continually reminds us that being carries with it the possibility of not being, desire implies a lack. Certainty relies upon the possibility of uncertainty.

> We lack, yet cannot fix upon the lack:
> Not this, nor that; yet somewhat, certainly.
> We see the things we do not yearn to see
> Around us: and what see we glancing back?
> Lost hopes that leave our hearts upon the rack,
> Hopes that were never ours yet seemed to be...
> (VI, 1-6)

This compelling series of propositions and negations forms the opening to another sonnet of the *Later Life* cycle. It constitutes one of the most concentrated examples, plainly articulated in straightforward etymology, of the collapsing of certitude in Rossetti's verse. From the very outset, the text is wholly unable to 'fix upon' the concept, 'lack', which forms its fundamental premise, 'We lack'. Grammatical certainty is simultaneously nudged as the verb becomes a noun within a single line. The second line, with its ironic 'certainly', does nothing to assuage the quandary of its predecessor, awkwardly stringing together a staccato succession of partial significations. Perception, given as sight ('We see') is also partially realized and leaves desire, with its implication of lack still pronounced, unfulfilled; 'We see the things we do not yearn to see'. The second attempt at perception is even more unsuccessful than the first as we see

'Lost hopes' that never 'were' but only 'seemed', leaving 'our hearts upon the rack' and the desire informing the poem unfulfilled. Kathleen Blake has observed how, in Rossetti's poetry, hope is often 'hope deferred', a hope never allowed into being and, thus, not hope at all.[20] Here, we look in vain for 'Lost hopes' in a sonnet which leaves us '(s)training dim eyes to catch the invisible sight, / And strong to bear ourselves in patient pain?' (VI, 13-4) This is a question unresolved, as I have demonstrated, in terms of the cycle as a whole. *Later Life* gives no single answer since its whole strategy has denied the possibility of such certitude.

In Rossetti's writing, then, we observe conscious scrutiny of the notion of certainty. This represents rejection of the stable subjectivity which some Romantic poetry had appeared to offer as a legacy to the Victorian writer and a marked alliance with the scepticism inherent in late Romantic writing as to that stability. The vital union between language and figure, the distinguishing feature of fully realized Romantic poetry, had successfully constituted a transcendent principle of order compensating for the collapse of natural and historical continuity which plagued the human spirit in the eighteenth century. A poem no longer evoked a pattern outside itself but constituted that pattern from within itself; the world constructed became inseparable from the poetic activity which made it; morality becomes activity, not a code or a system. Imagination assumed a redemptive role, the creative act generating an order inherent within its workings, no longer mimetic of an order outside itself but symbolically constituting that order through union of subject and object, letter and spirit. Hitherto incompatible orders of reality were fused in a spiritual celebration which language could constitute and form. Bloom and Frye have analysed the 'internalization' disclosed in this manner of writing and the programme of spiritual decline and recovery it began to instil in texts of the Romantic period. The symbolic projection of the internal landscape of the psyche onto that of the external world fused the two realms together in a subject/object unity of sense. Meaning could be generated from the ordering principle of this new stable subjectivity, epistemology was vouchsafed by a newfound manner of certitude.

The second-generation Romantics (Shelley in particular) had already exhibited anxiety towards this confidence in the absolute strength of the imagination - the apocalyptic despair of 'Alastor' and the solipsistic unquiet of the *Defence of Poetry*. Rossetti's early lyrics, in a manner becoming increasingly impatient in sustained pieces such a *Later Life*, form a continuity between Romantic ambivalence and Victorian doubt. Initially appropriating areas of Romantic expression and latterly emphasizing the inconsistencies and unease already inherent in those areas through her own discomfort with complacency, Rossetti discloses scepticism towards any manner of surety, self-conscious concern with the subject/object relationship and anxiety as to the very nature of 'reality'. On one level, the easily dogmatized Romantic assertion of stable subjectivity, fusion of subject and object brought about by communion of inner and outer, might be read as an attempt to abolish the problem of the object world. The object is overcome as 'other' by deft relocation within subjectivity and inner consciousness: rather than annihilating the issue, this manipulation simply presents the Victorian poet with the task of redefining the subject/object relationship from within a new framework.

In attempting to abolish the problematic object, Romanticism only succeeded in suppressing it inside a fresh epistemological system, thereby summoning later scepticism in poets such as Wordsworth towards such a reductive procedure. The whole nature of reality, not simply the status of one element (the object) within that version of existence, had been qualified by what critics held to be the initial Romantic assertion of stable subjectivity and the battlefield for late eighteenth-century commentators (and those of today) which that area became. Idealism, based upon a fundamental unity of the perceiving mind, had in fact been urged by the Romantics as a new philosophical position.

Many Victorian writers took this Romantic idealism to task not as a model of basic subjectivity (as it had been offered to them) which had internalized and drawn the external object world under its friendly wing, but as a model of total perception and, therefore, still involving the subject/object *relationship* as an essential formative element. Christina Rossetti, undoubtedly, was one such writer. Isobel Armstrong has summarised a concern that I believe to be fundamental to Rossetti's work:

> Criticism of nineteenth-century poetry often presupposes a transcendent account of the subject, in which the unity of subject and object is achieved, and in which the relationship between consciousness and the world is mystified, through the personalising and subjectivising of the free autonomous self and its agency. A study of the language of nineteenth-century poetry suggests rather that it works to demystify the relation between subject and object, and does not assume a primal unity on the part of the receiving mind. Indeed, it struggles with the problem of the relationship itself.[21]

It is this very hypothesis that my reading of Christina Rossetti here will explore and extend. This 'problem of the [subject-object] relationship itself' is addressed, as we shall see, in an intertextual manner that calls into question literary-historical tradition, issues of gender-bias and sexuality, and, behind these, matters of belief and faith, and matters of language. One of the areas in which notions of stability, instability, and 'relationship itself' are confronted by Rossetti, again in a manner that acknowledges areas of Romantic speculation and ambivalence, is in poems dealing with dreams and dreaming, to which I now intend to turn my attention. Here we will witness a subtle but complex usage of language that prefigures in effect certain advanced strategies that we will find in the longer poems to be examined later in this study.

3

I ANSWER NOT FOR MEANING: DREAMS AND DREAMING

There are sleeping dreams and waking dreams:
What seems is not always as it seems.
Christina Rossetti, 'A Ballad of Boding'

What can it mean? you ask. I answer not
For meaning, but myself must echo, What?
Christina Rossetti, 'My Dream'

I

In attempting an investigation of Christina Rossetti's treatment, discussion, and narration of dreams and dream sequences, I hope to pursue further the notion that a main function of her writing is shrewd exposition of the belief that meaning, at all levels, is not a fixed, but a relative thing. I wish to illustrate - before consolidating the case with examination of pieces such as *The Prince's Progress* and the *Monna Innominata* cycle - that the poetics of the Rossetti text where language and signification are concerned serve repeatedly to stress the non-unified nature and potential uncontainability of the self. To facilitate this, it will first be necessary to give a general introductory statement concerning the treatment of dream experience in poetry of the Romantic period, attempting to show the manner in which this outlook provides an invaluable position from which to assess the strategies at work in Christina Rossetti's verse, especially that dealing openly with 'other-worldly' experience. I intend to show that Christina Rossetti's interest in dreams and their meanings is a predictable step in the unified strategy of her written output, an extension of the concerns located in the poetry looked at in the previous chapter.

It will then be instructive to provide a discussion of the treatment of the dream as an occurrence itself in the Rossetti canon, rather than the events contained therein, and the difference in this treatment between the 'devotional' and the 'secular' poetry. A selection of poems will be compared and contrasted in order to highlight the (often subtle) differences in treatment of the dream at narrative and symbolic levels resulting from Rossetti's manipulation of modes of writing inherited from the Romantic period. This will preface a study of the open presentation of dream narrative and how this relates to the wider concerns of Christina Rossetti's lyric writing, as I interpret it, and the lexical and symbolic arrangements exhibited therein. The aim will be to isolate a working strategy relating to the manner of symbolism and causality employed, to illustrate what this might tell us about the attitude of Christina Rossetti's verses towards dreams, their narratives and ideas of meaning in general. In particular, I wish to illustrate the ways in which Rossetti dramatically reworks the Romantic attitude towards dreaming and the imagination, hence towards poetic creation and the reading process itself.

Midway through Tom Stoppard's play *Rosencrantz and Guildenstern are Dead*, discussing the nature and importance of 'order' as opposed to the 'shambles' implied by any intrusion of 'spontaneity' onto things, Guildenstern declares that a 'Chinaman of the T'ang Dynasty - and, by which definition, a philosopher - dreamed he was a butterfly, and from that moment he was never quite sure that he was not a butterfly dreaming it was a Chinese philosopher. Envy him; in his two-fold security'.[1] Afforded a misleading degree of flippancy by its being couched in an epigrammatic form rather redolent of Wilde, Guildenstern's is an interesting, and certainly a provocative starting point in a discussion of the treatment of dreams and dreaming in literature. Whereas the butterfly is given no temporal restrictions and typifies the timeless world of nature, the Chinaman is fixed in time and geography; he is from China and, being 'of the T'ang Dynasty', is thus ascribed to a particular historical period. He is the subject of every clause of the sentence - the first of the passage - which delights in equating his fortunes with that of the small insect; in other words, we see the riddle from the perspective of the subject, the Chinaman, who is to be respected since he is 'a philosopher', and in being called to 'Envy him' we are urged towards some kind of identification with him. The scenario is a loaded one. The Chinaman seemingly represents 'real', existence as we know it; the butterfly (in Greek, as Aristotle pointed out, ψυχή/psyche can mean butterfly and soul), a suitably delicate and vulnerable image, emblemises the 'unreal', less substantial world of the dream. The 'philosopher' partakes uncertainly of both spheres of meaning. In doing so, he recognises the 'reality' of imagination whilst simultaneously describing a potential dichotomy between the two.

So, seen conventionally, Guildenstern's argument would appear to be weighted in favour of the typical pre-Romantic, pre-psychological view of the dream and its pertinence to waking reality. The seeming flippancy of his observation does not only reside in its construction: his conclusion, that we should 'Envy' the Chinaman 'in his two-fold security' seems at odds with these premises. We might expect to be encouraged to scoff at the philosopher's bewilderment, not to be jealous of the 'security' it allows him to assume. The admirable principle of 'order' Guildenstern deduces from the fable can only stem from the co-existence of two alternative spheres of being, thus creating the sense of 'two-fold' stability attained by way of simultaneous alternatives which appear to be contraries. Whatever the terms of the argument itself as portrayed, where the 'dream' is clearly just that and the 'dreamer' is firmly rooted in an identifiable 'reality', the conclusion hints heavily that the two areas of existence might just be differently constructed views of the world, neither having superiority, which, when understood as compatible versions of what might be termed 'real', allow us a subtler vision.

But this conclusion is one very much of Stoppard's epoch, the twentieth century, rather than of that period inhabited by Guildenstern within the fiction of the drama. It is a viewpoint whose conception and history are worth tracing, since it is one that forms a major feature of Christina Rossetti's treatment of dream experience. One commentator has noted that '[D]ream is the commonest challenge to everyday reality ... Dreams ... create new models of reality'.[2] It might be debatable whether dreams 'create' or are the creation of 'new models of reality', but the point is a valid one nonetheless. The revolution that took place in the field of scientific knowledge during the seventeenth century was matched by the Protestant loss of certitude as to the literal truth of Christian cosmology. Prior to this, in ancient and mediaeval times, literal faith in Christian myth - in the existence of demons and angels and the possibility of spiritual visitation - had meant that dreams were taken literally by philosophers as physiological proof of the actuality of the spiritual plane. The rise of rationalistic thinking during the reign of Queen Elizabeth I meant that dreams were relegated 'into an intellectual limbo', regarded as unscientific, unclassifiable and no longer objectively tenable as evidence of a now widely doubted spiritual 'reality'.[3] Shakespeare's *A Midsummer Night's Dream* draws much of its energy from an investigation of the worth of various alternative perspectives onto what might be regarded as a stable 'reality'. In the play, the waking weaver, Bottom, muses:

> I have had a most rare vision. I have had a dream
> past the wit of man to say what dream it was. Man
> is but an ass if he go about to expound this dream.
> Methought I was - there is no man can tell what ...
> The eye of man hath not heard, the ear of man hath
> not seen, man's hand is not able to taste, his tongue to
> conceive, nor his heart to report what my dream was.[4]

The repeated confusion of agent and qualifying verb form here - 'eye/heard', 'hand/taste' - stresses the incompatibility (in Bottom's low but worthy opinion) of the dream experience with any value codes established from common experience (though, on one level, the grammar is the code and the comedy lies in our suspicion that there is a kind of sense in Bottom's words). Elsewhere, Duke Theseus concludes:

> Lovers and madmen have such seething brains,
> Such shaping fantasies, that apprehend
> More than cool reason ever comprehends.
> The lunatic, the lover, and the poet
> Are of imagination all compact.[5]

The joke, again, is in the failure of the speaker to see that he, too, is a figment of the poet's dream, and that without the imagination of the poet he would not 'exist'. In hindsight, the lovers themselves view the strange night-time events in the wood as 'small and undistinguishable, / Like far-off mountains turned into clouds'.[6] All these comments seem to urge a lack of trust toward any type of non-real experience: dreams and visions are all very well, but only when seen as such, as abnormal interludes, and what a relief it is to have both feet back upon the solid turf of reality. But, typical of the Shakespearean text, born of a period when notions of dreams and their value were shifting, there is another argument implicit within the drama. In pragmatic terms, the confusion of the illusory and the real might well be undesirable, but could not the correlation of the two prove educative in offering new perspectives and widening our notions of the two prove educative in offering new perspectives and widening our notions of ourselves? The theatre is the dream of life. Hippolyta, Queen of the Amazons and in many ways the essence of a sympathetic, feminine nature within the context of the play can see this:

> But all the story of the night told over,
> And all their minds transfigured so together,
> More witnesseth than fancy's images,
> And grows to something of great constancy;
> But howsoever, strange and admirable.[7]

'Constancy' has grown from the 'transfiguration' (this unusual term is surely not casually placed) in perspective afforded to the lovers by the dream-like events of the night. As one critic of the play puts it, '[t]he illusory has its part in the total experience of reality'.[8] With Theseus's telling admission that

> …as imagination bodies forth
> The forms of things unknown, the poet's pen
> Turns them to shapes, and gives to airy nothing
> A local habitation and a name… [9]

one is reminded of the essential point that, representing the imagination untethered to guideposts of consecutive reason, dreams offer endless possibilities to the 'poet's pen' or to the conception of (not just fantastical) literature itself. The psychologist H. J. Eysenck has remarked that 'the major part in dreams is played by visual images' and 'conceptual thought appears to be resolved into some from of plastic representation.[10]

This recalls both Ezra Pound's references - in a discussion of the ways in which language may be charged with meaning - to what is termed 'phanopoeia … which is a casting of images upon the visual imagination',[11] and Dryden's famous declaration that '[I]maging … is in itself the very height and life of poetry'.[12] The possibilities that the world of dreams presents to the poetic imagination is immediately apparent. Equally apparent, from even the most superficial of surveys of the varying attitude towards what might be called 'other-worldly' experience in the literary field, is the fact that, whilst logic and rationality have at times been posited dogmatically as the only objectively 'true' norm, there have also been other standpoints which have contradicted this opinion and have actively sought to promote the significance and wholesomeness of dreams and the life of the unconscious.

With this in mind, I propose now briefly to examine the attitude towards the imagination - and the relevance specifically afforded to dream experience in this quarter - displayed in the work of the Romantics. I believe that there are important ways in which Christina Rossetti's treatment of dreams and dreaming is specifically conditioned by her inheritance of Romantic values and, furthermore, by her desire to rework these modes of thought into a personalised manner of articulating other-worldly experience. Romantic thought is, both historically and ideologically speaking, crucially relevant to Rossetti's poetry, providing a context within which her treatment of dreams may be considered. It would be wrong, however, to assume that the legacy of literary and philosophical thought available as raw material to Rossetti is adopted idly. Like many Victorian poets, Rossetti is involved in a conscious rewriting of the radical shift in thought brought about by the Romantics in antagonism to the earlier stress on the principle of reason, and the neglect of what they were to elevate as the creative power of the imagination.

A note made by Coleridge on his voyage to Malta in 1804 is of interest here, questioning the value of the traditional distinction between dream and supposed actuality to the disparagement of the former:

> Poetry a rationalised dream dealing (? with) to manifold Forms (? of) our own Feelings, that never perhaps were attached by us consciously to our own personal Selves ... O there are Truths below the Surface in the subject of Sympathy, and how we become that which we understandly (sic) behold and hear, having, how much God perhaps only knows, created part even of the Form.[13]

This hypothesis involves an open recognition of what we might term the dream-like nature of the form and feeling of poetry, negotiating an important connection between the process of perception and the simultaneous assimilation (and/or production) of meaning where we 'become that which we... behold and hear'. Such a collapse into one another of spheres previously conceived of as separate areas requires us to admit that boundaries between the conscious and the unconscious are far from clearly defined. Poetic conception, the rationalisation of the dream, is held to be a partly unconscious function - 'below the Surface' - but these energies must then be modified and shaped by the conscious mind. As this *Notebooks* and *Biographia Literaria* show, Coleridge was profoundly interested in the psychology of dreams and dreaming, and frequently turned his attention to analysing the likely degrees of control that the conscious mind might have over these seemingly unconscious manifestations. One commentator notes that

> between the normal modes of mental activity and the passivity of dreaming there are various states in which the usual controls imposed by the will and the reason are relaxed in differing degrees, and to these Coleridge applied the term 'reverie'. It included not merely ordinary day-dreaming but ... opium reveries and nightmares as well.[14]

Consequently, it is fair to read *The Rime of the Ancient Mariner* - a work purportedly inspired by an actual dream of Coleridge's friend Cruikshank - as a piece possessing all the splendour and unrestricted fluency of a dream which is then, by means of an embedded narrative technique and traditional balladic presentation, subsequently submitted to the strictures and ordering principles lent by the operations of the conscious mind. The Latin epigraph to the poem, adapted by Coleridge from Thomas Burnet's *Archaelogiae Philosophecae* (1692) draws attention immediately to this facet of the work's strategy:

> Facile credo, plures esse Naturas invisibiles quam visibiles in rerum universitate ... Harum rerum notitiam semper ambivit ingenium humanum, nunquan attigit. Juvat, interea, non diffiteor, quandoque in animo, tanquam in tabula, majoris et melioris mundi

imaginem contemplari: ne mens assuefacta hodiernae
vitae minutiis se contrahat nimis, et tota subsidat in
pusillas cogitationes. Sed veritati interea invigilandum
est, modusque servandus, ut certa ab incertis, diem a
nocte, distinguamus.

[I readily believe that there are more invisible than
visible natures in the universe … The human mind
has always sought the knowledge of these things, but
never attained it. Meanwhile, I do not deny that it is
helpful sometimes to contemplate in the mind, as on a
tablet, the image of a greater and better world, lest the
intellect, habituated to the petty things of daily life,
narrow itself and sink wholly into trivial thoughts.
But at the same time we must be watchful for the
truth and keep a sense of proportion, so that we may
distinguish the certain from the uncertain, day from
the night.][15]

The concern is undoubtedly with the blending of conscious and
unconscious sides of the psyche (the Chinese philosopher and butterfly
as one), the fusion of the two levels in the service of poetic creation,
wherein poetry becomes indeed representative of a 'rationalised
dream'. Similarly in Coleridge's most famous 'opium reverie' poem,
'Kubla Khan', whose subtitle is 'A Vision in a Dream', the atmosphere
is that of a dream landscape renegotiated in the light of conscious
inventory and evaluation of its contents. 'Could I revive within me /
Her symphony and song, / To such a deep delight 'twould win me', [16]
muses the speaker of 'Kubla Khan', recalling the dream vision of the
'damsel with a dulcimer'. The poem thus retrospectively attempts to
distance the 'I' which now speaks from the inhabitant of the 'vision…
once I saw', an operation which appears far from straightforward
once one considers the questions which arise related to divisions
(conscious/unconscious and otherwise) within the articulate self at

other levels in the text. 'Kubla Khan' functions at several levels: it is, simultaneously, a statement about imagination and the creation of art, an erotic drama, and a political statement (echoing Coleridge's earlier poem 'The Fall of the Bastille', whilst the implications of the 'pleasure dome' are nearer to the great houses of Europe threatened by revolution - the 'underground' - and so, archetypally, Versailles). However, importantly, on another symbolic plane, the subject of this piece may be taken as being the (con)fusion of conscious/unconscious forces engaged in the act of creative activity, and it is the nature of this operation which the poem itself may by taken as imaging. The sinister 'caverns measureless to man' from which the 'sacred river' emerges to rush through Khan's 'gardens bright with sinuous rills' vividly propose the idea of the differing levels of creative energy involved in the dreamlike act of poetic production, and, moreover, the several levels of reality which become fused in this process, causing subject and object to collapse into one another, the outer world becoming the inner. Adair summarises this feature of Coleridge's artistic strategy which became symptomatic of the whole Romantic approach to poetry:

> The schism which science had made between subject and object, man's consciousness and the surrounding world, Coleridge struggled all his life to close, both in poetry and philosophy. But he only really succeeded in his greatest imaginative poems, and then only for a brief period. In *The Ancient Mariner* and 'Kubla Khan' the inner and outer world become one: the idea and the image are fused in the waking dream.[17]

Coleridge's substantial exploration of this aspect of poetic creation, in part influenced by the conception of the subconscious offered in German Romantic philosophy in general and Schelling in particular, strongly demands that the notion of symbolic imagery as fundamental to poetry be accepted without reservation. A new mythology is born, guaranteed not by the conventional and calculated employment of classical allusion, but rather stimulated by the realisation that the imagination's deepest subconscious patternings must be taken as archetypal, symbolic and thus 'mythopoeic' in character. Poetry was no longer to be regarded as mimetic of an external 'reality', where imagery fulfilled a constitutional rhetorical function, but, in its fusion of subject and object, its potential to disrupt so called certainties as to levels of consciousness and linked ability to reconcile opposites, the image becomes emblematic of truth newly created through art. The internal is made external and imagination finds itself elevated from the position of begrudged irresponsibility to the status of commanding spirit. The image - its authenticity arising from depths more profound than the simpler fields of memory, wit or fancy - may communicate more than the consciously intended meaning of the work or the writer, creating as it does a fresh reality of its own positioned beyond the areas of intelligibility conventionally divulged in utterance.

This idea is deftly conveyed in a sonnet of Christina Rossetti's written in the winter of 1856 entitled 'In an Artist's Studio' (*Poems*, III, 264): 'One face looks out from all his canvasses, / One selfsame figure sits or walks or leans: / We found her hidden just behind those screens'. Coincidentally and significantly addressing the notion of the male-monopolised construction of female identity in art (to be tackled, as we shall see, at length in *Monna Innominata*), this fascinating sonnet makes clear the notion that the medium by which the 'nameless girl' is translated into art upon the canvas cannot detract from the significance engineered by considerations beyond the superficial representative qualities of the painted image: that instant upon which intentionality seizes and thence decrees the pictorial nature of the image. All signs point to that which remains constant behind these 'screens':

A queen in opal or in ruby dress,
A nameless girl in freshest summer greens,
A saint, an angel; - every canvass means
The same one meaning, neither more nor less.

The varying external images are all devices by which the 'same one' essential concept is imparted, the constant object of inspiration which the artist 'feeds upon... by day and night' and which, in turn, may affect the artist in manifold ways, 'Fair as the moon and joyful as the light'. Just as different ways of seeing are involved in the totality of perception, the truth created by the fusion of the manifold images may appear as concealed or deliberately reflected, but remains the same elemental truth, represented by and yet ever beyond the image of itself which we are allowed to view: 'We found her hidden just behind those screens, / That mirror gave back all her loveliness'.

The mirror 'gave back' the 'loveliness' of the figure and, by verbal association, the subject of the paintings 'looks back' on the artist, becoming a mirror to reflect his being, enabling a construction to be made on the other side of actuality - 'Not as she is' - reflecting and externalising the non-rational impulses of the artist. Conclusively and crucially, turning the sonnet into much more than a study in artistic representationalism, the figure appears 'Not as she is, but as she fills his dream'.

The parallel proffered here in the Rossetti text between the mechanism of the artistic image and the symbolism of neurotic and unconscious fantasy, by extension dreams and dreaming, is an important allusion to the study made in this area by the Romantics, a study fuelling a great deal of the poetry of that period. Above all, this correlation should have us refer to one of Christina's favourite poets, Coleridge. The Romantic ideal was the resolution of all earthly antitheses: a fusion of subject and object fuelled by a belief in the continued existence of the past and the marvellous potential of its revival:

> They wanted to reflect in their poetry not the fixed splendour of God's eternity, but their own personal, confused apprehension, in the here and now, of a human timelessness. They took hold of the idea of eternity; but they removed it from its empyrean world

into their own. In brief, paradoxically, they brought
Eternity into Time.[18]

The positing of a collective, universal unconscious (later to be redefined
in the works of Jung and his followers) had occupied sections of
Coleridge's *Biographia Literaria*, making the soul into a treasure trove,
a centre the component parts of which could be reflected by external
images, and from which inassimilable source arises poetic creation.
The careful acknowledgement of these factors in the work of the
Romantics leads inevitably to a fundamental questioning of authority,
by Rossetti and used as a central motif in the poetic text, and in
particular in her treatment of dreams and dreaming. Andre Beguin
summarises the new awareness as follows:

> If anything distinguishes the Romantic from all his
> predecessors and makes him the true imitator of
> modern aesthetics, it is precisely that he is always
> highly conscious of the bonds that link him with
> the dark realm inside himself. The Romantic poet,
> knowing that he is not the sole author of his work,
> having found out that poetry is primarily a song risen
> from the abyss, tries deliberately and in complete
> lucidity to induce the mysterious voice to rise. It is
> not the source itself nor the method of his writing
> which is very different, for the act of poetic creation
> is in these respects fixed from all eternity; the only
> real difference lies in the poet's attitude to these laws
> of spiritual fecundity.[19]

The Romantic believes that, on one important level, everything is
centred upon the self, and yet a lack of confidence concerning the
stability and unity of the self continually nags at this faith. The
awareness that this internal matrix is reflected by poetry's outward
summoning wholly renegotiates the relation between perceiver and that

which is perceived, and the realm of other worldly, dream experience becomes a model upon which this representational dilemma may be played out. In *The Unmediated Vision*, Geoffrey Hartman declares that one of the functions of Wordsworth's poetics is unsuccessfully to locate a position where that 'kind of imperceptible cognition' which is the poetic imagination can be true both to itself and to the external world. Wordsworth fails to resolve this dichotomy, since 'although it can be argued that his final tendency is toward an imageless vision, he claims the necessity of the external world for this end'.[20] Momentum is felt in much Romantic verse toward that point where 'the statement of a relation' may exist 'in such immediate terms that no incitement to relational thinking remains'.[21] It is my belief that the analysis of dreams and dreaming contained in certain poems of Christina Rossetti forms a sustained re-interpretation of this condition.

II

Any literary text which revels in examining its own conception, motivations and status may wish to take advantage of the widened scope of reference and causality permitted by the investigation of dream and suchlike areas of experience. The work of the nineteenth-century thinker Sir Francis Galton (who introduced the principle of 'association' to psychology) and, of course, Sigmund Freud and Carl Gustav Jung, successfully applying scientific methods to the study of dreams, gradually made an interest in dreams 'intellectually respectable'.[22] Freud was highly aware of the manner in which dreams represented a 'transfiguration' of one code of reality into another, noting the following in *An Outline of Psychoanalysis*:

> Dreams, as everyone knows, may be confused, unintelligible, or positively nonsensical, what they say may contradict all that we know of reality, and we behave in them like insane people, since, so long as we are dreaming, we attribute objective reality to the contents of the dream. [23]

Or, as Coleridge put it: 'In ordinary dreams we do not judge the objects to be real; - we simply do not determine that they are unreal'.[24] The frame of meaning generated within a dream may indeed seem to 'contradict all that we know of reality', and yet be judged by that 'reality'. This idea is expressed in a very brief and very charming manner in a poem from Christina Rossetti's 1872 Sing-Song collection of children's verse:

> "I dreamt I caught a little owl
> And the bird was blue -"
>
> "But you may hunt for ever
> And not find such an one."
>
> "I dreamt I set a sunflower,
> And red as blood it grew -"
>
> "But such a sunflower never
> Bloomed beneath the sun."   (*Poems*, II, 45)

This little verse simultaneously unifies and separates imagination and 'reality'. But if this serves to remind us on waking that the 'reality' we might be tempted to hold up as the 'norm' is actually just one of many possible self-contained frames of reference, then it is a positive step. In 'An Old-World Thicket' (*Poems*, II, 123-8), with its Dantean epigram - 'Una selva oscura' [A dark forest] - and mysterious setting, Christina Rossetti transports us to a fantastical realm, disengaging our certainties by the hypnotic repetitions: 'Awake or sleeping (for I know not which) / I was or was not mazed within a wood... / (Asleep or waking, for I know not which)'. The poem's intriguing opening, whilst clearly echoing the final couplet of Keats's 'Ode to a Nightingale' - 'Was it a vision, or a waking dream? ... Do I wake or sleep?'[25] - distinctly recalls the moment, in Shakespeare's *A Midsummer Night's Dream* when the confused lovers emerge from the wood:

LYSANDER. I shall reply amazedly,
Half sleep, half waking. But as yet, I swear,
I cannot truly say how I came here…

DEMETRIUS. Are you sure
That we are awake? It seems to me
That yet we sleep, we dream.[26]

The pivotal point in Rossetti's poem, marking a shift in tone from awe and wonder to sharp anxiety, comes with the dreamer-speaker's realisation, contemplating a paradisal scenario of accentuated natural surroundings, that, to cite a phrase from another Rossetti poem, 'all that was but showed what all was not' (*Poems*, II, 125). In other words, the acceptance of one sphere of reality, with its own codes acceptable upon its own terms if not by the values we are accustomed to respect, simultaneously represents the admittance that more than one 'version' of reality is possible: 'Their meat was nought but flowers like butterflies, / With berries coral-coloured or like gold…'.

By comparing and contrasting the implications inscribed within these separate models of existence, the poet is able to move toward conclusions concerning the generation of modes of discourse and the hidden assumptions upon which they rely for their self-justification. Literature of dreams can illustrate to us, by means of the assertion of the complete substantiality of the 'other' or 'non-real' experience, the loopholes in what we might consider a watertight rationality. And if we can come to accept the declaration, forwarded by Breton in the *Manifestoes of Surrealism*, that dream as a mode of being may tell us as much about ourselves as 'real' life, then the possibilities for an investigation of the relative nature of reference and meaning are significantly increased.[27]

Sir Maurice Bowra, in his seminal work *The Romantic Imagination*, acknowledges of Christina Rossetti:

In her we see truly Romantic temperament, trained
to look for beauty in mysterious realms of experience,

> and able to find it without any strain or forcing of
> herself ... so great were her gifts for the interpretation
> of strange corners of life and fancy ... She was often
> enough content to withdraw into fancies and dreams
> and to find a full satisfaction in the world of her
> imagination.[28]

This 'temperament' provides the energetic inquisitiveness we will (in chapters to follow) see operating behind such generously uninhibited works of the imagination as *Goblin Market* and *The Prince's Progress*. Rossetti's excursions into the area of 'fancies and dreams' were never simply an escapist withdrawal, but rather a positive attempt to broaden the referential capacities of her poetry. Yet there is a constant fixation in her work with an attempt 'to see what the other world is really like'[29] which does not manifest so openly in the colourful dream-like narrations of the two works cited above, but functions on an altogether more subtle level. Of the eleven hundred poems of Christina Rossetti hitherto published, roughly ten per cent concern themselves, often wholly, with some kind of attitude towards dreams and dreaming (see Appendix). Sometimes, as in 'An Old-World Thicket' (*Poems*, II, 123-8), 'A Ballad of Boding' (*Poems*, II, 79-85) and 'My Dream' (*Poems*, I, 39-40), the actual substance of the other-worldly experience is set down, questioned, interpreted or simply left to speak for itself. But there are many more lyrics where it is not the substance, but rather the idea of the dream itself that is the subject at hand.

Charles Rycroft, in a study entitled *The Innocence Of Dreams*, notes that '[n]o dreams dreamt by Christ are recorded in the New Testament', and suggests that it is therefore 'tempting to correlate the lack of any record of Christ's dreams with the fact that dream interpretation plays no part in Christian religious theory or practice'.[30] Not surprisingly, one does detect a difference in approach to the topic of the dream in Christina Rossetti's outwardly devotional lyrics - where, indeed, dreams and dreaming do crop up less regularly than in the more secular pieces. (In fact, and significantly, there is no mention of dreams in any of the poetry Rossetti composed after 1866, about which period she began the production of predominantly exegetical devotional writing with which she closed her poetic career.) But it must be noted that the dichotomy of treatment is not at all as clear cut as might at first be expected, and the frequent usage by the poet of the notion of 'sleep' as euphemistically denoting death (a literary convention itself: one recalls the 'To be or not to be...' soliloquy in Shakespeare's *Hamlet*, and Keats's 'Sonnet to Sleep') further complicates matters.[31] Stressing the importance to her art of Christina Rossetti's evangelical background, Jerome McGann ambitiously unleashes the sweeping claim that the Adventist notion of 'soul sleep' is the 'single most important enabling principle' in Rossetti's verse.[32] Many of Rossetti's early poems do adopt the doctrine of soul sleep as a metaphorical starting point from which to examine the relative values of the profane and the divine, but the premillennialist motif is, again, just one strand in a complex intertextual approach, and to state, as does McGann, that 'no other idea contributed so much to the concrete and specific character' of Rossetti's writing is to miss the rich interweaving, the eclectic interrogation of inherited positions which characterises Rossetti's poetry.[33]

The two separate states, sleep and death, may be categorised together as manners of 'Rest' in traditionally Christian Salvationist terms. This is the proposition offered by the opening lines of an early poem, 'The Dream' (*Poems*, III, 104-5), directly recalling Hamlet's plaintive 'Rest, rest, perturbed spirit':[34]

> Rest, rest; the troubled breast
> Panteth evermore for rest:-
> Be it sleep, or be it death,
> Rest is all it coveteth.

The expected distinction between the two modes, the orthodox view of death as 'dreamless' sleep, is forthcoming in the devotional and secular poems. The pious verse, 'There Remaineth therefore a Rest for the People of God' (a very slight misquotation of Hebrews 4. 9, substituting 'for' for 'to') presents death as a 'blessed ... secret ... heavy dreamless sleep' (*Poems*, III, 216-7). 'Autumn', written in 1858, describes the death of a 'solitary swallow':

> One latest, solitary swallow flies
> Across the sea, rough autumn-tempest tossed,
> Poor bird, shall it be lost?
> Dropped down into this uncongenial sea,
> With no kind eyes
> To watch it while it dies,
> Unguessed, uncared for, free:
> Set free at last,
> The short pang past,
> In sleep, in death, in dreamless sleep locked fast.
> (*Poems*, I, 143-5)

This final line is poignantly, though probably unwittingly recalled in what is generally reckoned to be the last poem Christina Rossetti wrote before her own death, the beautifully resigned 'Sleeping at Last' (the title is William Michael's, not Christina's), which pictures the lost one within her grave beneath the 'purple thyme and the purple clover': 'No more a tired heart downcast or overcast, / No more pangs that wring or shifting fears that hover, / Sleeping at last in a dreamless sleep locked fast' (*Poems*, III, 339-40). But Rossetti, characteristically, is not content idly to adopt this one conventional system of articulation as an ultimate certitude. From the perspective of this single frame of reference death may well be metaphorically imaged as 'dreamless sleep', but this proposition is not casually accepted. 'Days of Vanity' (*Poems*, I, 192-3), and here we recall the Chinese Emperor of Stoppard's play, performs the inversion: 'A dream that waketh ... Such is life that dieth'.

Here one detects the Platonic view ('Among very great authors, none ... seemed to appeal to her more than Plato' (*Works*, lxx)) of

life on earth as a mere pale reflection of the higher from of existence
to be enjoyed hereafter. This attitude is wholly compatible with a
Christian standpoint, of course, and yet the vital ambivalence in
the symbolic possibilities offered - death as 'sleeping' yet also as
resurrective 'waking' - becomes an invaluable point of release for the
poet investigating the relative nature of ways of allocating meaning.
To envision death as 'in a dreamless sleep locked fast' forces external
description to be a terminus - imaginative potential dies along with
the sleeper's unpermitted vision. The tension aroused by this dilemma
operates at a latent level in 'Life and Death' (*Poems*, I, 155), both of
whose stanzas open in rather too prosaically dogmatic a manner, as
if the speaker is vainly trying to convince us of the validity of these
simply voiced (all but one word are monosyllables) maxims:

> Life is not sweet. One day it will be sweet
> To shut our eyes and die …
> Life is not good. One day it will be good
> To die, then live again;
> To sleep meanwhile …

All is not well here. Within the matrix of meaning generated by the
poem as a semantic device there resides a contradiction, which the
contents of the verse fail to resolve. 'Life' is defined as 'not sweet' and 'not
good' - two negative instances - and thus it 'will be sweet / To … die'.
This is fine, but if '[L]ife is not good' then to state that 'it will be good /
To … live again' (invoking a characteristic New Testament paradox)
represents, within the framework of meaning constructed by the terms
of the poem, a glaring non sequitur. Matters are not assisted and little
comfort is offered by the fact that the rest of the poem consists (bar
the final couplet) of a repeated chain of negative constructions 'Nor …
Nor … Nor' - hence associated grammatically with 'Life' which was
guaranteed as a negative essence - each one a luxuriant descriptive image
of those aspects of life which will be forsaken in death. The 'flitting
butterfly … happy lark that soars sky-high … the waxing wheat … Rich

ranks of golden grain' - all these natural images are linked grammatically and essentially with 'Life'. The 'sleep meanwhile' of death represents a renunciation of all these elements. Standing as pictures of abundance, the natural vignettes are surely desirable and so it truly would 'be good / To ... live again'. But in this case the assertions that 'Life is not sweet ... not good' become contradictory to the strategy that the rest of the work follows. After the invocation to 'sleep meanwhile' the second stanza begins to deal not with the absence of plenitude, but more so with the absence of absence; in sleep we will 'not ... feel'

> the wane
> Of shrunk leaves dropping in the wood...

> ... Nor mark the blackened bean-fields,
>   nor where stood
> Rich ranks of golden grain,
> Only dead refuse stubble clothe the plain...

On more than one level, the poem (originally titled 'An Escape') does not seem able to make up its own mind where its emphasis ought to lie. From the relinquished fecundity of the first stanza we move to the scarcity of the second. Both presence and absence will become absent in sleep, and the usage of the word 'dead' in 'dead refuse stubble' only adds to the confusion. The tension between opposing forces implied in the poem's title 'Life and Death' is rapidly superseded by the energy created by the text's endeavours to challenge its own premises. By the time the final line of the poem is reached, the reader's feeling is one of unease with the overall philosophy of the piece. In hindsight, the glib opening statement, 'Life is not sweet', rings hollow since the events, semantically and grammatically, of the poem have destroyed all certainty as to the truth of the work's initial premise. We would like to 'live again' since we have been convinced that to 'die' would leave us asleep to the things that are good in life. The final line strikes, then, an ambiguous note:

where stood
Rich ranks of golden grain,
Only dead refuse stubble clothe the plain:
Asleep from risk, asleep from pain.

'Risk', the potential for ambivalence of result as opposed to direct
certitude, and 'pain' as opposed to harmonious complacency and
pleasure, are elements we find consistently motivating the poetry of
Christina Rossetti. The similarity to Keats here is, again, striking:
specifically rekindled are the sentiments of 'La Belle Dame sans
Merci' in which some commentators have, rightly, located the implicit
importance of risk and pain in a world which is a 'vale of soulmaking'.[35]
Forever striving to illustrate the relativity of meaning and referentiality,
Rossetti's verse continually moves towards areas of 'risk' and 'pain'
in its attempts to examine, and often deconstruct and even blow
asunder, its own strategies and methods of construction. When we
shift attention to a detailed examination of the *Monna Innominata*
sonnet cycle (*Poems*, II, 86-93) we shall witness the quintessence of
this drive. Where Rossetti's attitude to traditional notions of dream,
sleep and death is concerned, the eye for dualities is ever alert: 'I must
unlearn the pleasant ways I went, / Must learn another' (*Poems*, III,
207). Thus the speaker of 'A Discovery', and in the same way the
Rossetti text repeatedly seeks to 'unlearn' the inscribed presuppositions
it relies upon for its (at least literal) integrity. A poem mentioned earlier,
'The Dream' (*Poems*, III, 104-5), - whose main theme, like 'A Ballad
of Boding' (*Poems*, II, 79-85), is 'that which is not … but seems!' -
makes clear the yearning to demonstrate the sub-textual implications
manifest in what is, seemingly, an inoffensive discussion of the nature
of dreams:

Tell me, dost thou remember the old time
We sat together by that sunny stream,
And dreamed our happiness was too sublime
Only to be a dream?

At a central point in this poem, and making a shift in tone, comes a revelation: 'now that thou art gone'. Thus (as is the case in *Monna Innominata*) it is clear that the speaker is addressing an absence. In the idyllic and temporally non-specific setting afforded by the second stanza (above), the speaker recalls proving that something could not simply be 'a dream' by dreaming of that very something. The attempt is to dream something into reality, and this is in effect achieved by the realisation, in a dream, that the 'happiness' must be more than a dream itself. Thus dreams are relegated, on a Platonic type of hierarchy leading to ultimate truth, to a level below that of the reality of the situation in which the speaker and addressee are conceived of as being. And yet it is by means of a dream that the speaker is able to gain this insight. 'Maiden May' (*Poems*, II, 98-101) being as a simple ballad, as pretty as the 'bower' in which May sits:

> Maiden May sat in her bower,
> In her blush rose bower in flower,
> Sweet of scent;
> Sat and dreamed away an hour,
> Half content, half uncontent.

But the dream that May is permitted becomes the key to all sorts of knowledge and revelation, as she contemplates nature and the universe, we would scarcely think possible judging by the poem's humble opening:

> Wherefore greatest? Wherefore least?
> Hearts that starve and hearts that feast?
> You and I?
> Stammering Oracles have ceased,
> And the whole world stands at "why?"

This poem dramatically illustrates the possibility that 'dream' may be able to unfold new and unexpected perspectives upon that which we might otherwise ignore or take for granted. This, in turn, is a sharp reminder of the relativity of frames of reference, a theme in which we detect a purpose running through too many of Christina Rossetti's works for it to be random.

Another prominent theme in Rossetti's poetry is the investigation, literally and symbolically, of the inner processes leading up to and constituting the creative function in the artist. How might the attention to dreams relate to this other concern? The following passage comes from Charles Darwin's *The Descent of Man*, published during Christina Rossetti's lifetime in 1871:

> The Imagination is one of the highest prerogatives of man. By this faculty he unites former images and ideas, independently of the will, and thus creates brilliant and novel results … Dreaming gives us the best notion of this power; as Jean Paul (Richter) … says, 'The dream is an involuntary kind of poetry'.[36]

Bearing this Coleridgean idea of Darwin's (similarly arrived at via German thought) in mind, we may now move to an assessment of Christina Rossetti's use of the notion of the dream and how this is interwoven with another of the major concerns of her work, the inquiry into the machinations of the creative psyche.

The 1857 poem 'Fata Morgana' (*Poems*, I, 49-50) conveys the speaker's sense of despair at compulsively and forever pursuing the elusive, shape-changing Fata Morgana, a figure from mythology traditionally associated with healing, magic and fertility but also with the more threatening and sinister person of Morgan le Fay, ominous, elusive sister to the king in Arthurian myth, repeated in Tennyson's *Idylls*.

> A blue-eyed phantom far before
> Is laughing, leaping toward the sun:
> Like lead I chase it evermore,
> I pant and run.

In Christina Rossetti's poem it quickly becomes clear that the 'blue-eyed phantom' may be regarded as a symbol of the speaker's imaginative self, the poet's spirit (in both senses of the term) of creativity. Further to facilitate and substantially reinforce this identification the fleeing vision is directly - and this is as much Rossetti's own invention as an idea inherited with the Morgana myth - associated with 'singing' and 'song' in the poem's second stanza:

> It breaks the sunlight bound on bound:
> Goes singing as it leaps along
> To sheep-bells with a dreamy sound
> A dreamy song.

On one important level, the poem becomes a self-reflexive testimony to the poet's search and desire for inspiration, with the sought after creative energy crystallised into the vibrant and vivid image of the attractive phantom. The potential for artistic endeavour offered by the Fata Morgana muse - the 'song', which is sung - is twice described as being 'dreamy' and the use of this adjective is not simply casual.

The moment of poetic fruition, and artistic creation in general, is a subject frequently investigated by Christina Rossetti's verse at literal, or more often (as here) at symbolic level. It is a topic which, like dreams themselves, does not lend itself to empirical, scientific categorisation; of the hazy, twilight realm of experience, the creative process lends itself well to expression, metaphorically, in images of 'dreamy' connotation. One recalls H. J. Eysenck's statement, cited earlier, that 'the major part in dreams is played by visual images, and ... conceptual thought appears to be resolved into some from of plastic representation'.[37] Thus the dream itself my be taken as not unlike poetry in its conception and articulation. The peculiar sense of privacy which surround dream as experience, the mystery therein, and the impossibility of paraphrasing without distorting the dream vision provide further relationships with the creative, artistic function. In Christina Rossetti's poem, the experience of chasing the source of inspiration, the Fata Morgana, indeed becomes, in the third and final stanza, an address made by the speaker to his/her own self.

> I laugh, it is so brisk and gay;
> It is so far before, I weep:
> I hope I shall lie down some day,
> Lie down and sleep.

Consciousness of the self here, as in so many of Rossetti's lyrics, marks the simultaneous confession - implicit, as we have seen in certain Romantic texts - that the self is in a state of division. The ambiguous state is splendidly conveyed by both the structure and import of the first two lines of this stanza. 'I laugh … I weep' - the two opposing ideas, two versions of the 'I' pronoun the fractured state of the speaker at differing moments in time, are indeed split apart in the syntax of the lines. And that which causes the plausibility of, and calls attention (metaphorically and syntactically) to this dichotomy is the image of the 'blue-eyed phantom' - 'it is so brisk and gay; / It is so far before'. Confronted by this knowledge of the division in the self revealed by attention to the poetic muse, the speaker brings the poem to a fairly inconclusive close by voicing the desire to 'Lie down and sleep'. Such a climax reveals a desire perhaps to relinquish the pursuit of inspiration (giving finality to this single text), and yet also to enter the domain of dreams to seek new instructive visions. The whole poem might be described as dream-like in its avoidance of external reference, its visionary quality and close concern with the speaker's wish to 'sleep' affords a degree of circularity to its import; the speaker sleeps to dream anew, the text begins itself again and will never achieve finality except in the final dreamless 'sleep' of death. In a thematically similar sonnet of 1849, 'Two Pursuits' (*Poems*, III, 176), textual continuity rather than finality is overtly the concern of the poetry. The speaker interacts with two separate muses within the same work.

The sonnet begins: 'A voice said: "Follow, follow:" and I rose / followed far into the dreamy night'. The speaker goes in impassioned

pursuit of this vague image of the creative aspect of the self in the
same way that the speaker chased the Fata Morgana in the poem of
that name. But it rapidly becomes apparent that this first muse is a less
than fruitful source of poetic inspiration:

> It led me where the bluest water flows,
> And would not let me drink …
> It left me, wearied out with many woes.
> Some time I sat as one bereft of sense:

The potential creative energy of the first 'voice', which gave urgency
and substance to the initial section of the poem, has been exhausted.
In its ambivalent presentation, the muse of 'Two Pursuits' at this stage
is akin in effect to the powerful and enigmatic figure of Moneta in
Keats' *The Fall of Hyperion: A Dream* - the 'tall shade veil'd in drooping
white' - who instructs the dreaming speaker:

> Thou art a dreaming thing;
> A fever of thyself - think of the earth;
> What bliss even in hope is there for thee?
> What haven?[38]

In 'Two Pursuits', as in *The Fall of Hyperion*, the poetry finds itself in
a state identical to that of its speaker - 'bereft of sense'. A new impulse
is required to resuscitate the energy of the poetry: 'But soon another
voice from very far / Called: "Follow, follow:" and I rose again'. The
speaker (thus the lyric) begins again, its continuity guaranteed by the
presence of this newfound inspirational energy which the speaker
assures us, 'will not leave me till I shall go hence'.

'Echo' (*Poems*, I, 46), another deceptively simple poem, also clearly
alludes to the association between the creative act and the world of
dreams. The literal allusion is to the legend of Echo, who fell in love
with Narcissus only to pine away with her lack of success in coping
with his giant ego, till she had nothing left but a voice. On one level,

then, the piece would seem to ask to be interpreted as a love lyric whose speaker yearns for the company of a lover who is no longer present. In this respect, the poem is typical of Rossetti. The vocabulary used is characteristically simple, and yet the poem's elusive, vague qualities do, I think, counter the plausibility of the straightforward biographically determined interpretation, which some critics have preferred. Packer believes the verse to be addressed to William Bell Scott who - and this is only the most superficial of objections - can hardly have been said to have had 'soft rounded cheeks' (he had a prominent beard) and even 'bright' eyes, judging from portraits of Scott, seems a little optimistic.[39] A much more fruitful reading of 'Echo' may be produced if, akin to 'Fata Morgana' and yet from a different perspective, it is regarded, with all its subtle allusions, as a symbolically articulated invocation to the poetic muse.

> Come to me in the silence of the night;
> Come in the speaking silence of a dream;
> Come with soft rounded cheeks and eyes as bright
> As sunlight on a stream;
> Come back in tears,
> O memory, hope, love of finished years.

This forms a summons to the energies within the unconscious self - to 'memory, hope, love', those functions defying empirical measurement, to return 'in tears', coupled then with the emotional, feeling function of the inner self. The sense here is somewhat akin to that voiced by Wordsworth's maxim in his 'Preface' to the *Lyrical Ballads* that poetry 'takes its origin from emotion recollected in tranquillity'.[40] But the Rossetti text beckons further to inspirational energies, which are imaged in the form of a vogue, childlike (perhaps angelic) figure afforded no name, gender, nor external history. Like the 'Fata Morgana' muse-figure (and Keats' Moneta), the essence at the heart of 'Echo' is associated with 'sunlight', the light of positive, generative energy, and in a draft stanza of the poem included in the notebook manuscript in the Bodleian Library but omitted from the published version, the muse in 'Echo' is directly associated with utterance and articulation (as the Fata Morgana instilled 'song' into the verse): 'Come with the voice whose musical low tone / My heart still hears tho' I must hear no more: / Come to me in my weakness left alone' (*Poems*, I, 247). In the same manuscript version, the speaker's 'soul' is compared to 'a tired bird at close of day' whilst the addressee is conceived of as being an 'oasis' and 'Dearer than daylight'. It is clear that the speaker (thus the lyric itself) is frightened of being exhausted of song - then, as in the case of Echo, reduced by love to nothing but a voice, she would be nothing, not even having song. Consequently, the poet sends these words to the elusive - like an 'oasis' - source of poetic inspiration. From the point of view of one lacking in inspiration, the poem narrates a symbolic tale of what it is to have inspiration come to the self. The muse is imaged as absent and so the words of the poem become (in fact the poem itself becomes) talisman to the presence of creative energy. With a smart circularity reflected in the lyric's deliberately enigmatic title, 'Echo' (which enhances the verse even assuming no knowledge of the Echo myth), the poem becomes a monument to its own conception, a shrine to the unconscious motivations that it attempts dramatically to portray. Again, the inspirational impulse is closely associated with the realm of dreams. 'Come in the speaking silence of a dream', beckons the speaker: this emphasises the potential for articulation inherent in an alternative version of reality, the new frame of reference afforded by consultation of the dream experience, forbidden by the constraints of the rationality our waking life teaches us to honour.

The dream sphere represents a world of instinctive (thus unconscious) rather than conditioned (conscious) response. Coleridge recognised this important fact: 'The language of the Dream/Night is contrary to that of Waking/the day. It is a language of Images and Sensations, the various dialects of which are far less Day-Languages of Nations'.[41] With this fundamental notion in mind, the second stanza of 'Echo' moves on to offer an image of the 'bitter sweet' dream itself:

Oh dream how sweet, too sweet, too bitter sweet,
Whose wakening should have been in Paradise,
Where souls brimful of love abide and meet;
Where thirsting longing eyes
Watch the slow door
That opening, letting in, lets out no more.

This very concentrated passage expresses at once the desire and despair of the speaker, looking to the 'speaking silence' of the dream sphere for a harmonious union with the energy of inspiration addressed in the first stanza. The same effect may be found in the third sonnet of the *Monna Innominata* cycle (*Poems*, II, 86-93), which begins: 'I dream of you to wake: would that I might / Dream of you and not wake but slumber on; / Nor find with dreams the dear companion gone'. The speaker longs to remain in the realm of 'happy dreams' since the radiant presence of the soul-mate there 'makes day of night': 'Thus only in a dream are we at one'.

Like the speaker of 'Echo', the 'Unnamed Lady' who provides the voice in the *Monna Innominata* sequence craves unity from her currently divided state. Again, this symbolic conjunction with the inspirational energy offered by the absent muse, may be found in the non-empirical world of the dream. But the qualifying tone of 'only in a dream' suggests that the harmonious state offered by the dream sphere is by no means an absolutely stable position, since the process of waking will ultimately render the unity a fleeting image and return the speaker to a state of division. 'I dream of you to wake' is the crucial admission made in the *Monna Innominata* sonnet, illustrating the Rossetti text's maintenance of notions of relativity in this investigation of the relationship between dreams and the creative act. The waking of the speaker is necessary if the contents of the dream are to be interpreted adequately and fully. Thus the speaker of *Monna Innominata* begs to 'slumber on', but cannot, and in describing the dream process sets herself outside it, finding the unity therein envisioned to be only a transient image, 'the dear companion gone'.

Faced with the prospect that 'only in a dream we are at one' the disheartened sonnet speaker comes to a despairing conclusion, and one which contradicts the notion of death-as-dreamless-sleep which we encountered earlier (although even there it was challenged rather than passively accepted): 'If thus to sleep is sweeter than to wake, / To die were surely sweeter than to live, / Tho' there be nothing new beneath the sun'. Presented with the notion of the 'bitter sweet' nature of dreams - offering harmony, which from an alternative perspective may not be so attractive - the speaker of 'Echo' seemingly accepts a compromise. Dreams at least offer some salvation (only escapist in the sense that it is an escape into creativity), some vital opportunity for union with the spirit of inspiration, no matter how controversial this might appear in hindsight: 'Yet come to me in dreams, that I may live / My very life again tho' cold in death'.

The 'speaking silence of a dream' may bring the possibility of utterance to that which had hitherto been considered unutterable, new 'life' to that which had been thought 'cold in death'. 'In dreams' the speaker (and hence the lyric) may be instilled with new pulse, new breath; the premises of the 'bitter sweet' dream world are nevertheless accepted and the poem ends with implied communion between speaker and muse. The lyric has written itself.

> Come back to me in dreams, that I may give
> Pulse for pulse, breath for breath:
> Speak low, lean low,
> As long ago, my love, how long ago.

One might almost say that 'Echo' ends upon a note of satisfaction - a poem has written itself around the notion that no inspiration was at hand. A foreshadowing of Ted Hughes' 'The Thought Fox', or Seamus Heaney's 'Digging', perhaps? But Rossetti, as we have noted, is always concerned with exploring all sides of an argument. 'Fata Morgana' demonstrated that the acceptance of poetic inspiration in terms of a frame of reference constructed around notions of 'dreaming' necessarily involved the admittance that the self was split, that there were differing levels of being. 'Echo' dramatises the acceptance of the dream realm as a feasible alternative to everything else we have, since the possibilities offered there are better than 'silence' even if they be a dislocated version of our waking 'truths'. Silence to 'Echo' (the mythical figure and the poem) would be non-existence, since a voice is all she has - fitting the idea of the eternal for the poet being his/her power to sing as expressed by Keats' mortal nightingale/super-poet and its immutable song, and Yeats' golden bird of Byzantium that can only sing eternal songs to the dying, mortal world.

In direct contrast to the relieved acceptance of 'Echo', the appropriately titled 'Mirage' (*Poems*, I, 55-6), composed in June 1860, conveys a sceptical and saddened view of the entry into the world of the dream in the search for inspiration.

> The hope I dreamed of was a dream,
> Was but a dream; and now I wake
> Exceeding comfortless, and worn, and old,
> For a dream's sake.

Here is none of the bold persistence displayed in 'Echo', and the speaker's words are afforded added import by virtue of the fact of his/her speaking in hindsight. The pursuit of an empty dream has left only a sense of bitterness, and the poem's mid-section marks a relinquishment of the title and aspirations of poet on the part of the speaker:

> I hang my harp upon a tree,
> A weeping willow in a lake;
> I hang my silenced harp there, wrung and snapt
> For a dream's sake.

Yet the rhythm and repetition within the third and final stanza's opening couplet, which forces the verse relentlessly on, seem to go against the desire of the speaker to establish a state of inertia with a 'still' and 'silent heart'. With a much fiercer sense of irony than that subtly placed in the drama of 'Echo' here is a poem writing itself about the rejection of inspiration. It forms another perspective onto the same issue, imbued with the resentment that the pursuit of a dream sphere of reference has brought about the coincident revelation that the speaker's self is divided: 'Mirage' soberly and astutely puts forward the argument, needed alongside all the other notions concerning these models of reality, that dreams may leave us just as 'comfortless' as the waking world from which we sometimes seek to escape. Yet the whole tone of the poem, reinforced by the repeated line that closed each stanza, stresses just how powerful a concept in the speaker's mind the notion of the dream has become. In however unsavoury a manner, the dream has provided the poet with inspiration and the poem is testimony to this: 'Life, and the world, and mine own self, are changed / For a dream's sake'.

Rossetti's description of the dream as a 'speaking silence' - donating the possibility of utterance to that hitherto unsaid - is perhaps at the heart of her concern with dreams as a poet. Forever exploring new frames of reference with which to express or challenge ideas of poetic creativity, investigating areas of 'other-worldly' experience, the world of the dream is a prime sector for consideration. When silence can speak, new possibilities open up, what was thought dead may live again, meaning explodes. The speaker of that fascinating poem, 'The Convent Threshold' (*Poems*, I, 61-5), after interpreting two fantastical dreams which she has experienced, remarks on the potential of the hidden meaning of dreams, their 'speaking silence':

> For all night long I dreamed of you:
> I woke and prayed against my will,
> Then slept to dream of you again.
> At length I rose and knelt and prayed:
> I cannot write the words I said,
> My words were slow, my tears were few;

But thro' the dark my silence spoke
Like thunder.

It is clear then that dreams are regarded with great respect in the
poetry of Christina Rossetti. They offer new ways of interpreting the
world, and thus new manners of utterance. The treatment of dreams
in the poetry is by no means a settled constant: on the contrary, it is a
shifting perspective itself which is always alert to, and stressful of the
relativity of ideas. This notion of relativity is neatly conveyed in the
overt attempt to narrate a dream vision that makes up the 1855 piece
'My Dream' (*Poems*, I, 39-40). Christina Rossetti herself writes in
the margin of an 1875 edition of her poems that the episode was 'not
a real dream' (*Works*, 479) and, indeed, this heavily symbolic poem
has baffled many critics, who, like William Michael Rossetti, have
been forced to conclude: 'As it was not a real dream, and she chose
nevertheless to give it verbal form, one seeks for a meaning in it, and I
for one cannot find any that bears development' (*Works*, 479).

On one level the poem tells of a dream wherein the speaker finds
him/herself standing 'beside Euphrates while it swelled'. The river
begins to change hue and then suddenly from it come a 'crew' of infant
crocodiles, rapidly increasing in stature, each wearing 'massive gold /
And polished stones'. One regally attired crocodile grows larger than
the rest, assumes dominance over the lesser creatures and manifests
this newfound superiority by eating every single one of his fellow
crocodiles in sight. The cannibalistic reptile then sleeps, dwindling 'to
the common size' as he does so. A ship appears, sailing down the river,
waking the crocodile who, at the sight of the 'winged vessel' repents,
'shed appropriate tears and wrung his hands'.

'What can it mean?' asks the speaker. Packer, of course, concludes
that the majestic and gargantuan crocodile represents William Bell
Scott - he so lately of the 'soft rounded cheeks' - and sees the poem as
a desire for some sort of domination on Christina Rossetti's part.[42] It
is certainly a feat of the imagination of a league with the fantastical
scenario of *Goblin Market* ('My Dream', not Packer's interpretation,

although that too is fantastical), and no sources of its narrative are known. William Michael Rossetti rightly praises the visionary qualities of the work:

> If anything were needed to show the exceptional turn of mind of Christina Rossetti - the odd freakishness which flecked the extreme and almost excessive seriousness of her thought - the present poem might serve for the purpose. It looks like the narration of a true dream; and nothing seems as if it could account for so eccentric a train of notions except that she in fact dreamed them. And yet she did not... (*Works*, 479)

We know from the *Rossetti Papers* that the poem was more than likely inspired by 'a drawing of various crocodiles ... by the French artist Ernest Griset'.[43] It is framed as a dream vision by the introductory and concluding (but never conclusive) comments of the speaker, opening in enigmatic fashion: 'Hear now a curious dream I dreamed last night, / Each word whereof is weighed and sifted truth'. A seemingly calculated and empirical sentiment resides here, eager to assert the 'truth' of that which follows, though it is admittedly 'curious' and a 'dream'. The incidents recorded are later described as 'facts'. Far from being randomly generated (which we might expect from a dream narrative), the images which follow are 'weighed and sifted', carefully chosen and arranged, the means to an end: 'I stood beside Euphrates while it swelled / Like overflowing Jordan in its youth: / It waxed and coloured sensibly to sight'. The Nile of Shakespeare's *Antony and Cleopatra*, in particular the discussion of fertility and crocodiles aboard Pompey's galley which Christina would have known in her 'deep ... supreme' reverence for the bard (*Works* lxx), seems influential here.

> ANTONY. The higher Nilus swells,
> The more it promises; as it ebbs, the seedsman
> Upon the slime and ooze scatters his grain,

And shortly comes to harvest.

LEPIDUS. Y' have strange serpents there.

ANTONY. Ay, Lepidus.

LEPIDUS. Your serpent of Egypt is bred now of your mud by the operation of your sun: so is your crocodile ... What manner o' thing is your crocodile?

ANTONY. It is shaped, sir, like itself, and it is as broad as it hath breadth; it is just so high as it is, and moves with it [sic] own organs. It lives by that which nourisheth it, and the elements once out of it, it transmigrates.

LEPIDUS. What colour is it of?

ANTONY: Of its own colour too.

LEPIDUS. 'Tis a strange serpent.

ANTONY. 'Tis so; and the tears of it are wet.[44]

'Humour, in its inner essence, she could enter into', William Michael reveals of his sister's 'intellectual' appreciation of Shakespeare (*Works*, lxx). The above passage would no doubt have appealed to Christina. Indeed, its gently mocking tone itself is similar to that end-framing 'My Dream', as the speaker enigmatically refrains from disclosing the 'meaning' of her narrative.

The river of Rossetti's poem, imaged in terms of another river 'in its youth', becomes the archetypal river of life: described in terms of actual physical response, 'sensibly to sight', it may represent the ongoing stream of conscious experience. The reptilian (dragon, serpent) is a recurrent image of fear of the primeval, with which we need to come to terms, thus an object of both fear and wonder: 'Till out of myriad pregnant waves there welled / Young crocodiles, a gaunt blunt-featured crew, / Fresh-hatched perhaps and daubed with birthday dew'. From the depths of the flowing representation of consciousness is born the 'blunt-featured' mass of strange creatures; these present a suitably imposing image of the unconscious function, within and yet encroaching beyond the consciousness. The 'Young crocodiles' represent the birth of a dream.

The speaker is indeed dreaming 'a curious dream' since the events narrated symbolically enact the workings of the dream process itself. The crocodiles are 'girt with massive gold' and there are many of them, marking the grains of embroidered narrative, largely incoherent (newly born) to begin with which initiate the dream experience. And then comes the macabre vision of the kingly reptile devouring his kin, an aptly bizarre dream-image, the logic of which, like the crocodile 'knew no law, … feared no binding law': 'He battened on them, crunched, and sucked them in… / ground them with inexorable jaw: / The luscious fat distilled upon his chin'. At one level of interpretation, this episode marks the symbolic portrayal of the most fiercely motivated part of the unconscious self gaining dominance over, and assimilating the potential of all other unconscious impulses. The dream gradually achieves a dominant theme (a theme, rather than a narrative's 'binding law') and the struggle relaxes, the lord and master crocodile sleeps.

This is where the poem shifts in tone and emphasis, alerting us to the fact that a new point is to be made, and this point would appear to have to do with the relativity of experience. The crocodile, who has represented the dream in symbolic terms thus far, himself sleeps and experiences a manner of dream visitation:

> In sleep he dwindled to the common size,
> And all the empire faded from his coat.
> Then from far off a winged vessel came…
> …white it was as an avenging ghost.

The other-worldly appearance of this 'avenging ghost', sailing down the river of consciousness may be taken as a new dream metaphor, suitably different in connotation to the crocodile symbol, arriving to lend a new perspective to the symbolic presentation recently established: 'It levelled strong Euphrates in its course; ... seemed to tame the waters without force'.

This new apparition brings calm to the conscious part of the self, undoubtedly troubled by the recent symbolic occurrences, and, just as notably, allows the dream image, the crocodile, to be viewed from a new vantage point:

> The prudent crocodile rose on his feet
> And shed appropriate tears and wrung his hands.
>
> What can it mean? you ask. I answer not
> For meaning, but myself must echo, What?
> And tell it as I saw it on the spot.

The poem tells, not, in the words of Henry James, 'in any literal vulgar way' but on a subtle symbolic register.[45] Concerned with the relativity of meanings as much as with meaning itself - 'I answer not / For meaning', disclaims the speaker - 'My Dream' is an example of Rossetti's writing presenting in vivid images that which elsewhere its strategies constantly relate.

I have aimed to show, thus far, that the early, and best, poetry of Christina Rossetti is involved in a constant, post-Romantic debate with itself as to the non-fixity of meaning and identity as expressed in poetic language. Rossetti's best known, and most admired piece, *Goblin Market*, casts notions of sexuality and innocence into the ongoing equation. By doing so, the poetry takes up and extends the concerns I have already located in the Rossetti text, putting them to the further service of exposing the iniquity towards women of traditional poetic expression.

4

SUGAR-BAITED WORDS: MODES OF TEMPTATION IN *GOBLIN MARKET*

With its iterated jingle
Of sugar-baited words...
Christina Rossetti, *Goblin Market*

Although *Goblin Market* was not specifically intended for children, it is, on one level, a 'fairy tale'.[1] Rossetti's production of a mature work of child-like fantasy, her direction of fairy lore toward the adult reader, itself indicates a desire to re-address and hence re-assess a literary tradition. It also tells us something of a (former) role of the fairy tale which Rossetti's imagination attempts to resurrect. Von Franz speaks of this function:

> Until about the seventeenth century, it was the adult population that was interested in fairy tales. Their allocation to the nursery is a later development, which probably has to do with the rejection of the irrational, and the development of the rational, outlook - so that they came to be regarded as nonsense and old wives' tales and good enough for children.[2]

But the dominant ideology that had condemned fairy stories to imprisonment in the nursery (only allowing them probation in the company of 'old wives', females dealing in 'nonsense') was forged upon male subjectivity. Writing as a woman, Rossetti constructs an adult fairy tale in order to expose the partiality of the judgement outlined by von Franz, and re-establish the potential for articulation of experience still alive within a form of writing held by men to be irrational nonsense, fit only for infants and women, an inferior code.

Goblin Market opens with a description of the perpetually passive listening process 'maids' must perform when faced with male (goblin) directives. There is no choice:

> Morning and evening
> Maids heard the goblins cry...
> Evening by evening
> Among the brookside rushes,
> Laura bowed her head to hear,
> Lizzie veiled her blushes...

This passive hearing act is a submissive, embarrassing - one feels, almost degrading - affair, a retreat from activity or natural expression. The goblin men are singers of song - troubadour poets of a sort - whose rhyming (literally) expresses a desire to hold women captive. The sisters, in the poem's first seduction, have been tempted into craving such subjugation. But by the end of the poem the girls' situation has changed. The 'pleasant days' of innocence may be 'long gone' but the time of their hardship at the hands of 'little men' is 'not-returning time' and, in the presence of 'children of their own' indicative of an ongoing harmony, woman's right to self-expression has been reclaimed - the girls become the owners of their (his)story - in an image recalling the oral tradition of storytelling:

> Laura would call the little ones
> And tell them of her early prime,
> Those pleasant days long gone
> Of not-returning time...

This redirection of emphasis, I want to show, is achieved not through aggressive reversal of male-oriented ideology (which would be as sinister and subversive as that it attempted to counter) but through a clever interweaving of textual strategies illustrating the dangers of promoting one reading at the expense of alternatives, advocating plurality of interpretation as, I have argued, does much of Rossetti's poetry.

I have mentioned Rossetti's adoption of fairy-tale terminology. The folk-tale idiom is a highly self-reflexive register, acutely drawn towards its own limits as a discourse, traditionally repeating stock motifs and devices rather than inventing particulars. Rossetti employs these conventions sedulously. For example, the sisters inhabit an ahistorical setting with no specific geographical location. The (feminist) independence which this affords them is embroidered into description of their daily routine, an existence couched in the least specific pastoral terms:

> When first the cock crowed his warning,
> Neat like bees, as sweet and busy,
> Laura rose with Lizzie;
> Fetched in honey, milked the cows,
> Aired and set rights to the house,
> Kneaded cakes of whitest wheat.
> Cakes for dainty mouths to eat,
> Next churned butter, whipped up cream,
> Fed their poultry, sat and sewed;
> Talked as modest maidens should…

It is with the considered employment of this stock manner of visualizing the world of the 'modest maidens' that the strength of *Goblin Market* as a treatise emerges. An aggressively anti-phallocentric work would do more than quaintly ironise the phrase 'modest maidens', but Rossetti disturbs such ideological ordering in a more subdued fashion, letting the text as a whole function as a critique of its components. *Goblin Market* works with and within fairy tale discourse to construct its own thesis at another level. Wendy Mulford has stated of women's writing:

(W)e must break through our silence. But we cannot create a language. We can make a lexical selection, designed to exclude, for example, the obvious phallic metaphors of penetration, thrust etc., for forceful action, for energy and desire. Such a lexical pruning… is part of the process of thinking in our language, realizing its subtle articulations of male dominance, making some redress and calling the feminine into presence in verbs, quantifiers, substantives and pronouns.[3]

Goblin Market seems to be formulated along such lines with one important qualification. Because Rossetti's poem operates not least at a symbolic level, its manner of 'lexical pruning' is necessarily a delicate and complex affair. In *Goblin Market*, awareness of the plurality of readings offered by positing a signifier outside its customary parole necessitates a tolerance of one loaded metaphorical possibility in the belief that other symbolic readings (those neglected by the masculine ideology whose bias the text seeks to identify) are equally permissible and valuable. Simply, for *Goblin Market* to eschew all words, images, symbols carrying potentially phallocentric import would be to acknowledge - to bow and bashfully hear, as Laura initially does - rather than to overcome that ideology masquerading as truth which has silenced woman's voice for so long. Such base 'pruning' would merely mark submission to the pervasive power of the male tradition, rather than a more effective remanagement of the premises which have long supported that one-sided tradition.

Goblin Market, then, attempts to reconstruct a lost feminine mode of expression from raw materials stamped with male prepossession:

> Golden head by golden head,
> Like two pigeons in one nest
> Folded in each other's wings,
> They lay down on their curtained bed;

> Like two blossoms on one stem,
> Like two flakes of new-fall'n snow,
> Like two wands of ivory
> Tipped with gold for awful kings.

Thus the sleeping sisters are described after Laura's experiences with the merchant men. The progressive quartet of similes offers visually diverse images of the girls linked thematically by desire to express purity (yet the 'curtained bed' provides tantalizing concealment). We find traditional articulations of purity - cooing birds, delicate blooms, snow, ivory; the most striking thing about these similes is their lack of originality. They are stock images familiar from fairy lore. Yet is their employment here not unsettling? Two objections spring to mind. First, why describe the girls in traditional terms of absolute purity when, in the terms of the main narrative, Laura has symbolically fallen and is no longer pure at all? Secondly, the girls are not differentiated - 'Like two... Like two... Like two' - but the text has thus far chiefly functioned to demonstrate their *differences*. The building up of similes, a device used five times in the course of the poem, implies consolidation, reinforcement of a single idea, but simultaneously admits contradictions. The images are linked smoothly if we accept conventional readings that will unite them under the heading of purity. However, there are further visual dimensions to each image that do not coincide and so reduce the effect of sequential consolidation. The notion of two blossoms (perhaps we read 'white' by conditioned response?) may be akin visually to 'two flakes of... snow' but what of the following image: 'Like two wands of ivory / Tipped with gold for awful kings'? This image, with its suggestion of mythic iconography, introduces a deliberately jarring effect into the visual chain. White 'ivory' may suggest purity, but the image is extended into a phallic arena - 'wands of ivory / Tipped with gold' - immediately reinforced by the proposition of male as tyrant - 'for awful kings'.

Underwriting notions of specific signification, complacent assimilation of the sequence of similes here is disrupted, as seeming thematic unity is shown to contain contradiction. Lizzie is as she was, but Laura has fallen: difference, and not absolute purity, is signified here, and this can only be discerned from the imagery if we delve further than the tradition reading process encourages. The sisters are together but also apart in the terms of the narrative; the text has offered them as a unit (sisters) yet also cast them asunder: the language of the above passage symbolically mirrors this ambiguity, begging to be interpreted at different levels, as internally complementary yet simultaneously marking out difference. Thus Rossetti exposes the limited vision of a tradition by manoeuvring within the very confines of that tradition, stretching its presumptions into areas which highlight the contradictions within the coding.

This desire to redirect tradition from within is furthered in *Goblin Market*'s symbolic treatment of sexuality and eroticism. Again, the use of the fairy tale form is notable. Stephen Prickett has observed that fairy stories 'offer a surrogate language of sexuality'.[4] This function, involving in *Goblin Market* a subversion of patriarchal values, arises in part from the mythic resonance of the fairy tale mode, its capacity to 'reduce…mythical themes to more human proportions'.[5] A text such as *Goblin Market*, considering the freedom to arrange archetypes anew which the production of an original fairy tale allows, is able consciously to disturb a symbolic order we accept as fixed and neutral. Just as the language of Rossetti's poem dislodges certainty of reference in the area of simile, its discussion of sexuality also examines complacency in its deconstruction of the way sexuality and eroticism are usually portrayed.

It has been said of *Goblin Market* that 'much of the imagery is unmistakably and openly sexual'.[6] This reckoning should, I think, be regarded as a prefatory remark rather than a conclusion. To state that a term is unmistakably sexual implies that there is a settled, predetermined view as to what is sexual and what is not. It is precisely this manner of preconception that *Goblin Market* sets out to expose as ideology disguised as truth. *Goblin Market* is a fable of temptation, succumbed to and overcome. But the concern with temptation does not end at the narrative level. An integral function of the poem is to illustrate how a text may tempt a reader into blinkered acceptance of one interpretation at the expense of other equally plausible readings. It is satisfying to recall how many times critical opinion has been tempted and seduced, by a poem warning of the dangers of temptation and seduction, into pigeonholing its many layers of meaning into one compartment. The poem has been read as allegorical, sexual, Christian, feminist, social, pornographic, artistic and psychological in import.[7] Recently, with the application of critical methods less eager to produce one consummate meaning, it has been acknowledged that *Goblin Market*, rather than demanding unilateral explanation, deserves 'perception and participation in its whole vision'.[8] So, whilst it is fair to say that 'Laura's "fall"... can be well enough understood in sexual terms', such a pronouncement must be weighed against the patterning, symbolic and moralistic, woven by the poem as a whole.[9] Plurality of response is clearly demanded.

In the first description we have of the sisters, Laura and Lizzie are pictured '[c]rouching close together':

> With clasping arms and cautioning lips,
> With tingling cheeks and finger tips.
> "Lie close," Laura said,
> Pricking up her golden head;
> "We must not look at goblin men,
> We must not buy their fruits;
> Who knows upon what soil they fed
> Their hungry thirsty roots?"

The picture of innocence? That is surely all that this passage purports to be. And yet the language brims with a sensuousness suggestive to the point of salaciousness: 'close together... clasping... tingling... Pricking... fruits... hungry thirsty roots'. This register exploits precisely the gap between innocence and loss of virtue, which the text proceeds to narrate. There is nothing inherent in this collection of words that should make one read them as prurient or pornographic in import; any such interpretation relies upon the supply of such references brought to the poem from a predetermined tradition of reading. Language itself has experienced the fall from an innocent state, long before *Goblin Market* comes to describe Laura's fate at the hands of sweet temptation. 'Sweet tooth' Laura's fall, indeed the whole poem, serves ironically to illustrate a potential return to an untouched state for language, or at least an understanding of how language might illustrate its own potentialities. In an 'iterated jingle / Of sugar-baited words', the language of *Goblin Market* repeatedly functions to tempt one reading (sexual, conditioned) over potential others, a constant reminder of how bias in signification becomes insidiously naturalized within discourse. The goblin men function as a symbolically fractured unit, 'signalling each other' yet diversely described, prefacing these increasingly intensifying passages as the girl submits further:

> (Laura) sucked their fruit globes fair or red:
> Sweeter than honey from the rock,
> Stronger than man-rejoicing wine,
> Clearer than water flowed that juice;
> She never tasted such before,
> How should it cloy with length of use?
> She sucked and sucked and sucked the more
> Fruits which that unknown orchard bore;
> She sucked until her lips were sore…
> And knew not was it night or day
> As she turned home alone.

In the act of sustaining this highly sensuous atmosphere, the terminology cannot but fail to assume its erotic dimension. The Eucharistic description of Laura abandoning herself to sensuousness becomes simultaneously sensual. This careful assimilation of provocative, loaded terms, from the phallic 'fruit globes fair or red' to the rhythmic, unpunctuated repetition of 'sucked and sucked and sucked', lures us into certainty that the sexual interpretation of this incident must surely be the right one. But this is not so, and, just as Laura leaves the scene knowing 'not was it night or day', the text here resides inside the same suspended, twilight state by showing how the elevation of one reading to authoritative status leaves behind other potential signifieds, relegating the text to a limbo realm of painful inaction.

This is patently not the ultimate function of *Goblin Market*, yet it is a temporary step along the road to the resurrection of language. Laura's fall, imaged as it is, invites a sexual reading. Lizzie's sacrifice later in the poem leads to employment of the same language register as that which narrated Laura's abandonment to sensuality. Lizzie returns from her intercourse with the goblins:

> She cried "Laura," up the garden,
> "Did you miss me?
> Come and kiss me,
> Never mind my bruises,
> Hug me, kiss me, suck my juices…
> Eat me, drink me, love me;
> Laura, make much of me:
> For your sake I have braved the glen
> And had to do with goblin merchant men."

These lines are as loaded with sexual connotation as the previous passage cited. Laura's orgasmic response, 'as one possessed', links the passages by syntactic, rhythmic association: '(s)he hung about her sister, / Kissed and kissed and kissed her'. And Lizzie's exit from the glen is expressed in a manner consciously recalling Laura's departure: 'In a smart, ache, tingle, / Lizzie went her way; / Knew not was it night or day'.

But this portion of the text is describing acts of charity and loving kindness. Laura's fall bespake lust; Lizzie's intercourse with her sister here is not a lesbian, sexual act, but one of pure love and selflessness. The poem's use of the same language which so suggestively related Laura's fate with the goblins at a later point in the narrative where suggestiveness is far from appropriate further encourages the hypothesis that the text is deconstructing its own codes, illustrating the inadequacies of the language with which the poet is trying to write anew. *Goblin Market* utilizes the same register at conflicting points in the narrative to show how reductive it is to allocate one set of signifieds alone to a code. So, Jeanie '(f)ell sick and died' because she met the goblins and '(a)te their fruit' then 'pined and pined away' to taste the fruit again until, unable to find the goblins once more, she 'fell with the first snow'. Yet later it is plainly stated that Jeanie died because she had prematurely experienced 'joys brides hope to have'. So, again, how do we read Lizzie's act, how interpret the goblin fruit? No *consistent* degree of symbolic motivation can be identified in the poem. The language tempts us toward the certainty of one interpretation only to follow this seduction with the embarrassing revelation that such 'sugar-baited' singular interpretation is wholly inefficient for a complete understanding of the poem.

Thus far, I have attempted to show here just how *Goblin Market* negates the possibility of complacent assimilation of its images. By simultaneously inviting and subverting a (set phallocentric) symbolic order, thereby exposing the ideological bias upholding such an order, the work demonstrates that language is not a transparent medium reflecting some pre-ordered sense of reality somewhere, but constitutes that reality itself. In the Romantic sense, *Goblin Market* is a self-conscious, self-reflexive text, continually investigating its own status as poetry. In a post-Romantic sense, the work's ultimate concern is to do with the structuring and order of language itself. By repeatedly sparring with our notions of what language ought and ought not to do, fantasizing an attack upon a received symbolic order from within the fairy tale form, Rossetti forces us to reconsider what we regard as 'truth'. Fantastic literature is free from 'realistic' restraints and utilizes this liberty to articulate the struggle against the context, literary and social, within which it will be determined. Furthermore, fantastical literature offers itself to the female creative instinct as an 'appropriate medium for suggesting a sense of estrangement, of alienation from "natural" origins'.[10] *Goblin Market* is, then, not an exercise in escapism, but a striving towards expression: the critique of language offered by the poem stems from this desire. Such an investigation may be prefaced by a discussion of sexuality and tradition, since these are matters arising out of language, but the final thrust of *Goblin Market*'s argument inevitably centres upon language itself. Thus, after avoiding their call for so long, we must now examine the function of the goblin men, consider their song and the role of their fruit, so far as the strategy of *Goblin Market* as defined above is concerned.

The poem's title, *Goblin Market*, is significant here. It may be read as oxymoronic, juxtaposing the 'goblin' image, something primitive, animal of instinct, outside man's law and untethered to rules of worldly logic, with the concept of a 'market', an idea formulated by man's law-making, a system of ordered commercial interchange. It is from this implied fusion of primitivism and materialism that the work's symbolic treatment of language may be gauged.

McGillis has remarked that '(w)hat the goblins are selling is language'.[11] In the world of *Goblin Market*, it is the goblin men who offer language at its most colourful and opaque (in fact, at its most deceptive), and therefore at its most obvious as a medium, and the 'modest maidens' who must barter with the merchants in market terms. The linguistic register the goblins hawk is attractive; it is meant to be so, since we can only know their fruits by their descriptions of them. Language writes the world of the poem, just as language writes the world for us, and the goblins' language is singular and alluring:

> "Come buy our orchard fruits,
> Come buy, come buy:
> Apples and quinces,
> Lemons and oranges,
> Plump unpecked cherries,
> Melons and raspberries,

Bloom-down-cheeked peaches,
Swart-headed mulberries,
Wild free-born cranberries,
Crab-apples, dewberries,
Pine-apples, blackberries,
Apricots, strawberries..."

The rhythmic '-berries' repetition here is literally mouth-watering, and the settling of metre, from the odd, arresting irregularities of line length into a regular repeatable pattern from '[s]wart-headed mulberries' constitutes a hypnotic, enticing incantation. The goblins are advertisers, putting language together unit by unit in order to create a commercially attractive proposition. A highly ambiguous phrase - 'Sweet to tongue and sound to eye' - both outlines the quality of the fruits and describes the language which constructs the wares. If 'to tongue' and 'to eye' are infinitives, then the fruits are discussed as objects. However, if 'tongue' and 'eye' are nouns prefaced by the 'to' preposition, then the phrase operates at another level. The fruits are 'sweet to tongue' as linguistic items and 'sound to eye' (with sound changing from adjective to noun) as sound-constructs in appearance. Again, the goblins become dealers in language. Laura and Lizzie are recipients of this discourse, and the awareness of its visual (language creating the vision) impact is emphasized. 'We must not look,' says Lizzie, wisely.

But '[c]urious Laura' does look, is tempted. The goblins offer a new, appealing manner of signification and expression, which seems to free language in its difference from the norm, just as the diversity of appearance of the merchant men is appealing in its non-conformity to uniform standards.

One had a cat's face,
One whisked a tail,
One tramped at a rat's pace,
One crawled like a snail...

Impressed by these various guises, Laura is convinced that the male goblin code, seemingly diverse and outside customary speech patterns, will allow fresh expression:

> The whisk-tailed merchant bade her taste
> In tones as smooth as honey,
> The cat-faced purr'd,
> The rat-paced spoke a word
> Of welcome, and the snail-paced even was heard;
> One parrot-voiced and jolly
> Cried "Pretty Goblin" still for "Pretty Polly";
> One whistled like a bird.

This passage is important. The diverse forms of the merchants ought, by simple projection, to indicate potential for pluralistic expression. In fact, this is not the case. They purr and whistle, communicating nothing but self-gratifying sound patterns, and the 'parrot-voiced' cries an unnaturally reflexive, narcissistic 'Pretty Goblin'. What the goblins offer is a perversion of language, just as naturalized male-ordered traditions of writing are perversions of neutrality. The goblins are tricksters because they parade mutated linguistic codes in order to deceive others into participation in their one-sided games; their words are truly 'sugar-baited'. Furthermore, the goblins attempt to purvey something natural which ought to be freely accessible to anyone; they load words with value as if it were their right to do so. And the values are deceptive. McGillis has noted:

> Instead of freeing language and releasing passion, the goblin words fix, enclose, suspend and exhaust those who listen to them...[12]

Laura has no 'money', the currency the goblin men seek. However, trading 'a precious golden lock', she attempts commerce with them, venturing innocently, naturally to participate in the male goblin discourse. Predictably, the results are disastrous. Laura sought a new manner of expression in the attractiveness of the goblin code, but, through entering into the male sphere unprepared, she loses the power of articulation. She becomes silent.

> She said not one word in her heart's sore ache;
> But peering thro' the dimness, nought discerning . . .
> So crept to bed, and lay
> Silent till Lizzie slept;
> Then sat up in passionate yearning,
> And gnashed her teeth for baulked desire, and wept
> As if her heart would break.
>
> Day after day, night after night,
> Laura kept watch in vain
> In sullen silence of exceeding pain.

The goblins, the men in this fairy land, have successfully silenced the female who desired to employ their ways as if they were natural to herself. Lizzie's approach is different, however, less impulsive and more calculated:

> (Lizzie) put a silver penny in her purse,
> Kissed Laura, crossed the heath with clumps of furze
> At twilight, halted by the brook:
> And for the first time in her life
> Began to listen and look.

Now, 'for the first time in her life', Lizzie is about to involve herself in the quest for expression. She succeeds where Laura failed because she meets the goblins on their terms, with a 'silver penny in her purse'. Unlike Laura, who was impetuous and had no a priori knowledge of the implications of the discourse into which she entered, Lizzie is forewarned and subverts the male creed from within, by shrewd manipulation of its own terms of contract.

> "Good folk," said Lizzie,
> Mindful of Jeanie:
> "Give me much and many:"
> Held out her apron,
> Tossed them her penny.

Lizzie has, in fact, two things with her which show her already coming to terms with the commercial coding she hopes to overcome: her 'silver penny' and the remembrance of Jeanie who died because 'she met (the goblins) in the moonlight'. Unlike Laura, who had 'no coin' and 'spoke in haste' with her 'last restraint…gone', Lizzie boldly and directly attacks the right to supremacy of the goblin law. She occupies the position of barterer, reversing the power relationship inscribed within the goblin code as we have hitherto witnessed it in operation. Lizzie takes control of the scene swiftly and incisively, meeting the men on their own terms.

> "So without further parleying,
> If you will not sell me any
> Of your fruits tho' much and many,
> Give me back my silver penny
> I tossed you for a fee."

Faced with this usurper of their code, the goblins resort to physical assault. The empty, half-realized nature of their discourse - '(b) arking, mewing, hissing, mocking' - which had just recently seemed so attractive, is all their commercially loaded system of language is reduced to, once someone has questioned, as Lizzie has, the relevance of its values. Lizzie's entry into discourse with the goblins is, notably, simultaneous with a relinquishment of the passivity of old. She will utilize the male logos on her own terms, but will not, as did Laura, be an idle receptacle for their register:

> Lizzie uttered not a word;
> Would not open lip from lip

Lest they should cram a mouthful in:
But laughed at heart...

When Lizzie (whose feminine traits - 'her stocking... Like a lily' - are emphasized during the struggle) has '(w)orn out the men, their exit from the poem (literally and symbolically) is predictable confirmation of how their code has faltered:

At last the evil people
Worn out by her resistance
Flung back her penny, kicked their fruit
Along whichever road they took,
Not leaving root or stone or shoot . . .

The penny, symbol of Lizzie's assimilation of and attack upon the goblin code, is returned to the girl: '[Lizzie] heard her penny jingle / Bouncing in her purse, / Its bounce was music to her ear'.

The penny gives the gift of expression (it sings music, literally, and symbolizes defeat of the men) to Lizzie, and, consequently, back to Laura. The goblin men, meanwhile, must kick away 'their fruit', the symbol of their trade, thus their discourse: we never hear the male voice again in the poem. Lizzie has shown that the goblin code is just that - a code - which can be underwritten, employed by a non-goblin voice. She has managed to cancel out any claim to supremacy that the male inhabitants of the poem might previously have made. Thus, by the end of *Goblin Market*, with Laura's recovery, discourse is reclaimed from the snatches of subversive ideology masquerading as truth (the goblins were masqueraders). Woman can now express her own desire, write her own story:

Laura would call her little ones
And tell them of her early prime,
Those pleasant days long gone
Of not-returning time:

> Would talk about the haunted glen,
> The wicked, quaint fruit-merchant men,
> Their fruits like honey to the throat
> But poison to the blood…

In narrating her story, Laura uses the fairy tale mode, the poem's reclaimed register perpetuating itself yet further. But this poem, which has continually warned against complacency, is not fully done. In terms alien to the rest of the work (it is cunningly placed inside apostrophes), the ending of *Goblin Market*, which many commentators have condemned as being idle dogma and an unnecessary closure device, ironically offers one pat interpretation of a text that has strenuously and repeatedly advocated plurality of response.

> "For there is no friend like a sister
> In calm or stormy weather;
> To cheer one on the tedious way,
> To fetch one if one goes astray,
> To lift one if one totters down,
> To strengthen whilst one stands."

Of course, this may be (and has been) read as a statement of feminism, but, in the terms of the whole poem, it has another function. Language has been reclaimed by women in the course of the meta-fiction of *Goblin Market*. Laura's closing remarks show that, in placing one dogmatic interpretation on the events she is re-narrating, the possibility for complacency exists as much in feminine discourse as it did in male ordered ideology. The struggle goes on, as the poem ends on a self-satisfied note clearly at odds with the rest of its revelations.

Goblin Market is an important, original and provocative poem. In its story of the sisters and the goblin men, it colourfully and symbolically dramatizes the struggle it encounters and negotiates at linguistic level. Literally and symbolically, the work illustrates the modes of temptation offered to the reader by male-ordained patterns of discourse, and the subsequent reclamation of signifying potential back to a condition of neutrality, thus freeing language. The displacement of signification embodied in the poem's use of simile and treatment of sexuality alerts us to the struggle within language being played out meta-textually beneath the fairy tale narrative. Like much of Christina Rossetti's poetry, *Goblin Market* portrays and refines its philosophical concerns through its ambiguities, images and plot, visibly deconstructing the tradition of writing within which it will be placed, thus establishing potential for a new, untraditional tradition to be born. Christina Rossetti's next significant work, which formed the title poem of her second major collection, *The Prince's Progress and Other Poems* (1866),[13] would ably confirm and meaningfully focus that potential. *The Prince's Progress* is a sophisticated piece, and marks a harnessing of textual and symbolic strategies we have seen at work in this poet's earlier writing, offering a groundbreaking investigation of poetic tradition, and exposing iniquities deeply inscribed in quest romance in particular, and in lyric poetry in general.

5

FOR MINDS SUCH AS MINE:
THE PRINCE'S PROGRESS

Of course, I don't expect the general public to catch these
refined clues; but there they are for such minds as mine.
Christina Rossetti, Letter to Dante Gabriel Rossetti, March 1865

I

William Michael Rossetti tells us that his sister's 'habits of composition
were entirely of the casual and spontaneous kind' (*Works* lxviii). But
Rossetti scholars have long regarded this statement with scepticism.
Examining available manuscripts, we know Christina Rossetti to have
been a scrupulous reviser of her work and, as Kathleen Jones has
observed, her brother Dante Gabriel

> bombarded her with suggestions for revisions of her
> poetry, some of which caused Christina what she
> described as 'stamping, foaming, hair-uprooting'
> paroxysms. But she endorsed many of them, deleting
> lines, altering rhymes and adding stanzas at his
> direction, not always with felicity.[1]

I am going to describe the composition of a single long poem, *The Prince's
Progress*, here in order to show just how in control Rossetti actually was of her
own methods of poetic composition and, furthermore, how intellectually
aware she was of the symbolic and psychological implications of such a
process where the notion of poetic creativity in general is concerned.

William Michael claims of the eighty-six stanzas comprising *The Prince's Progress* (*Poems*, I, 95-110) that:

> The original nucleus of this poem is the dirge-song
> of its close — 'Too late for love, too late for joy,' etc.
> This was written in 1861 and entitled 'The Prince
> who arrived too late.' When Christina Rossetti was
> looking up, in 1865, the material for a fresh poetical
> volume, it was, I believe, my brother who suggested
> to her to turn the dirge into a narrative poem of some
> length. She adopted the suggestion… (*Works*, 461)

This dates the initial *conception* of *The Prince's Progress* as it stands as sometime 'in 1865'. This is, I would suggest, erroneous. The above statements closely recall another note of William Michael's, appertaining to a letter from Christina Rossetti to her other brother, Dante Gabriel, in which the composition of *The Prince's Progress* is discussed, notably the characters of the Alchemist and hero Prince: 'The reference to "my Alchemist" and "The Prince" applies to her other poem *The Prince's Progress*. It was Dante Gabriel who got her to turn a brief dirge-song which she had written into that longish narrative, as a pièce de resistance for a new volume'.[2] The letter referred to was written from Hastings, dated 23 December 1864. Its contents affirm that at this juncture the Prince's narrative is already a well-established notion in the minds of both writer and recipient: 'True, O Brother, my Alchemist still shivers in the blank of mere possibility; but I have so far overcome my feelings and disregarded my nerves to unloose the Prince, so that the wrapping paper may no longer bar his progress'.[3]

The writing of the Prince's narrative, if not already under way, must have begun soon after this point. In a letter dated 16 January 1865, Christina Rossetti declares 'This morning out came the Prince, but the Alchemist makes himself scarce, and I must bide his time'.[4] As William Michael states, these comments 'must mean that Christina had composed some portion of The Prince's Progress' at this juncture.[5]

By 30 January 1865 Dante Gabriel had returned an 'annotated' draft of '*Prince*' to his sister and the 'Alchemist' section was written.[6] In February, Dante Gabriel sent Christina his illustrations for *The Prince's Progress* and in March Christina refers to the work as a finished item in another letter to Dante Gabriel from Hastings: 'I readily grant that my *Prince* lacks the special felicity (!) of my *Goblins*; yet I am glad to believe you consider with me it is not unworthy of publication.[7]

We have to conclude that the Prince's narrative was written between December 1864 and March 1865, whilst Christina was officially resting at Hastings after tuberculosis had been diagnosed. Any suggestion of Dante Gabriel's to 'turn the dirge into a narrative poem of some length' must have been made in 1864 before Christina left for the Sussex coast, possibly as early as May 1864, at which time Dante Gabriel was already 'urging his sister to prepare a new volume'.[8]

Matters of chronology aside, William Michael's relation of his brother's proposal is clearly an important starting point in an analysis of the construction of *The Prince's Progress*. Firstly, we may re-quote the *Rossetti Papers*, where it is claimed that it 'was Dante Gabriel who got her to turn a brief dirge-song which she had written into that longish narrative'. Next, in the *Poetical Works*, the 'Too late for love' song is named as 'the original nucleus' of the final text of *The Prince's Progress*: 'it was, I believe, my brother who suggested to her to turn the dirge into a narrative poem of some length. She adopted the suggestion'. To say that Christina *modified* the suggestion would surely be fairer. The six-stanza song which concludes *The Prince's Progress* is a virtually unaltered form of a short lyric written five years previously and published as a complete single work in *Macmillan's Magazine* in May 1863. To this degree, *The Prince's Progress* neither demands nor indicates internal re-management of the original dirge-song. The dirge-song is not restructured or remade into a narrative, but remains essentially unaltered itself as a song now *prefixed by* a narrative. The lyric makes sense in terms of (and directly comments upon) that narrative but, importantly, is not itself narrativised. This formulation of an eighty-stanza narrative affording specific context to a poem of six stanzas written a half decade earlier places Rossetti into an interesting position in relation to her own poetry.

Significant here are the uncharacteristically forceful objections made by Christina to another suggestion from the ever attentive Dante Gabriel concerning *The Prince's Progress*: namely that a 'tournament' scene might prove a healthy addition to the narrative — the tale of a laggard Prince's trial-laden journey towards his sleeping Bride — which was to preface the 'Too late for love' lyric. Clearly viewing this proposal as an intrusion upon the schema of the work at hand, Christina writes to her brother from Hastings on 10 February 1865:

> How shall I express my sentiments about the terrible tournament? Not a phrase to be relied upon, not a correct knowledge of the subject, not the faintest impulse of inspiration incites me to the tilt... You see, were you next to propose my writing a classic epic in quantitative hexameters or in the hendecasyllables which might trip up Tennyson, what could I do? Only what I feel inclined to do in the present instance — plead goodwill but inability... Also (but this you may score as the blind partiality of a parent) my actual *Prince* seems to me invested with a certain artistic congruity of construction not lightly to be despised; 1st, a prelude and outset; 2nd, an alluring milkmaid; 3rd, a trial of barren boredom; 4th, the social element again; 5th, barren boredom in a more uncompromising form; 6th, a wind-up and conclusion. See how the subtle elements balance each other and fuse into a noble conglom![9]

Such comments indicate a poet well-acquainted with the tools of her trade — 'quantitative hexameters… hendecasyllables… congruity of construction' — and, furthermore, support the hypothesis that in the construction of the Prince's narrative Rossetti was thinking directly and deeply about her own methods of poetic composition, examining and questioning her own powers of creativity. The considered manufacturing of an episodic narrative story, as described above by Rossetti in list form, to preface and explicate the 'Too late for love' dirge-song composed half a decade earlier, puts Rossetti into the position of interpreter and critic of her own work. In short, we witness her becoming involved in a thorough, thoughtful, and open examination of her own methods of writing. In a letter written in 1854 to William Aytoun, then editor of *Blackwood's* magazine, the 23-year-old Christina had avowed that 'poetry is with me, not a mechanism, but an impulse and a reality'.[10] The statements of the Hastings letter to her brother show her, eleven years later, reconciling the three areas — 'mechanism', 'impulse', and 'reality' — into a maturing intellectual thesis. Such a position is vastly removed from that proffered by William Michael, alluded to at the beginning of this chapter:

> I have said elsewhere, but may as well repeat it here, that her habits of composition were entirely of the casual and spontaneous kind, from her earliest to her latest years. If something came into her head which she found suggestive of verse, she put it into verse. It came to her (I take it) very easily, without her meditating a possible subject, and without her making any great difference in the first from the latest form of the verses which embodied it; but *some* difference, with a view to right and fine detail of execution, she did of course make when needful. If the thing did not present itself before her, as something craving a vesture of verse at her hands, she did not write at all … and still less had she, in the course of her work, invited any hint, counsel, or co-operation. (*Works*, lxviii-lxix)

This is just one clear instance of the protective William Michael's sundry subjective attempts to propagate and promulgate a mythic version of his sister: understandably well-intentioned and born of admirable brotherly bonding, but often bearing little relation to the Christina Rossetti we find revealed in her own writings. In opposition to William Michael's claims here, Christina's attempts to define and analyse her own 'system' of poetic production (for, contrary to William Michael's opinion, she most certainly followed a 'system', as we have seen and shall further see) can be found in many of her surviving letters coincident with the period during which, it has been shown, the main narrative of *The Prince's Progress* was under construction. On the first day of December 1863, finding inspiration lacking, Christina writes to her publisher, Alexander Macmillan to declare that 'if one conviction can go beyond another, I am yet more firmly convinced that my system of not writing against the grain is the right one, at any rate as concerns myself'.[11] Christina refers to this 'system' in letters written from Hastings during the period which was, we have demonstrated, that of the composition of the main narrative of *The Prince's Progress*. The central episode of the Alchemist proved troublesome in the construction of the dramatic tale, but when the section was finally written Christina, enclosing a copy of the relevant verses, writes to Dante Gabriel on 30 January 1865: 'Here at last is an Alchemist reeking from the crucible. He dovetails properly into his niche … He's not precisely the Alchemist I prefigured, but thus he came and thus he must stay; you know my system of work'.[12]

Two months later another direct and telling reference to this 'system of work' appears in the correspondence between the two siblings. This letter is itself undated but William Michael places it as being of March 1865. In part, it deals once more with Dante Gabriel's aforementioned 'tournament' suggestion. 'Not the faintest impulse of inspiration incites me', Christina had objected on 10 February 1865, and, now, once more urged 'to the tilt', she complains: 'I do seriously question whether I possess the working power with which you credit me; and whether all the painstaking at my command would result in work better than — in fact half so good as — what I have actually done on the other system'.[13] Prompted by 'not the faintest impulse of inspiration', the idea of a tournament is evidently offensive to 'the other system', a concept which, though left vague here and never plainly defined elsewhere, is surely to be judged as antithetical to notions of 'working power' and 'painstaking'. The 'system' would seem to owe some sense of its prefiguring to notions of poetic inspiration and artistic creation and their relationship to laboriously contrived literary endeavour. Cast in the rôle of interpreter of her own poetry — in the construction of an original narrative which would justify the terms of the original lament song — one detects a move on the poetess's part towards an assessment and investigation of the methods and processes involved in the formulation of a literary text.

As previously noted, the elegy which concludes *The Prince's Progress* — the last six stanzas of the final, published 1866 version — first appeared as a self-contained work in the *Manuscript Notebook* currently in the British Library. The poem is dated 11 October 1861 and titled 'The Prince who Arrived too Late'. It next appears without significant amendment as a single short lyric published in *Macmillan's Magazine*, VIII, May 1863, now re-christened 'The Fairy Prince who Arrived too Late'. Taken as a complete single work from the pen of Christina Rossetti, the lyric is characteristically vague in areas of import and external reference. The 'princess' is named as such only once (tellingly, she is denied an upper-case initial; the Prince always has one), and even then the placing of this appellation directly after, in fact as partner (enhanced by the repetition of 'enchanted') to an obviously metaphorical construction leaves the certainty of its reference — to an *actual* princess? — hugely open to debate.

> The enchanted dove upon her branch
> Died without a mate;
> The enchanted princess in her tower,
> Slept, died, behind the grate... (*Poems*, I, 109)

Yet the title of the lyric as published independently, along with later references to the 'crown' the maiden wears and her being 'Meet queen for any kingly king' make a consistent and coherent reading of the lyric as a traditionally elegiac lament over a dead princess immediately plausible and justifiable. According to the Manuscript Notebook, the 'Too late for love' poem was composed just eleven days before the semi-political narrative 'A Royal Princess' (*Poems*, I, 149-52), written on 22 October 1861, which shows Rossetti to be preoccupied with the image of an unhappy princess at this time. (The disillusioned royal in the latter poem is also conceived of in terms of the 'dove' metaphor, lamenting 'Me, poor dove that must not coo....'.)

Some of the description in the 'Too late for love' lyric seems to owe its tone to works such as 'Once' (*Poems*, III, 186) or 'Listening' (*Poems*, III, 236), a poem which transforms the simple dove image into a sustained, extended simile. Furthermore, despite the rejection of the eminently Arthurian jousting tournament, the 'Too late for love' song unashamedly inhabits another mediaeval convention in a very positive sense — that of the maiden, Elaine or the Lady of Shallot, dying in the tower. There are echoes of Coleridge's 'Christabel' (as there had most clearly been in *Goblin Market*) in the lyric's somewhat sinister atmosphere, and Keats's 'La Belle Dame Sans Merci' and 'Isabella' are certainly recalled. Another strong influence would appear to be Tennyson's 'Mariana', (published in 1830, the year of Christina's birth), itself a suggestive rather than referentially specific lyric poem. The image of the distraught, weeping female isolated in the 'moated grange', with its darkly Shakespearean echoes, whose lover will not come, would seem to be an obvious source of inspiration for the plot of *The Prince's Progress* in general. The language of Rossetti's lyric draws directly from another Tennyson poem, the maid's song from the book of *Guinevere* (1859) in the *Idylls of the King*, published as a separate poem in 1859: 'Late, late, so late! and dark the night and chill! / Late, late, so late! but we can enter still. / Too late! too late! ye cannot enter now'.[14]

This song, in turn, is a relation of the parable of the ten virgins from the *New Testament* book of Matthew, chapter 25. This story would of course be well known to Christina from her intensive biblical studies, but it appears that she favoured, considering the reversal of the plot (in the biblical tale, the 'bridegroom' is Christ and it is the virgins who are too late for the 'marriage') she effects in her own poetic production, the language of the episode over and above the strict religious parable: '5. While the bridegroom tarried, they all slumbered and slept. 6. And at midnight there was a cry made, Behold the bridegroom cometh; go ye out to meet him'.[15]

However few or various its sources, Rossetti's 'Too late for love' lyric communicates unproblematically at literal level. Similarly, the Prince's narrative also articulates coherently at the level of surface meaning as the description of a sequence of events whose consequence supports the general import of the lyric it prefaces. On that plain, fictive narrative level the hero Prince, '(s)trong of limb if of purpose weak', gradually surmounts the various obstacles and distractions along his route, reaching his goal, the 'enchanted princess', alas 'too late for joy', her death having directly preceded his arrival. These occurrences construct a perspective from which the lyric can be approached, giving the song a voice (literally, in the form of the 'veiled figures' that chant the dirge at the close of *The Prince's Progress*, but also metaphorically) and specifying a single reading of the vague funeral lament which otherwise could only have been speculatively inferred from the short, suggestive lyric (particularly its title) alone.

Aside from local influences, the Prince's narrative unequivocally draws heavily upon the traditional discourses of fairy tale and quest myth. The predicament of the hero Prince as he journeys towards the sleeping maiden openly recalls the tale of *The Sleeping Beauty* and, like *Goblin Market*, works well enough as a simple moral tract. However, a careful examination of *The Prince's Progress* makes it clear that, though the poem functions perfectly as a straightforward narrative, there are peculiarities in the imagery, language and structure of the poem which, in a manner typical of Rossetti's writings, suggest that more than a surface reading is invited. Christina Rossetti herself makes implicit this possibility in a letter to Dante Gabriel from Hastings of 3 March 1865 in which she says of *The Prince's Progress*: 'I think that the plot is now obvious to mean capacities without further development or addition'.[16] In the same letter, however, she goes on to argue against Dante Gabriel's specific objection to her use of the word 'aftermath' in stanza 47 of the poem, declaring of the term in question:

> I think it gives a subtle hint (by symbol) that any more delays may swamp the Prince's last chance. In the same way ... 'Now the moon's at full' seems to me happily suggestive of the Prince's character. Of course I don't expect the general public to catch these refined clues; but there they are for minds such as mine.[17]

These are significant admissions. Such comments — 'a subtle hint... suggestive of... refined clues... for minds such as mine' — denote a distinct authorial awareness that the poetic text is capable of working on more than one level and reveal a writer interested by the internal dynamics of a poetic text. The fundamental narrative plot is held to be 'obvious' whilst beyond this plane lies the 'refined' world of 'symbol'. This proposal forms a basic premise, I believe, for a fuller reading of the great majority of Rossetti's poetical works, and certainly for an understanding of *The Prince's Progress* in particular.

A coherent, consistent reading of *The Prince's Progress* may be achieved without difficulty at narrative level, but such a reading may only be partial. A more thorough interpretation involves sedulously delving beneath the poem's surface, a recognition that additional communication is effected by the text at the level of symbol. Thus the 'full moon' becomes not just the full moon, but may be a symbol of fecundity, the Mother-of-all; the questing Prince is not any Prince of history but may be read as an emblem of the 'strong' masculine conscious ego, and his prospective partner, the sleeping Bride, may symbolise the feminine unconscious function — the 'veiled bride' as she is termed in the text. All of these archetypes regularly feature in fairy tales, the form Rossetti had already re-invented to her own ends in *Goblin Market*, where temporal and spatial dislocation (the events of *The Prince's Progress*, like those of *Goblin Market*, are never specifically located in time nor in space, never directly aligned to our 'real' world) affords an eternal quality to the import of the text, encouraging symbolic, non-empirical readings. The self-confessed attention to and interest in symbols and their inter-relationships within the poetic text shows Rossetti to be a writer keenly aware of modes of construction available to a poet, supremely involved in ordering the text from within, supervising the relationship of parts to the whole as the poem evolves. A recent commentator has rightly noted that much of Rossetti's poetry 'reflects an acute sensitivity to the duality of experience'.[18] Christina Rossetti's awareness of the differing levels of import of her work is translated, in *The Prince's Progress*, into a concern with duality and ambivalence as the text begs that we be sensitive to its implicit, as well as explicit suggestiveness.

Another feature of *The Prince's Progress* that suggests that more than a surface reading is possible appears in the highlighting of the quest aspect of the tale. The change of title from *The Fairy Prince who Arrived Too Late* (1863) to *The Prince's Progress* (1866) indicates a marked shift of emphasis from the conclusion of the journey to the journey itself. The third stanza of the poem begins thus: 'In his word-end palace the strong Prince sat, / Taking his ease on cushion and mat, / Close at hand lay his staff and his hat' (*Poems*, I, 95). The introduction of the 'strong Prince' is coincident with the statement of his purpose — the 'staff' and 'hat', traditional materials of the quest, precisely placed and noted. The poem then moves through a series of trials that the Prince must undergo, cataloguing an episodic maturation of the 'youth'. These trials may be viewed as a sequence of symbolic re-births, each of which allows the Prince a potentially heightened level of awareness of self and surroundings, highlighting consecutive stages in the hero's development and the development of the quest itself. In a traditional quest epic, this would normally be the case, but it is crucial to an understanding of *The Prince's Progress* to grasp that Rossetti's Prince is a singularly inept, or at best unreliable interpreter of signs and situations. His incorrect reading of the situations he encounters brings about his own failure and, simultaneously, the death of the maiden.

Whether the Prince assesses them adequately or otherwise, the fact that the episodic rhythms of the narrative are to be read on a symbolic level, as Rossetti herself intimated, is conveyed especially well in the conclusion to the Prince's encounter with the Alchemist. (I will examine Rossetti's significant treatment of this archetype in some detail later in this chapter.) A death is left behind, in the form of the old 'atomy': 'Thus the dead man stayed in his grave, / Self-chosen, the dead man in his cave' (*Poems*, I, 102). Simultaneously, the Prince, having been confronted by this vision of mortality, emerges from the dark, womb-like cave — a blatant symbolic re-birth — carrying the 'Elixir of Life' for which the Alchemist's death was catalyst. Not for the first time in the poem, however, the Prince fails to learn from his experiences and the 'Elixir' is never used in the subsequent narrative. The Prince has been given the 'Elixir of Life' but he allows his Bride to die nonetheless. Peculiarities such as these — the highlighting of the quest and its patterns and the part they play in the story, coupled with the special emphasis placed upon symbolism — support Christina Rossetti's own wish that the text might communicate more than just surface meaning. Furthermore, these features establish, alongside the literal, a richly psychological frame of reference for the work, related to a wish on the part of the author (similar to that governing *Goblin Market*) to reassess myths and their often ambiguous psychological implications.

Folk tales are instinct with psychological symbolism. Bettelheim has noted that '(a)pplying the psychological model of the human personality, fairy tales carry important messages to the conscious, the pre-conscious and the unconscious mind'.[19] Marie Louise von Franz, a student of Jung, offers much illuminating work in this field, providing close readings of traditional tales, expressed in Jungian and post-Jungian terms, to confirm the view that fairy tales 'convey at the same time overt and covert meanings'.[20] Structured around a hierarchy of patterned symbols, fairy tales may be directly related to what are held to be the unconscious areas of the self. Never specifically located in time nor space, these legends are able with ease to assume a dream-like, eternal register, their figures and events not chained to overtly causal procedures, the offspring of the imagination rather than any factual rationale. Most frequently following (as did Rossetti's *Goblin Market*) the traditionally comic progression — from order through chaos to order re-established and seen to be of a more permanent nature — fairy tales frequently culminate in marriage, symbolic assertion of the achievement or restoration of harmony in the psyche. In *The Sleeping Beauty*, one of the most obvious influences upon *The Prince's Progress*, the slumbering maiden may represent the feminine part of the psyche, the feeling, emotional side, broadly speaking the unconscious mind. She is pricked to sleep by the phallic spinning-wheel needle, an offending because too forceful an assertion of masculinity, attempting aggressive dominance over the feminine but merely succeeding in extinguishing beauty through negative animus influence. The maiden sleeps and the castle also sleeps while it becomes surrounded by thorns — the psyche becomes barren and stagnant — so that the sleeping girl, symbol of the unconscious, is obscured, repressed, potentially lost forever. The masculine, conscious aspect of the self must now assert itself and attempt to redeem the fading unconscious or it, too, is condemned to stagnation and extinction, as the deaths of the early crusaders in the tale illustrate. Finally, the right questing male appears and his essential union with the princess, along with their happiness thereafter, symbolises the restoration of harmony in the psyche.

Of course, this does not happen in *The Prince's Progress*. Rather, Rossetti repeatedly re-investigates the ritual figures and procedures which, long cut off from their mythic origins, had become stock archetypes, and she improvises the plot of the romance to make it relevant to her own desires as a woman and poetess. The text borrows archetypes from fairy lore and quest myth — the questing hero, sleeping maiden, Alchemist, phases of the moon — yet, as was the case in *Goblin Market*, none of these devices is transplanted idly from whence it came. Each is re-managed and manipulated in the course of Rossetti's poem to reconstruct a new, notably more open-ended myth. *The Prince's Progress* concludes not in a pleasant marriage and the prospect of new life, but in a death and a song. The final dirge-song becomes, literally and symbolically, the deferred, surrogate, untraditional prize, that which arises as a result of the quester's failure to attain the quest-goal (the sleeping maiden) as initially, traditionally defined. The psychological implications of this re-invention of fairy tale patterns, coupled with the emphasis upon the quest motif, both linked to the idea of 'song' as the creative goal, constitute a post-Romantic internalised quest in the tradition of Coleridge's *Ancient Mariner*, Keats's 'La Belle Dame Sans Merci' and *The Fall of Hyperion*, and Shelley's *Alastor*, where a surface narrative may also embody symbolic patterns portraying a psychological landscape and relating to notions of identity, the self, and the act of poetic creation.

Significantly, by addressing principles defined in Romantic poetry, Rossetti actively allows the more sensitive and subtle male perspectives of poetic tradition to guide her own writing as it seeks to subvert other areas of that tradition. The particular species of quest articulated in *The Prince's Progress* is one which may be identified as Romantically demonic in so far as the subject goal of the crusade is eventually and sadly disclosed as being (superficially) delusive. But this has the result of encouraging an evaluation of voyage as more than equal to destination (one recalls the shift in emphasis from arrival to journey in Rossetti's title change). Hence the enshrinement of the resultant sense of loss, preserved in the quest vision that is synthesised into the literal quest, the poetic text, can be more than elegiac. English and German Romanticism had arrived at this point with its repeated fusion of romance and premonstration, admitting a historical modulation in consciousness and, most obviously in Wordsworth's *The Prelude*, achieving what Harold Bloom describes as an 'internalisation of romance' where 'the poet takes the patterns of quest romance and transposes them into his own imaginative life, so that the entire rhythm of the quest is heard again in the movement of the poet himself from poem to poem'.[21]

The fundamental search can now be acknowledged to be within the self, exploring and widening consciousness by means of an examinatory technique which projects itself into what are often held to be hidden regions of the psyche. The cost of this internalising process is the terrified awakening into self-consciousness, the discovery of a self that is far from unified, as Hartman metaphorically puts it: 'We dream, we wake on the cold hillside, and our 'sole self' pursues the dream once more. In the beginning was the dream; and the task of disenchantment never ends'.[22]

But, with this in mind, the internalisation allows a new, clearer understanding of the interplay connecting all the parts of the psyche, potential knowledge of the hitherto unknown, a manner of poetry whose main concern becomes its own status as a concrete manifestation of the abstract mental performance which gave it being. Poetry becomes its own subject, symbolically exposing and exploring the creative energy which caused it to be. In this quest the mediating (and meditating) ego grows ultimately concerned with its own structure and the relationships between the various parts of the self that combine to instigate poetic maturity. Through the poem, the poet maps the construction of the poem. This is certainly the case with *The Prince's Progress*.

However, there is one major qualification here. Christina Rossetti is on the side of the maiden. Rossetti sees that in the demonic Romantic quest the goal is relegated to inaction. If that goal is symbolic of the female aspect — as it is in almost all love poetry written by men — then woman becomes an empty symbol, devalued and forever silent. In quest literature such as *The Sleeping Beauty* woman is literally and symbolically reduced to silence and inaction as total emphasis is placed upon the hero's masculinity as embodied in the patterns of the quest. What, then, is her own quest, woman's goal? In terms of the traditional form, it is to be met, to achieve conjunction (which happens or does not happen regardless of her own efforts). Her representation is thus wholly in the service of the questing male's progress. And what, then, if the quester is inefficient, a bungler, and fails? Then woman's quest for representation necessarily fails too. She becomes an absence, silent and ineffectual. This is the injustice that *The Prince's Progress* seeks to expose.

As previously noted, *The Prince's Progress* concludes, significantly, not in a marriage but in a song. The song marks, literally and symbolically, the fruition of the poetic impulse. The poem as a whole evinces an interest in songs, their generation and their status. Each stage in the Prince's episodic (non-)maturation is instigated by a song. The very existence of this song, as much as its content, seems to spur the quester forward, re-establishing the quest and its purpose, keeping the poem alive. Emanating from the mysterious, disembodied 'sad glad voices' these summoning songs become noticeably more lyrical as the work progresses towards its final instance of song, the 'bride-song' of the 'veiled figures', also unidentified. One song ends and another begins, as 'the blossom of blossoms blow'. In *The Prince's Progress*, the initial and final states described (literally and symbolically) are decidedly disharmonious and non-unified. A manner of conjunction is achieved — the Prince does finally reach his destination — but the maiden is dead and the unsatisfactory, partial nature of this communion is posited as a necessary prerequisite to poetic creation, that is the final lament. Allowed a classical, closed ending where the Prince and his Bride join in blissful wedlock, the text could not fulfil its fundamental purpose, the location and dramatisation of the moment of inspiration which, in letter and spirit, brings forth the 'Too late for love' song. To this end, the narrative presents an examination of the conscious/unconscious relationship rendered by means of the symbolic evaluation of the conscious ego, its education and development, via the trials experienced by the hero Prince in the course of the quest. Another quest is involved too: the quest to demonstrate and counter the impossibility of free articulation that is woman's plight, trapped in silence as she is within a manner of poetry made by men on men's terms. By writing *The Prince's Progress* Rossetti symbolically addresses

110   Paul Hullah

this issue and maps out the problematic area that is poetic creativity as seen from a Victorian woman writer's perspective. In short, as intimated earlier, the construction here of an original and provocative narrative to preface the original 'Too late for love' song actively manifests a desire on the part of the poetess to explore the psychology and dynamics of poetic creation itself, simultaneously exposing, as does so much of Rossetti's writing, the difference between static (literary) tradition and active (female) experience.

Received literary codes discernible in the transtextual narrative of *The Prince's Progress* are not idly adopted, but rather actively adapted and remanaged by Rossetti as part of her own quest to find a radically new form of expression appropriate to female experience in a man's world. Thus the predicament of the hero Prince as he journeys towards the sleeping maiden may openly recall the tale of *The Sleeping Beauty*, but, crucially, in Rossetti's loaded retelling the bumbling Prince arrives at his destination too late. Similarly, the Prince's tardy trek towards his unfortunate object might, like *Goblin Market*, be passed off as a plain moral tract admonishing a reader against temptation and resultant sloth. But a sedulous examination of *The Prince's Progress* makes it clear that, however well it might advertise itself as a straightforward dramatisation of the *carpe diem* theme, there are prominent irregularities in the imagery, language, and structure of the poem that make the text truly proto-modernist (and undoubtedly feminist) in nature. To illustrate this point, I will now begin to analyse the poem's narrative in some detail, attempting to demonstrate it furtherance and consolidation of motives at work in *Goblin Market* and earlier 'secular' poems, where disturbance of the conventional reading process (facilitating some redress of the anti-female bias in conventional male-ordered literary address) is conscientiously and dramatically enacted. I will subsequently consider one of the traditional symbols supplanted from pastoral, fairy tale and quest literature by Rossetti: the milkmaid. I want to show how this archetype is reworked in *The Prince's Progress* and elsewhere, by the female poet as part of her ongoing revisionist manifesto. Thereafter I will consider another important archetype that appears in Rossetti's poem: the alchemist.

II

The Prince's Progress opens with a cascade of assonantal and repetitive forms:

> Till all sweet gums and juices flow,
> Till the blossom of blossoms blow,
> The long hours go and come and go,
> The bride she sleepeth, waketh, sleepeth,
> Waiting for one whose coming is slow; -
> Hark! the bride weepeth. (*Poems*, I, 95)

The emphasis here is notably upon long feminine vowel sounds and rhymes. The initial conditional clause 'Till all sweet gums and juices flow' is Keatsian and sensual, indeed *sexual* in import, denoting the immediate presence of a strong desire towards fruition. Anaphora and end stopping postpone the climax of the first two-line conditional prior to its being expanded upon: language itself is suspended in wait for the prospect of natural growth. Straightaway the poem establishes a reversal of the traditional summons to the poetic muse. Here, the female figure, traditionally the muse herself, must attend passively the arrival of 'one whose coming is slow', the questing 'hero' who will allow her the gift of articulation.

Temporal certitude is also rapidly dislocated (as it was in *Goblin Market*), not by means of a traditional 'Once upon a time...' device to signify this time and all time and thus outside any time, but here by the hypnotic blurring of chronometry in 'The long hours go and come and go', which, along with the repetitive 'sleepeth, waketh, sleepeth,' establishes the idea of flux (and also of extended time) in the text. This is a notion later thematically developed in a questioning of the containable nature of apparently disparate 'opposites': attention is repeatedly drawn to the areas of uncertainty that border any seemingly precise defining act, as the poem examines ways in which various parts of the self are autonomous yet complementary, with boundaries unclear and limitations of effect and influence hard, if not impossible, to establish. In fact the opening two stanzas of the poem adumbrate this concern of the entire text: though the second sestet is radical in being composed solely of dialogue, thus self-contained as a register, it is yet complement and partner to the first stanza, answering and developing ideas set out in those preceding lines alone. In this way, the structuring of the poetry already prefigures what will become a major symbolic aspect of the choate text.

The second stanza runs:

> "How long shall I wait, come heat come rime?"--
> "Till the strong Prince comes,
>   who must come in time,"
> (Her women say), "there's a mountain to climb,
> A river to ford. Sleep, dream and sleep:
> Sleep," (they say): "we've muffled the chime,
> Better dream than weep."

The charmingly simple 'rime/rhyme' pun here is critical and pivotal: it turns frost into formal poetic structure and, by association, makes 'heat' symbol of the fire of inspiration, the glow of creative energy. Fusion of these two can bring about the poetci fruition sought, which the yearnings for natural plenitude opening the poem figuratively foreshadowed. This will occur when the 'strong' conscious ego, our Prince, 'comes' to achieve conjunction with the maiden, 'veiled bride' to the conscious, thus symbol of the unconscious. The soft, reassuring tones of '[h]er women' (a concentrated expression of elemental femininity) at once define the objectives of the quest: 'there's a mountain to climb / A river to ford.'

So the opening of *The Prince's Progress* deftly enacts a dislocation of traditional quest directives. A female-oriented distinction is drawn between the male quest hero's conventionally active role, and the passive function undertaken by the quest's traditionally female object. In a manner we will see openly declared in Rossetti's remarkable 'Preface' to *Monna Inominata*, thence self-consciously practiced in that seminal work itself, this female writer takes inherited poetic conventions and assays to expose these received 'norms' as enormously weighted in favour of a dogmatic phallocentric reading.

In *The Prince's Progress*, the poem's progress, according to literary quest principles normalised by centuries of poetry, is *literally* controlled by the machinations and movements of the male subject, whilst a female object must passively attend for the male 'hero' to attain his 'goal'. The codes of the literary quest, like those of the poetics Rossetti inherits as a Victorian author) have been cast and wrought to male-ordained specifications. To participate in the quest (and in poetic convention) a woman must submit herself to an existence she has been rendered powerless to undo. Thus, early in the poem, her 'women' urge the princess to 'Sleep, dream and sleep: / Sleep... / Better dream than weep', seemingly recommending passivity over active articulation (weeping) of her plight. In Tennyson's 'Mariana' (1830) weeping is presented as potentially articulate activity – 'She wept, "I am aweary, aweary, / O God, that I were dead!"'[23] But such weeping will only express, and indeed emphasise, the unqualified hopelessness of woman's plight, trapped as she (conventionally is) inside her tragedy. No initiative is taken. To *initiate*, within these male-constructed confinements, can be to transcend the imprisonment, to become (for instance) Eve the seductress and submit oneself to a history of religious and social disapproval (this issue is specifically examined in the 'Esther' sonnet of *Monna Innominata*, to be discussed in a later chapter). Or, perhaps ideally, to become the female *poet*, and to write one's own self into being and identity. (But that would have to come later.)

Importantly, the imperative to 'dream' delivered in *The Prince's Progress* directly precedes the introduction of the figure of 'The Prince' himself, thus potentially and arguably positioning the subsequent quest drama as a dream narrative emanating from the perspective of the princess: the tragicomic pitiful failures of this quest might be read as her silent (unconscious) commentary upon the quest and its rituals. And, in so much as it occurs in a symbolic realm and, crucially, does *not* result in an awakening of the sleeping dreamer, we would have to accept this as a plausible reading. We must also recall (referring back to the third chapter of this study) Rossetti's insistence on a poetry intent upon blurring boundaries and confounding expectations, where a 'dream' may become as worthy a version of 'reality' as those other portions of the narrative that frame and describe that 'dream'. Freed thus from conditions of logic governing direct reportage, dream fictions may encourage a more intense and questioning vision than a realist discourse might produce. In *The Prince's Progress*, such pointed deflections of certainty challenge and unsettle the reader, disrupting confidence in any single dominant, definitive authorial voice, readying us for the prospect of a radical new voice to emerge through the tangle of woven perspectives.

We are introduced to the 'strong Prince... / Taking his ease' in his dream-like 'world-end palace', with the tools of the quest – 'his staff and his hat' – lying idly by as he waits for a full moon. Just three stanzas in to the work, it is clear that any sense of urgency to propel the narrative will come not from the quester himself, but rather from the object of the quest. In contrast to the 'pale kings, and princes' of Keats' 'La Belle Dame Sans Merci', who encourage inertia, mysterious admonishing voices persistently urge Rossetti's Prince forward to the '[s]pell-bound' (bound most of all by man-made quest conventions, surely) princess, a 'veiled bride' who can do nothing but be 'patient', trapped as she is 'for thy sake', unable actively to function in her poem-prison unless and until allowed to do so via the influence and actions of the questing male subject.

Rossetti's Prince is '[s]trong of limb if of purpose weak', and the early stages of the poem's episodic narrative seem little short of sarcastic in the lamely idyllic presentation of the dallying hero revelling in the certainty that all will be well, come what may:

> Forth he set in the breezy morn,
> Across green fields of nodding corn,
> As goodly a Prince as ever was born,
> Carolling with the carolling lark; —

Sure his bride will be won and worn,
Ere fall of dark. (*Poems*, I, 96)

The ineffectual Lancelot of Tennyson's 'Lady of Shallot' is recalled in the atmosphere here, travelling through similar 'barley-sheaves', unaware of his destiny and his desired female object's emotional condition: '"Tirra lirra," by the river / Sang Sir Lancelot'.[24] Complacency reigns in these effete and ineffective questers. 'So light his step, so merry his smile', begins the next stanza of Rossetti's poem, as the narrative voice never allows us to forget the lack of urgency in the Prince's journeying, emphasising his 'merry' mood in direct contrast to the pained confinement of the waiting maiden. 'Sure his bride will be won and worn': there is an ominous self-satisfaction about the Prince and his notion of woman as a passive object to be 'won' and 'worn' (as a prize, a trophy, a symbol of male dominance; yet also, from the maiden's perspective, worn *out*, usurped, extinguished).

In short, here is a quester willing unquestioningly to enjoy the ritual of the quest with no regard for the meaning of its goal nor any desire to assimilate new knowledge that his progression towards this goal may afford him. The poem's chorus of a 'hundred sad… glad voices' (all of them (doubly!) female: '[h]er women') have already warned the hero that 'Time is short… use to-day while you may', and yet, unheeding of their words, at the first sight of a distraction, the 'Prince, who had journeyed at least a mile, / Grew athirst at the sight'. Again the tone is one of sarcasm — 'at least a mile' — highlighting the hero's pathetic lack of tenacity as he falls at the first hurdle in the way of his progress. That first hurdle is a milkmaid.

In the Prince's intercourse (a sexual union is implied) with the stereotypical 'wave-haired milkmaid' of pastoral literature, we obtain our first real glimpse of the hero's (or, more properly, anti-hero's) total inability to read signs correctly and thus competently move towards his avowed goal: the male muse which woman (the sleeping maiden) has come to rely upon to allow her a poetic voice, mute as she has become within this literary tradition, is quickly shown to be an unreliable, and thus to Rossetti an unacceptable agent. No longer content to witness herself vicariously defined by men's writing which places woman as its passive receptacle and silent object of desires, Rossetti exposes the unfairness to woman of the heroic phallocentric quest narrative in the sustained image of the helpless, tragic heroine, powerless to alter her own fate, and the blinkered, bungling Prince who has the power but neither the urgency nor the vision to resurrect her.

The milkmaid episode forms the first step in the poem's exposure of the masculine hero's incompetence. It is a device Rossetti had employed six months previously in a short but interesting poem entitled 'A Farm Walk' (*Poems*, I, 159-61). In this piece, the speaker appears to be a London gentleman who has ventured North from the big city in order to escape his busy life. The 'comely milking maid' he briefly encounters stays in his mind afterwards as a symbol of pastoral innocence: effectively, the poem calls into question man's appropriation of symbols as empty shells for his own use, to be filled with meaning which will suit his own purpose alone. The maid is reduced to a passive, docile image, mirroring the male speaker's own desire (notably, her only words are exact echoes of the male speaker's own phrases). This is a male voyeuristic fantasy and, as such, places woman as passive participant, trapped within the phallocentric drama, replete with a rather unsettling image of 'pail' as vagina and all:

> I stood for a minute out of sight,
> Stood silent for a minute
> To eye the pail, and creamy white
> The frothing milk within it,
>
> To eye the comely milking maid
> Herself so fresh and creamy:
> "Good day to you," at last I said;
> She turned her head to see me:
> "Good day," she said with lifted head;
> Her eyes looked soft and dreamy…

The milkmaid here is 'comely' and 'dreamy' because she represents a fantasy towards which the male protagonist is (sexually) attracted. Significantly, at the end of 'A Farm Walk', when the speaker resigns himself to the fact that he will never see the maid again, he cannot work out that she was important to him as a symbol he sought to appropriate for his own ends. Rather, he prefers the equally male-oriented vision that she has been usurped by another man: 'Perhaps in farmhouse of her own / Some husband keeps her cosy... / Good bye, my wayside posy'.

In *The Prince's Progress*, the milkmaid episode is important because it presents the first distraction in the narrative, the first 'trial' faced by the questing hero and, thus, the initial test of his mettle. That Rossetti herself viewed the milkmaid as a key element in the poem's overall strategy is clear from that letter of February 1865 cited earlier in this chapter that she wrote to her brother Dante Gabriel, in which she outlines her conception of the narrative structure: 'my actual *Prince* seems to me invested with a certain artistic congruity of construction not lightly to be despised; 1st, a prelude and outset; 2nd, an alluring milkmaid ... the subtle elements balance each other and fuse into a noble conglom!'[25] As I have already argued (and, hopefully, already demonstrated), much of Rossetti's poetry may be taken as dealing with matters of reading and interpretation or, more precisely, misreading and misinterpretation. In *The Prince's Progress,* the prominent inclusion of the milkmaid early in the heavily symbolic narrative makes it clear that, like the maid of 'A Farm Walk', she is a cipher to be decoded, and like any symbol or any poem (as conceived of by Rossetti) she embodies the potential for plurality of meaning. She is ambiguously described as 'rosy and white'. 'Was she a maid, or an evil dream?' we are urged to ponder.

The milkmaid talks in riddles and is herself a riddle to be solved. A simple 'wave-haired milkmaid', she simultaneously boasts 'shining serpent coils'. She is thus both a pastoral maiden and a Medusa figure realised in diabolic terms, embodying starkly contrary aspects of the feminine. The Prince's failure to comprehend her correctly sets a precedent that the rest of his journey will confirm by repetition. As a symbol, the milkmaid has been assimilated into the patterning of the traditional literary quest but still she may dupe the Prince here due to her own active (unlike that suffered by the 'veiled bride') unwillingness wholly to submit to male dominance and desires. The milkmaid demands reciprocal equality — '"Give me my fee," she said' — and indeed obtains it, yet ultimately (Rossetti once more going for subtle subversion rather than reductive upheaval of received literary conventions) she remains caught up and left behind in the quest world, illustrating further the predicament of woman conceived of as secondary citizen in a male-ordered version of experience. Like the biblical figure of Esther which Rossetti recontextualises to great effect in *Monna Innominata* (see *Poems*, II, 90), the milkmaid must become, in part, Eve-like seductress in order to gain temporary equality within a traditionally male-dominated structure.

The use of language in the milkmaid episode is notable. The scenario it creates might be termed neo-Edenic, verging on the surreal. The 'apple-tree', 'heaven lowered black' with 'fire-cloven edge', and the 'cunning… shining serpent coils' in the maid's hair are the most obvious danger signs missed by the Prince as, like Laura in *Goblin Market*, he succumbs to temptation without hesitation. These images beg that the incident be superficially understood as a coyly realised biblical fall myth, a simple allegory (again, as much of the imagery in *Goblin Market* initially appears to function), but further clues to a fuller reading of the passage may be located in the strange register employed at this point in the poem, particularly in the dialogue sequences. '"Whitest cow that ever was calved / Surely gave you this milk"', offers the Prince, but his speculative comment is a glaring instance of non-logic, for a cow's colouring does not influence the colour of its milk, which deftly conveys the Prince's naive misunderstanding of symbolic causality investigated elsewhere in *The Prince's Progress*. Playing on the Prince's gullibility, the milkmaid seeks further to expose his lack of understanding of signs:

"Give me my fee," she said. —

"I will give you a jewel of gold." —
"Not so; gold is heavy and cold." —
"I will give you a velvet fold
Of foreign work your beauty to deck." —
Better I like my kerchief rolled
Light and white round my neck."

This Prince clearly does not understand woman's desires. He has no idea what woman wants. When the milkmaid says 'Give me my fee', she may as well be demanding, 'Understand me as a quest symbol, tell me my worth, *interpret* me!' The word game that follows recalls the charged conundrums of Lewis Carroll's *Alice* adventures and puts the unwitting male quester at the mercy of woman's sharper wit. The Prince is quick to admit defeat:

"Nay," cried he, "but fix your own fee." —
She laughed, "You may give the full moon to me;
Or else sit under this apple-tree
Here for one idle day by my side;
After that, I'll let you go free,
And the world is wide."

In language echoing Keats' 'La Belle Dame Sans Merci', the maid, herself a secondary device in the traditionally phallocentric quest hierarchy, manages to subvert the tradition from within by gaining this little victory over the artless Prince. He is subtly cajoled into letting the female decree her own worth, her 'own fee'. Her statement of value is at first enigmatic and then plain. Requesting that she be given the full moon — that which was harbinger, catalyst to the Prince's own quest — she slyly demands that the premise for the quest be handed back to woman. Latterly, she asks for the Prince's attendance upon herself 'for one idle day by my side'. Unlike the masculine, proprietary ethic where partners are concerned, the female advocates a less aggressively possessive, more libertarian approach: 'After that I'll let you go free'.

The Prince chooses the latter alternative. He will not hand over the full moon to a woman, since to do so would be, symbolically to relinquish man's hold upon the quest and all its implications. His reasons are typically selfish: 'For courtesy's sake he could not lack / To redeem his own royal pledge'. No thoughts are spared for the waiting bride-to-(not)-be: the formal conventions of the quest ('courtesy', a 'royal pledge'), and not its object, are uppermost in the quester's mind. At least the milkmaid, herself trapped to a certain extent inside the parameters of male-ordered quest tradition, has displayed the power to deconstruct and subvert, by means of her 'subtle toils', the codes of the quest from within, taking an active role in the narrative. In sad comparison, the mute, passive princess has become a redundant symbol within the narrative taken from a male perspective, so that fulfillment of the rites of the quest itself, regardless of their loaded implications, becomes the priority of the Prince, over and above any authentic concern for the waiting maiden who, literally, relies upon his resolve, attention and progress for her very life, her continued existence.

The milkmaid actively decrees the Prince's (lack of) progress at this early stage of the narrative:

> So he stretched his length in the apple-tree shade,
> Lay and laughed and talked to the maid,
> Who twisted her hair in a cunning braid
> And writhed it in shining serpent coils,
> And held him a day and night fast laid
> In her subtle toils.

The Prince has succumbed to temptation and, emphasised by neo-biblical fall-myth imagery, is truly fallen, relinquishing at this point any hope of control over his own subsequent progress. The episode of the milkmaid thus marks a little victory for woman, the first small step in bringing about the ultimate failure of the Prince's quest. Manipulated by Rossetti, the stereotypical milkmaid figure is revealed to be a far from dead symbol, but still potentially alive, containing long-forgotten, untapped power. Just one example of the author's persistently innovative treatment of symbols and archetypes, Rossetti's milkmaids serve to remind us of their creator's own artistic quest to expose the one-sidedness of male-ordained literary conventions, giving hope to those who similarly seek to subvert and reinvent literary traditions, originating fresh ways of describing a world which for too long has failed woman's needs and been the property of others.

III

As part of her overall drive to subvert male-ordained codes of expression in her writing and find for her sex an appropriate mode of articulation, Christina Rossetti is repeatedly involved in the subtle but calculated remanagement of codes, ideologies, myths, and symbols inherited and borrowed from literary tradition. This might be termed her prime 'system of work' as a Victorian woman writer. *The Prince's Progress* offers unusually clear evidence in support of this theory. Rossetti's deft manipulation and strategic recontextualisation of the milkmaid persona from pastoral literature sufficiently supports such a notion, but as further evidence, I want to examine another archetype skillfully and knowingly re-invented by Rossetti in *The Prince's Progress*: the figure of the alchemist.

Maureen Roberts points to 'evidence in alchemical literature that the alchemists were aware of the ultimately psychic nature of their procedures', adding that the 'quest for unity or wholeness' is 'central to both alchemy and Romanticism'.[26] Roberts succinctly identifies precisely why alchemy would offer fertile figurative and philosophical ground to Rossetti's own post-Romantic quest to challenge and redefine inherited notions of 'unity' and 'wholeness', and to investigate their relationships to experience, imagination, and the self from a radically female proto-feminist perspective:

The introspective, radically symbolic and mythic language of hermetic philosophy of all ages, as well as its affirmation of a meaningful correspondence between mind and Nature, puts it - alongside Romanticism and the Platonic tradition - within a mode of thought and perception which draws its creative inspiration from a perennial substratum of innate archetypal ideas. Western alchemy, which flourished in Europe through to the end of the Renaissance, gradually faded into obscurity during the eighteenth century as a result of its incompatibility with the hypostasis of reason that characterized the spirit of "enlightenment." Romanticism, then, as a metarational reaction to empiricism, entails a reconnection to the archetypal realm and a corresponding reactivation of alchemical themes and symbols.[27]

Roberts cites the claim of the Renaissance alchemist Paracelsus (Theophrastus von Hohenheim, 1493-1541, who internalized principles of alchemy and applied them to human medicine, his work being a significant influence upon William Blake): 'Everything in external nature points to something internal'.[28] This idea could itself be a motif for much of Rossetti's poetry, and is certainly pertinent to the landscapes and characters we encounter in *The Prince's Progress*. Paracelsus had sought to explicate the human body in alchemical terms, and the Romantics further extended this revision of alchemy's domain into the realm of the Imagination, seeing alchemy as potential spiritual unifier of outer and inner. Rossetti, re-evaluating the subject-object relationship from a post-Romantic woman writer's viewpoint, and always aware of the ever-present disunities necessary for unity to have meaning, turns to alchemy as one of various available paradigms inherited from literary tradition whose parameters and principles she can usefully subvert and remanage in the course of her own poetry.

An alchemist, then, prominently inhabits and 'dovetails properly' into that compelling section of the Prince's narrative directly following dalliance with an earlier archetypal figure from pastoral tradition, the fair milkmaid who has just deftly seduced our willing hero. Awoken again by the lark, symbol of the poet in song, who (like the 'sad glad voices' first encountered in the seventh stanza of the poem, now less 'meek') urges him to proceed and admonishes him for his ably demonstrated anti-heroic 'sluggard' nature, the flawed, bungling protagonist Prince eventually resumes his interrupted journey. Immediately, the pastoral landscape is left behind and the atmosphere becomes one of pervasive sterility:

> The grass grew rare…
> A blight lurked in the darkening air…
> Behind his back the soil lay bare,
> But barer in front.   (*Poems*, I, 98)

This barren, apocalyptic landscape, a 'lifeless… loveless land', deliberately and directly recalls the vale of death described in Blake's 'The Argument' from the *Marriage of Heaven and Hell*. (In truth, Rossetti's 'loveless land' is also borrowed almost verbatim from an earlier sonnet of her own, 'Cobwebs' (*Poems*, III, 240-1).) This is an arena of inertia and frozen attitudes, offering the severest unfriendly terrain and presenting our protagonist 'of purpose weak' with a stark image of the implications of his own lack of vital resolution.

> A land of neither life nor death,
> Where no man buildeth or fashioneth,
> Where none draws living or dying breath;
> No man cometh or goeth there,
> No man doeth, seeketh, saith,
> In the stagnant air.

> Some old volcanic upset must
> Have rent the crust and blackened the crust;
> Wrenched and ribbed it beneath its duct
> Above earth's molten center at seethe,
> Heaved and heaped it by huge upthrust
> Of fire beneath. (*Poems*, I, 99)

To borrow a phrase memorably used by Rossetti herself when lamenting her own lack of poetic inspiration, the 'fire has died out' here.[29] The 'fire beneath' this earthy crust was once so potent that it '[w]renched and ribbed' the surface and came forth. Now, all is sterile and lifeless. Like the questing Prince, and like the codes of the quest itself, all the life force has been removed: only the barren picture remains. The Prince has truly awoken into 'solitude': the awakening is a painful one, but one which might be his salvation if he could (or would) only begin to read signs correctly and learn from them. The visible signs of nature — the changing, symbolic landscape of the poem — and the trials he undertakes continually, repeatedly present intimations of the spiritual world, with all its noble potential. Equally, they emblematize the imbalance in the nature of the male-ordered quest, the approaching apocalypse of hope and the tragic predicament of the princess, all signs which are ignored or misread by the Prince and only acknowledged by the female voices (or those symbolic utterances of nature) which persistently urge him forward with mounting alarm.

The perilous journey through a wasteland is a chief aspect of the major adventure in quest romance. In myth, the entire purpose of this expedition was to bring about the revitalisation of nature. Here, however, as in many post-Romantic quest poems — from Browning's 'Childe Roland to the Dark Tower Came' to Eliot's *The Waste Land* — this 'land / Of rugged blackness' is not only imaged as a phenomenon of external nature, but as a state of mind as well, making implicit the notion that the quester's search is one for spiritual renewal.

Perhaps most notably, there are definite, strong echoes here (and not only in this section of *The Prince's Progress*) of Keats' 'La Belle

Dame sans Merci'. Where Keats has 'on thy cheeks a fading rose / Fast withereth', Rossetti offers 'up rose the Prince with a flush on his cheek', and Keats' description of his hero '[a]lone and palely loitering' finds a more accusatory but similarly rhythmic reprise in Rossetti's '[y]ou loitered on the road too long'. Though there are obvious correlations in the two works, both being quest narratives, the difference in treatment of the mode is marked. Keats' disillusioned hero who, like Rossetti's Prince, moves against the bare, blighted landscape of solitude, is at least granted the visionary power to interpret and explain his sad predicament. Keats' whole poem begins with a question — 'O what can ail thee…?' — that it then becomes the business of the 'knight at arms' satisfactorily to answer. Though Keats' hero appears to have little chance of recovering his anima, his 'lady in the meads', his 'latest dream' at least presents him with an explanation of his loss:

> I saw pale kings and princes too,
> Pale warriors, death pale were they all;
> They cried - "La belle dame sans merci
> Hath thee in thrall!"[30]

This image of all the other 'pale kings' who have sought and lost the same vision of beauty lets the knight of 'La Belle Dame sans Merci' know his own projected fate. The 'horrid warning' might have come too late, but it does establish a degree of certitude towards which, in structure, the poem strives:

> And this is why I sojourn here,
> Alone and palely loitering,
> Though the sedge is withered from the lake,
> And no birds sing.

Keats' hero is a sad figure, but not directly culpable in his own fate. In direct contrast, Rossetti's Prince is continually allowed the prospect of redemption and recovery of innocence, but he does not accept these offered reprieves. Keats' knight concisely explains the barren wasteland he occupies in terms of the forced negation of his quest: Rossetti's quester is permitted the vision of bleak sterility whilst there is still opportunity to correct the progress of his journeying. Of course, he again misreads the signs around him, still believing himself to be on the 'right' road:

> Rueful he peered to right and left,
> Muttering in his altered mood:
> "The fate is hard that weaves my weft,
> Though my lot be good.'
>
> Dim the changes of day to night,
> Of night scarce dark to day not bright,
> Still his road wound towards the right,
> Still he went, and still he went…   (*Poems*, I, 99)

Throughout the poem, Christina Rossetti's Prince is a dumb participant in the death(s) surrounding him on his journey, making implicit symbolically what is made explicit in terms of the plot at the poem's close: his guilty complicity in bringing about the demise of the princess, original and still ultimate object of his mission. As D'Amico observes, Rossetti's 'strong Prince' is 'a fantasy creature of romance who [does] not exist'.[31] The flawed Prince moves idly through a series of what Rossetti, writing as a Victorian woman, sees as being redundant quest conventions, always blind to the fate he is actively inviting, a fate which must be painfully and passively submitted to by the helpless princess. Unlike Keats' hero, Rossetti's quester is given warnings in advance of the dreadful circumstances that await him, warnings which become progressively stronger and more explicit as the poem continues. Significantly, the Prince heeds none of them.

Compounding his plight, then, Rossetti's knight fails to make any positive deductions from the barren landscape he finds himself traversing at this point in the narrative. In fact, he directly disobeys the admonishments afforded to him subsequent to his recent dalliance with the seductive milkmaid.

> "Up, up, up" called the watchman lark,
> In his clear réveillée: "Hearken, oh hark!
> Press up to the high goal, fly to the mark.
> Up, up O sluggard…   (*Poems*, I, 98)

Similarly urged by the 'sad glad voices' to go '[u]p, up, up,' to ascend, the Prince, by now predictably, chooses to *descend* below the ground. Unlike that of Keats' Endymion, and in turn Homer's Odysseus, this Prince's underworld descent, through a cave down to depths labyrinthine, is one of escape. The other questers are prompted by the possibility of discovery in the nether world, to find or achieve some thing spiritual in import. The Prince of Rossetti's poem is hunting refuge in the cave 'world of trouble'. By now, he is drifting aimlessly on the tides of the quest, merely going through the motions and rhythms thrown up by the journey, having relinquished any real conception of his original goal.

The initial description of the cavern the Prince enters is notable in that it strongly delineates the place as a 'grave', and, moreover, a version of hell. In other epics, the cave jointly symbolizes a tomb of death and a womb of life, but it is clear which reading is to dominate the Prince's experience of the underworld:

> Out it flashed from a yawn-mouthed cave,
> Like a red-hot eye from a grave.
> No man stood there of whom to crave
> Rest…   (*Poems*, I, 99-100)

Retreating into this hellish catacomb, the Prince faces the prospect not of rebirth but of further compounding his predicament, his symbolic descent from activity. He escapes from the vision of solitude into a vision of the confused searching that his own quest has come to represent. He meets a mirror version of his current self, a toiling alchemist:

> In he passed and tarried not,
> Groping his way from spot to spot,
> Towards where the cavern flare glowed hot:-
> An old, old mortal, cramped and double,
> Was peering into a seething-pot,
> In a world of trouble.   (*Poems*, I, 100)

As the Prince is a quester, so the alchemist is also a searcher. The central positioning of this alchemist episode in *The Prince's Progress* reflects the centrality of its symbolic import in the overall 'system' of the poem and show us Rossetti once more reworking a recognizable traditional literary archetype. Interestingly, D. M. Stuart insists that *The Prince's Progress* was 'originally christened *The Alchemist*' — an appealing claim to which no source is given nor does any real evidence appear to exist: the notion is, however, indicative of the influence of the alchemist section over the rest of the poem's events.[32] Concerning the 'science' of alchemy and its actual practice in mediaeval times, Fred Gettings has made the following observations:

> The gold [an alchemist] sought was not really a metal
> at all. Rather than taking the path to worldly riches,
> the alchemist was seeking an inner secret, looking
> for a way to develop his own inner world of vision
> and understanding ... The genuine alchemists were
> concerned with spiritual things. They did not look
> into the dross metals ... Indeed they looked into the
> dross of man, that ordinary, untransformed inner life
> of man which they visualized as a sort of dead weight,
> containing more riches of miraculous powers than
> anyone could ever imagine ... The serious alchemist

sought to discover a secret whereby the wonderful
powers he could feel in his own inner being might be
released into the world in their full glory.[33]

In this sense, there are clear fundamental similarities between the
alchemist and the poet, both of who devote themselves to a quest
to relate their inner world to the 'dross' of everyday existence. From
her own father's substantial work in the area of the occult, its codes
and symbolism, Christina Rossetti cannot but have been aware of
the significations and implications in a creative sense attached to
the practice of alchemy: indeed, her learned father made original
research and wrote on this very subject.[34] Certainly, alchemy's links
with the strivings of the poet and its mythical potential as a *symbolic*
quest, as I have already mentioned, would not have escaped a writer
whose life's work, as I have argued elsewhere, revolved greatly around
an investigation of patterns of symbolism and their ideological
implications. Of this function, Chetwynd has noted:

> True symbolism is not fantasy, though both are
> the products of the imagination. Symbols attempt
> to express such fundamental principles that are
> synchronistically true for the outer world of matter
> *and* the inner world of the psyche, both of which
> stem from the same source and consequently behave
> according to the same principles. Over the years
> alchemy provided ample proofs to substantiate this
> duality, since its practitioners continually applied
> archetypal symbols to a microscopic universe, and
> time and time again the symbol demonstrated its
> validity to both spheres, the psyche and matter.[35]

In this way, then, alchemy takes on the mantle of a major archetypal
symbol itself, a quest emblematizing *any* quest. Given alchemy's
insistence upon the importance of a symbolic appreciation of elements

in any identifiable 'outer' pattern, the clearly internalisable timbre of the discipline, it is patently clear why Christina Rossetti sought so vehemently to include the alchemist encounter as central point of her reworked quest epic (an epic in which her own anti-hero's (mis) appreciation of symbolic input is pointedly much to the fore).

In Rossetti's considered and deliberate scheme of things, then, we may confidently propose that the alchemist achieves a post-Romantic position symbolic of the poet's (in particular the *female* poet's) ongoing struggle to make elemental sense from out of an unruly world in which all things are no longer pure, and where a biased ideology others have made comes masquerading as truth. Of course, like the milkmaid and the moon, the alchemist must partly and initially function within the terms of the quest and obey the *a priori* 'rules' of the literary tradition Rossetti ultimately desires to subvert by way of highlighting its several inadequacies in the course of her feminist treatise. In this manner, Rossetti's alchemist thus embodies the poet's *raison d'etre*, seeker for inner-to-outer connections and truths: but, caught in the predetermined world of the quest, he cannot simply make order from the chaos around him and becomes, poignantly, a microcosmic, telling reflection of the Prince. Such important potential for ambiguity of interpretation is commented upon at the moment of the old man's death:

> Thus the dead man stayed in his grave,
> Self-chosen, the dead man in his cave;
> There he stayed, were he fool or knave,
> Or honest seeker who had not found
> (*Poems*, I, 102)

Like the Prince, the 'old, old mortal' alchemist figure reworked from tradition into *The Princes Progress* finds the object of his quest too late, and the result is death. This represents an emphatic statement from Rossetti the female Victorian artist at this point in her development as a writer, concerning the way in which the poetic search for 'truth' within the present frame of reference afforded by poetic tradition in general is an impossibility. The aged alchemist expires without achieving his goal. His own death bathetically provides the final ingredient in his unviable mission to create elixir of life. This magnificent ambiguity must have seemed especially poignant to Rossetti, struggling to articulate woman's experience in a medium designed to denaturalize, repress and stifle it, at this early stage of her writing career.

Alchemy deals with the separation of the various ingredients of life and the consequent recognition of the complicated relationships between these elements. It is a notion concerned with transformation and is on this level an investigation of dualities, the awareness of viable alternatives to any set given. As such, on one crucial level, it can be appropriate metaphor for Christina Rossetti's 'system of work', her pre-Modernist post-Romantic way of declaring, simultaneously, the impossibility of free expression of female experience and 'truth' within the hitherto male-ordered poetic tradition, and the need to address and redress this imbalance if any kind of acceptable 'verity' is to be reclaimed for future generations of poets and women.

In *The Prince's Progress*, the reiteration of traditional quest patterning instanced by the alchemist's death functions to deliver fresh sustenance to the male quester: the Prince emerges hugging his 'phial of Life', seemingly re-energised. But his complacency and forgetfulness of his original goal remain, as he manages (lines 263-82) to sleep through another 'summons' to action, finally to resume his journey albeit 'drowsy' and, once again, 'though late'. Presumption pervades the knight's own words as he leaves the alchemist behind: "'Come what will of wind or weather, / This draught of Life when my Bride is won / We'll drink together.'" (*Poems*, I, 102) Our Prince permits no conditional mode into his self-constructed quest-narrative; a smug affirmative 'when' and never 'if'. Nonchalantly riding a quest tradition that, by its own terms and premises, exists to guarantee him successful passage, the Prince never countenances the possibility of failure. That is left to the female voices that entreat and implore him urgently and ominously throughout the poem:

> He can sleep who holdeth her cheap,
> Sleep and wake and sleep again,
> Let him sow, one day he shall reap,
> Let him sow the grain.   (*Poems*, I, 102)

The Prince sets off 'late' once more, clutching his 'phial of Life'. This vital elixir must, of course, be read as primarily symbolic, more so since, as an actual device in the subsequent narrative, it is redundant and never empirically put to the test. Again, the Prince appropriates meaning to suit his own ends, taking this elixir as a sign that his quest is proceeding naturally to its certain conclusion. Encouraged by the leaving of solitude behind, once more this hapless anti-hero's enthusiasm grows in inverse proportion to the portentous warnings he receives. All urgency is now gone from him: the Prince has all but forgotten his proper purpose here. Unmindful of time, he embarks now upon a leisurely nature ramble and decides to have a bath:

> By willow courses he took his path ...
> Loitered awhile for a deep-stream bath,
> Yawned for a fellow-man ...
> It's oh for a second maiden, at least,
> To bear the flagon, and taste it too,
> And flavour the feast. (*Poems*, I, 103)

The baptismal, partial drowning that occurs hereafter is, like most of the 'trials' along his route, the result of the Prince's own choosing and, by now characteristic, lack of foresight. (Like that of the old alchemist, this Prince's fate is '[s]elf-chosen'.) It also (akin to the alchemist episode) allows yet another symbolic rebirth to be purposefully misread by the quester. As a life-or-death scene takes place by the waters, pointedly abrupt interruptions to the telling remind us of the other struggle still going on beyond this main narrative. The resuscitation of the hero is punctuated by further parenthetical commentary from '[h]er women', only now they are resigned to the fate that lies in store for the princess.

They no longer admonish; now they merely passively observe the lack of progress. Like the princess, they have been rendered ineffectual, redundant by traditional conventions of quest literature.

All is lost now. Imagery itself becomes unfathomable: it is unclear whether the Prince – now laid beneath a willow – is dead or alive, uncertain whether his saviour is a Christ figure or an idealised anima, or both:

> Oh, a moon face in a shadowy place,
> And a light touch and a winsome grace,
> And a thrilling tender voice that says:
> "Safe from waters that seek the sea -
> Cold waters by rugged ways -
> Safe with me."   (*Poems*, I, 104)

Evidence here is deliberately inconclusive: as the princess has been left to fade away, so the quest is, quite literally, losing meaning. Even our unreliable interpreter Prince himself has abandoned a search for meaning, no longer even bothering to 'weigh' or 'scan':

> Had he stayed to weigh and to scan,
> He had been more or less than a man:
> He did what a young man can,
> Spoke of toil and an arduous way...
> (*Poems*, I, 105)

These lines might be read as indicating that, to the male forgers of the quest tradition (and those who choose to uphold its codes), there has come a point at which its values and rhythms have been assimilated into the mode as absolute *truths*. A 'man', customarily, will not 'weigh' or 'scan' the ideologies inscribed within quest myth, its abnegation of female expressiveness, and its assumptions of male dominance, but will accept all these without question. Such falsehoods masquerading as truths will be perpetuated by the masculine speaking of 'toil and an arduous way', thus reaffirming the phallocentric quest regardless of the plight of its female object.

Two beautifully poised and poignant lines confirm this: 'The promise promised so long ago, / The long promise, has not been kept.' (*Poems*, I, 105) As the Prince has relinquished his promise of fidelity of attention to the princess, so quest tradition has become unfaithful to woman's needs, rendering the female sex helpless, speechless non-participants in a loaded game invented and played by men. Within the biased rules of this convention, woman can only express herself by submission ('She in her meekness, he in his pride...' (*Poems*, I, 107)), subversion, or by, literally, becoming an absence in death, unattended by the male 'hero'.

The Prince's final burst of positive energy is ironic: he is 'stung' into action finally by the poem's certitude that hope is lost. Yet still his complacency reigns:

> Light labour more, and his foot would stand
> On the threshold, all labour done;
> Easy pleasure laid at his hand,
> And the dear Bride won.   (*Poems*, I, 107)

As The Prince's Progress comes to a conclusion with the original 'Too late for love' lyric, the princess is finally, albeit indirectly and partially, given a voice. It is a disembodied, fragmented voice, the voice of an absence. Within the terms of the set patternings of the phallocentric quest, woman's quest for representation fails or is, at best, only partial: her death, at least, brings about a 'song' (as the symbolic 'death' of woman in traditional lyric poetry brings about Rossetti's *Monna Innominata*, but that is a take for a later chapter), and, thus, at last this tragic princess manages to alter a male-decreed fate (narrative closure and a symbolic 'happy' ending in marriage) which centuries of unsubverted literary tradition have decreed for her.

By shrewd manipulation of the codes and ideologies that quest myths have relied upon for their apparent coherence and dramatic

impact since earliest texts, Rossetti goes some way towards reclaiming
another poetic tradition back from the male monopoly. She shows
woman as trapped: imprisoned in a permanent silent hiatus, a coma,
within a literary form (the quest narrative) that premises male as active
seeker of truths he is sure of finding and sure to find. In *The Prince's
Progress*, the form (like the bungling Prince himself) is shown to
be flawed, irrelevant and inadequate to woman's genuine needs and
desires. If woman is to appear as anything other than silent object
in such a tradition, her expression must forcibly be one of lack, of
desire unfulfilled, and of hope at best deferred, regardless of her own
endeavours. (And such is the energy behind the 'death-wish' yearning
which many unwittingly-tempted male commentators hasten to
identify in Rossetti's poetry.)

The final coup of Rossetti's quest poem lies in its final imaging
of that which it has argued, now in terms directly applicable to the
repressed female within English Victorian society. Rossetti is at last,
on one powerful level, describing her own predicament, and that of
so many women: anxious princesses trapped in an agony of forced
inaction and conditioned to accept non-expression as a norm. There
is palpable anger beneath a matter-of-fact surface diction here:

> We never heard her speak in haste;
> Her tones were sweet,
> And modulated just so much
> As it was meet:
> Her heart sat silent through the noise
> And concourse of the street.
> There was no hurry in her hands,
> No hurry in her feet;
> There was no bliss drew nigh to her,
> That she might run to greet.   (*Poems*, I, 109)

As Eliot, in *The Waste Land*, uses a mythical landscape (indeed the
'mythical method') to render the fragmented, disordered surface of

modern sensibility, so, in *The Prince's Progress*, Rossetti reworks the recognisable patterns of quest romance so that they form a metaphor not for movement towards stable identity and regeneration, but rather as an illustration of the inarticulation afforded to the feminine aspect (the feminine *subject*, potentially) by traditions of male ordering and male interpreting of myth and legend. Eliot himself describes Joyce's employment of this 'mythical method' in *Ulysses* thus:

> [The mythical method] is simply a way of controlling, of ordering, of giving shape and significance to the immense panorama of futility and anarchy which is contemporary history.[36]

In *The Prince's Progress*, and in many other poems, Christina Rossetti gives shape and significance to woman's position as silent 'other' in the male-ordered worldview repeatedly amplified by literary tradition in general and by quest poetry in particular. With this (what Lynda Palazzo has termed) 'deeply internalised gender prejudice' thus skilfully exposed via the ominously satirical fictional machinations of Rossetti's Prince's failed journeying, woman's *real*, desperate, and despairing quest for unfettered expression can be more directly documented, intensified, and significantly reframed in what I think is Rossetti's finest poem, *Monna Innominata*, this brave poet's most sustained articulation of the strain felt at being made marginal to an inherited tradition manufactured by partially-sighted others. In this truly remarkable and complex sequence of formal sonnets, we can witness the intertextual and trans-textual literary-historical aspects of Rossetti's art intensified to radically confrontational proportions, and observe the religious faith that would singularly occupy her late poetry addressed in a most open and provocative manner.

6

WOMEN ARE NOT MEN: APPROACHING *MONNA INNOMINATA*

Here is a great discovery, "Women are not Men"…
Christina Rossetti, letter to Dante Gabriel Rossetti, April 1870

I

Poetry in general, and in particular the Western sonnet tradition, from Dante and Petrarch through Sidney and Ronsard to more recent writers, dogmatically dictated that the love poem proceed from the subjectivity of a male speaker. Characteristically, the male poet addresses the goodness and beauty of an (usually) unavailable female object, which becomes at once his muse and the means by which his own identity is defined in song. The female is the muse, the male the maker. The speaker and addressee are not normally named, thereby ensuring that the poetry take on an eternal dimension - the female object representing a visionary essence over and above any specific personage from history. The verbal wooing which constitutes the traditional courtly love poem is underwritten by a repeated patterning which seeks to define identity through confession of desire which simultaneously maintains the gender placings of lover as male and loved one as female. All these set conventions of love-poetry define the male as subject and the female as 'other' and, thus, make the mode a problematical area for the woman writer. For the female poet, to inhabit the male-ordered tradition of sonneteering is to upset long established notions of subjectivity, to be forced to interfere with a set equation which has traditionally (with a few exceptions) held woman prisoner as the silent, passive object of male desires since its formulation.

But it is precisely this notion of the misrepresentation at work in the poetic forms which, as a woman poet writing in the nineteenth century, she inherited, that gives energy and bite to the poetry of Christina Rossetti, *Monna Innominata* (*Poems*, II, 86-93) continues the female poet's interest in redressing the iniquity towards woman inscribed in poetic tradition by working another subversion of a received mode - this time the courtly love sonnet sequence. With its bold prefatory remarks outlining the strategy of the piece in no uncertain terms, *Monna Innominata* forms the most overt statement of Rossetti's dissatisfaction with the position allocated to woman by the gender division perpetuated by the literary canon. Like *Goblin Market* and *The Prince's Progress*, *Monna Innominata* allows a comfortably assimilable reading at literal level. Suzanne Walden's pronouncement that this 'sonnet sequence fails both as a story of love and as a story of spirit' is, as we will see, predicated upon a misjudgement of Rossetti's motives and poetic technique.[1] The work gives a platform for the hitherto unsung feelings and thoughts of the muse to whom the tradition of courtly love poetry has been addressed: 'Had such a lady spoken for herself, the portrait left us might have appeared more tender, if less dignified, than any drawn even by a devoted friend' (*Poems*, II, 86).

The implication is obvious: woman has persistently been misrepresented and must now speak 'for herself'. Answering the distortions perpetrated by the poems specifically of Dante and Petrarch and, notably, the female Victorian writer Elizabeth Barrett Browning, the speaker of the fourteen sonnets paints a bleak picture of woman's lot. The scant, sedentary plot open with the speaker's reaction to the man's absence, continues with her musings upon the relationship between secular and holy love, and ends with the man's total disappearance, leaving 'Youth gone, and beauty gone' for the poetess as heroine, and 'Silence of love that cannot sing again' (XIV,

1, 14) for the heroine as poetess.[2] Founded upon contemplation rather than action, the literal level of *Monna Innominata* does cohere perfectly well but, again as with so much of Rossetti's work, one detects an equally coherent subtext at work in the poetry. The note preceding the sonnets unmistakably alerts the reader to the thesis of the sequence: the unfulfilled longing described in the bare narrative of *Monna Innominata* functions in the service of an equally strong desire to invert stereotypical conventions of poetic address, thereby exposing the injustice to woman in the traditional literary canon.

The circumstances of the composition of *Monna Innominata* are not at all well documented. With characteristic lack of precision, William Michael Rossetti gives the date of completion of the sonnet cycle as 'before 1882' - which seems distinctly probable since the sequence of fourteen poems was first published in 1881 in *A Pageant and Other Poems*. Her brother acknowledges his uncertainty about the date of the poems:

> The MSS, of Christina Rossetti's poems, up to 11 June 1866, are, with few exceptions, extant and dated in notebooks; but after that time, although several MSS. exist, few precise dates are traceable. Christina published the Prince's Progress volume in 1866 - the Pageant volume in 1881. The reader will understand that, in saying 'before 1882' - in this instance, and the like in several others – I do not imply that the composition was written shortly before 1882, for it may date at any time between June 1866 and 1881. I am seldom, in such cases, able to approximate the true date nearer than this. (*Works*, 462)

A letter sent to William Michael indicates that Christina Rossetti sent the poems to be included in the *Pageant* collection to her publisher Alexander Macmillan in April 1881: 'At last I took the plunge and sent in some poems to Macmillan, who before he saw accepted them, - for

I wrote first on the subject and he closed with them forthwith'.[3] It may be assumed that *Monna Innominata* was among the poems forwarded. Three months later - one day after the proposed publication date of the Pageant volume, postponed owing to binding problems - the sonnet cycle is directly referred to (and given a name for the first recorded time) in another of Christina's communications, this time to Dante Gabriel Rossetti: 'William [Michael Rossetti] saw the sonnets before you, merely because calling one day he downright asked to look at book, (sic) - a nervous moment for me, though I braved it out. Those he means are *Monna Innominata*'.[4]

We may only conclude, then, that the sonnet sequence was completed before 28 April 1881. It is impossible to be more precise. Yet instances of biographical vagueness such as this may be taken as pleasantly appropriate once the strategy of Christina Rossetti's poetic work is fully considered. As I stated at the very beginning of this study, historical determination as to the correspondence between poet-life and poet-writings has plagued criticism of Christina Rossetti's work. *Monna Innominata* translates as 'Unnamed Lady' and, in her own note prefacing the cycle, the author speaks of 'donna innominate', the unnamed women who formed the conventional object matter of Italian courtly love lyrics of the thirteenth century. She refers, significantly, to two poets of this period who actively broke with tradition by consistently naming the addressees of their lyrics - Dante, who wrote to his Beatrice, and Petrarch whose Laura of the *Rime* is also pronounced a real person by the poet. Beyond the narrative of the Rossetti sequence, these indicators suggest that there are other energies - with the notion of 'naming' and its implications where historical actuality or psychological structures are concerned - at work in the text. The 'Unnamed Lady' is interested in matters of signification.

As we have seen, *Monna Innominata* works an inversion of the typical renaissance lyric, allowing the woman to speak, as the 'Unnamed Lady' becomes the specified point of origin of the song, the poetic subject. The addressee is said to be male, but tellingly is also left unnamed. This lack of specific external reference is characteristic of Rossetti's work. Speaker and spoken to are hardly ever named as figures from actuality; in the great majority of her lyrics the 'you' addressed is undetermined as to gender or number. Even when a proper name is supplied, as in the poem "'No, Thank You, John'" (*Poems*, I, 50-1), one must be wary of jumping to historical conclusions. Dante Gabriel regarded this poem as overly personal,[5] and William Michael conjectures: 'I think I understand who John was; he dated, so far as my sister was affected, at a period some years prior to 1860'.[6] William Michael thought that the John of the poem was the painter John Brett, who displayed affection for Christina in 1852 (eight years before the verses were written, making the poem's protestations rather belated). This speculation, which a number of critics have supported down the years, along with any other guess as to the identity of 'John', is countered by Christina Rossetti's own written insistence that 'no such person existed or exists'.[7] Another mystery, another irrelevance?

Whatever, consistent, marked avoidance of direct external reference in the poetry has worked to the detriment of the author where criticism of Rossetti's poetry is concerned. As I have already stated, Christina Rossetti was (at least outwardly) reticent and withdrawn. Her adult life was a sad one of much illness, and she found it necessary, upon religious grounds, to decline two offers of marriage which, had it not been for the differences in devotional outlook, she would almost certainly otherwise have accepted. The first offer came in 1848 from the painter and Pre-Raphaelite Brotherhood member James Collinson, the son of a Mansfield bookseller, who reverted from Catholicism to the Anglican Church in an attempt to sway the High Anglican Rossetti; the second proposal occurred in 1866, coming from Charles Bagot Cayley, the linguist and translator of Dante. Both episodes were understandably painful experiences which deeply affected Christina Rossetti, Predictably, as a result of this unusual life history, much past criticism of Christina Rossetti's poetry has concentrated itself largely upon establishing historical correlatives for the poems, noting the date and place of composition and thence speculating as to whom the addressee or event referred to could possibly be. Such biographical detective work has its place but seems a highly reductive method of literary criticism. Certainly, it strives to attach one consummate meaning to each single text, thus, presumably, making the critic who 'discovers' that meaning the ultimate critic of the text in question. This process of historical detection is not only an uninspired way of reading poetry, but also a highly vulnerable one. As we know, Packer based the whole four hundred and fifty pages of her 1963 study Christina Rossetti upon the 'tentative hypothesis' (Packer's own words) that, from the age of seventeen onwards, Christina was passionately, secretly in love with the Scots painter William Bell Scott, a married man. Packer speculates upon the substance of meetings which it is claimed took place between the two, recording dates and circumstantial evidence, and concludes with wearying insistence: 'It is unlikely that a poet as subjective as Christina would conceive this [impassioned love] poetry in an emotional vacuum; consequently, we can only surmise that it was addressed to someone who does not appear on the record. The evidence I have uncovered points to the name of William Bell Scott'.[8]

Packer's work appears more scrupulous than it in fact turns out to be. Unfortunately for her, less than a year after the publication of her study, the Bell Scott theory was deftly blown asunder by a paper in Victorian Studies by William E. Fredeman, totally discrediting Packer's hypothesis, showing that her data was at best largely supposition and at worst fabrication, and noting furthermore Packer's lack of attention to vital documentation, discovered at Penkill Castle, of Scott's movements. The caustic, condemnation of Packer's work is telling: 'Circumstantial evidence derived primarily from the poetry makes impossible the precise documentation of a theory for which there is not a scrap of positive and direct proof'.[9]

Apart from ruining the friendship between the two academics, Fredeman's paper had the effect of rendering Packer's book (ironically one of the few substantial works of the twentieth century to take Christina Rossetti seriously as a poet) no more than an exercise in conjecture or imaginative biography bordering on romance fiction.

The episode illustrates the precarious position of the critic of literature who follows solely the path of biographical determinism. An all-consuming eagerness to place poems in strict biographical context seems to me unlikely to be productive of valuable literary criticism since, above all, it denies the primacy of imagination. All praise to the critic who deduces that the addressee of T. S. Eliot's 'A Dedication to My Wife' is Valerie Eliot. This revelation is of little relevance once we involve ourselves with a study of the poetry itself, its form, use of language and how that language works to create emotive effects, its debt or relationship to tradition, its symbolic structuring and tone, and so on.

Only in the last couple of decades has criticism of Christina Rossetti's work ventured meaningfully beyond historical considerations. With the advent of structuralist and feminist critiques, interest in the poetry at last overtook interest in its author's life and personal circumstances. It is no longer necessary to regard Rossetti's verses as a diary or a series of confessional letters directly addressed to Collinson, Cayley, Bell Scott or the next man through the door at 38 Charlotte Street, the Rossetti family home in London's West End. There is no reason why the unnamed figures which appear with substantial regularity in the poems - the strong lover, the golden haired maiden, the spectre, the sisters, the absent loved one - should have historical counterparts and their occurrence in the lyrics may or may not have been the consequence of actual events in the lifetime of the author. The case cannot usually be proven either way: Christina Rossetti, when alive, was keen, in correspondence, to deny the existence of external referents for the personae that inhabit her writing. In the devotional prose work, *The Face of the Deep* (1892), this topic is addressed openly and succinctly:

> Far from being necessarily an insurmountable disadvantage, I think that ignorance of the historical drift of prophecy may on occasion turn to a humble but genuine profit. Such ignorance entails (or wisely utilised might entail) that a general lesson, a

> fundamental principle, essence not accident, will be
> elicited from the abstruse text. Further, instead of
> attention being directed to the ends of the earth, our
> eye must be turned within…[10]

This is the case with Rossetti's poetic productions. The prominent and recurrent stock figures of address demand to be read as emblematic expression of urges within the self crystallized into seemingly identifiable forms, concrete expression of otherwise abstract notions. Thus the unnamed male addressed in *Monna Innominata* need not be Bell Scott, Cayley, or Collinson, but an intertextually wrought product of her reading and her creative energies, an imagined male essence, *animus* or soul-mate to the feminine aspect that Christina Rossetti's poetry seeks to reclaim and redefine by its inversion of the love lyric mode. In the first sonnet of the sequence, it is made apparent that the addressee is conceived of as a vision, or 'essence not accident'; 'For one man is my world of all the men / This wide world holds; O love, my world is you' (I, 7-8). Elsewhere, the loved one is described as truly a part of the speaker: 'O my heart's heart, and you who are to me / More than myself myself' (V, 1-2).

   In short, the text of *Monna Innominata* consistently encourages a reading having a psychological frame of reference. The contemplative sonnets are self-reflexive in tone and this, coupled with a prefatory note deeply conscious of the literary tradition in which *Monna Innominata* lies, should alert us to the main strategy of the cycle. The poetic text functions as a map of the self, executed in emblematic fashion: an essentially symbolic construction ordered in a supra narrative manner. As vagueness of external reference and literary reflexiveness are indicators toward this way of writing, then so is the open-ended nature of the typical Rossetti poem. *Monna Innominata* is the epitome of all these areas. The text precludes certitude and complacency in favour of interrogation and ambiguity as, by stretching modes of discourse until the ideology inscribed within them is revealed, traditional conventions and patterns are rewritten to make a new story, woman's story.

II

Monna Innominata is a poem painfully conscious of its own stance as poetry. Subtitled 'A Sonnet of Sonnets' - fourteen poems to match a sonnet's fourteen lines, the volta coming with the eighth sonnet as it arrives in the eighth line of every poem in the series - it utilises a favourite poetic form of Christina and Dante Gabriel Rossetti, the sonnet. To appreciate the full implications of the *Monna Innominata* series, then, it is essential to consider the tradition of writing, the love lyric and sonnet tradition as exemplified in the work of Dante and Petrarch, invoked by Christina Rossetti in the prefatory remarks to her work. The love lyric, and notably the sonnet (with its rigid structure and established pattern of argument and denouement), allows a platform for inquisitive contemplation. Housed within the set framework of the lyric we find philosophical musings already in the Southern European troubadour poetry of the thirteenth century (examined in detail later in this chapter); this is another broad tradition of the love lyric, realised through a combination of subsidiary images and terms, which transfers itself to the sonnet cycle tradition itself, which then becomes a base for intellectual explorations. This process instigates a self-referential tendency in the tradition that never leaves the discipline. Paul Oppenheimer writes provocatively, in his study *The Birth of the Modern Mind*, of the self-introspection, which becomes an integral part of the sonnet tradition.

> Modern thought and literature begin with the invention of the sonnet... As such it is the first lyric of self-consciousness, or of the self in conflict... The sonnet seeks to catch and echo the melodies 'unheard' of the human soul, to use Keats's' phrase, melodies both passionate and silent, both intimate and celestial.[11]

If early European poetry is referred to here, Oppenheimer's point is a debatable one, but his remarks do emphasise the intellectual appeal of the sonnet. The pleasure that Christina Rossetti drew from her exercises in the form - and the compulsiveness of her nature in this area - is indicated by the family's favoured choice of parlour game: bouts-rimés sonneteering was one of the Rossetti family's favourite pastimes. Crump notes this:

> When Christina was seventeen she played a literary game with her brother William. The game was known as bouts-rimes (sic) because each player received a series of rhymed line endings, which he had to use in writing a poem. In order to afford a greater challenge, the Rossettis often chose the sonnet form; moreover, a player was expected to complete his composition as quickly as possible. Christina was quite successful at this game. She was usually able to produce a creditable sonnet in less than ten minutes.[12]

Anyone who has looked at the sonnets Christina Rossetti produced in this way (a number were published in the *Collected Poems*) will recognise the understatement of Crump's 'creditable'. Christina was a remarkably talented, as well as a prolific sonneteer.

Both Christina and Dante Gabriel Rossetti produced sonnet cycles. Indeed the term 'sonnet sequence' was first coined by Dante Gabriel Rossetti in a letter to his writer friend Hall Caine, who was in the process of preparing a sonnet anthology (which included works by Dante Gabriel and Christina Rossetti): 'A Sonnet Sequence from Elder to Modern Work, with Fifty Hitherto Unprinted Sonnets by Living Writers. That would not be amiss. Tell me if you think of using the title A Sonnet Sequence, as otherwise I might use it in the House of Life'.[13] Hall Caine did not accept Dante Gabriel's suggestion. He called his anthology *Sonnets of Three Centuries*. Dante Gabriel went on to call his *House Of Life* a 'Sonnet Sequence' and the phrase soon became established.

In his illuminating study of the Victorian sonnet, *Scanty Plot of Ground*, William T. Going notes that it was 'the Victorian poets... who broadened the tradition of the sonnet sequence and added new complexity and significance to an old genre'.[14] This is certainly the case with Christina Rossetti, and nowhere are there better examples of this 'new complexity and significance' than in *Monna Innominata*. In writing the sequence from a woman's perspective, Christina Rossetti not only 'broadened the tradition' in which she was working, but inverted, and thereby subverted the mode. To show just how the subversion works, it is necessary to outline the particular poetic implications of the form that Rossetti isolates in her subtle commentary. An examination must be made of the poetics of the love lyric, of Dantean and Petrarchan adaptations in particular; only then can *Monna Innominata* be approached with confidence and read in a manner akin to that which its author intended and, in her own note to the poem, indeed begged.

> Beatrice, immortalized by "altissimo poeta... cotanto amante"; Laura, celebrated by a great tho' an inferior bard, - have alike paid the exceptional penalty of exceptional honour, and have came down to us resplendent with charms, but (at least, to my apprehension) scant of attractiveness.
>
> These heroines of world-wide fame were preceded by a bevy of unnamed ladies "donne innominate" sung by a school of less conspicuous poets; and in that land and that period which gave simultaneous birth to Catholics, to Albigenses, and to Troubadours, one can imagine many a lady as sharing her lover's poetic aptitude, while the barrier between them might be one held sacred by both, yet not such as to render mutual love incompatible with mutual honour.
>
> Had such a lady spoken for herself, the portrait left us might have appeared more tender, if less dignified, than any drawn even by a devoted friend...
> (*Poems*, II, 86)

These provocative remarks show that their author is acutely aware of
the ideological implications of the poetical form she is, by redrawing
'the portrait left us' by this male-constructed ideology, about to
readdress. *Monna Innominata* is a prime example of a text exploring
its own specified aims and overtly commenting upon the tradition
of poetry that it extends, rewrites and criticises. Again, within the
parameters of a poetic form synonymous with introspection, we may
witness the work of Christina Rossetti reflecting upon its own status;
openly recording its position in a literary canon made by men, the
woman's poem becomes a shrine to mark its own conception. Poetry
has become its own subject. But (as ever with Christina Rossetti) this
is not a dilettante, self-serving device. Consciously structured with
regard to the poetic form it modifies, *Monna Innominata* remanages
and manipulates tradition in such a way as to foreshadow a manner
of consciousness often said to be characteristic of modernist art and
literature. With this in mind, any literary-historical aspect addressed
here will primarily engage the manner of literary-interrelationship
summoned by the text of *Monna Innominata*. Simply put, *Monna
Innominata* looks forward and backward at once. In doing so, the
sequence sets up a tension between a version of the poetic self and its
(hi)story and a given pattern of language which, for the woman writer,
must raise issues concerning any and all narrative representation.
This undertaking revolves upon a major regard to the issue of
signification (in one sense, naming) obtaining between subjects and
predicates, selves and narratives which shows itself in the singularly
non-narrative element always at work whenever a poem of Christina
Rossetti's attempts to narrate a 'story' or posit chains of sequential
(i.e. e. historical) cause and effect. Echoing Romantic reasoning (as
epitomized in Wordsworth's 'Tintern Abbey'), Rossetti repeatedly
shows that the very attempt, the trying to come to a conclusion is more
important than the conclusion that is - or is not - reached. *Monna
Innominata* tells us little of incidents but deliberately (re)constructs the
character of the 'donna innominata' of the sonnet by allowing her the
'attractiveness' of a voice. In this, Christina Rossetti recalls a comment

made by Wordsworth: 'It seems to me that in poems descriptive of human nature, however short they may be, character is absolutely necessary ... incidents are among the lowest allurements of poetry'.[15]

As a close reading of the sonnets comprising the sequence will confirm, *Monna Innominata* is Rossetti's masterpiece because it repeatedly locates an insistence upon the priority of poetic relationships in their production of significance and, hence, in their presentation of poetic tradition or literary history. Poetry upholds its value-laden ideology by blinkered repetition. Christina Rossetti upsets the rhythm. Motivated by her sex, driven by a desire to investigate the signifying possibilities of (modes of) discourse, inverting patterns of symbolism, interrupting the notion of literary-historical coherence, Christina Rossetti produces her most complex and abstruse, yet richly rewarding work, *Monna Innominata*.

The embodiment of mental notions, noted earlier as a prime tenet of the love sonnet tradition, inevitably involves a simultaneous consideration - a calling into question of the notion of signification, the process of naming (and un-naming), the implication of and the reasoning behind such operations. Explicitly singled out for attention in Christina Rossetti's note prefacing *Monna Innominata*, Dante and Petrarch themselves broke with tradition by giving a specific name to the lady described in their lyrics, quite deliberately turning what had hitherto been an unattainable ideal figure into an historical personage. Prior to Dante and Petrarch, the unnamed, elusive lady of the love lyric had stood as a stock symbolic device, representative of the anima, soul-mate or feminine aspect to the male psyche, a personification of the feeling function with regard to the self, a crystallization of the emotional side of human nature and, an apt area for the lyric to address. Thus, Guido Cavalcanti, a contemporary of Dante, openly speaks of his lady as an inner, psychological function:

> My soul weeps through her sighs for grievous fear
> And all those sighs, which in the heart were found,
> Deep drenched with tears do sobbing thence depart,
> Then seems that on my mind there rains a clear

> Image of a lady, thoughtful, bound
> Hither to keep death-watch upon that heart.[16]

The object of address here is clearly more a visionary essence, the result of an emotionally state, than a person from actuality. In this manner, historical correlatives for the ladies who populated the lyric were neither necessary nor were they traditionally given, until the poems of Dante and Petrarch. Of course, the announcement of a proper name for the addressee of a literary work does not inhibit us from reading the works as turning upon psychological states, analyses of the state of love itself rather than of the loved one. Even though it has been shown that the figure of Beatrice may be rooted in identifiable temporal 'reality', she still stands as one of the most potent anima expositions in the history of world literature. Holmes' statement that Beatrice 'is an invention, but an archetypal one' seems to me not only empirically unstable, but also imaginatively unsound.[17] The two are simultaneous, certainly not incompatible. Beatrice is Beatrice; haply, she is also a metaphor for the divine, a neo-Platonic essence. And Laura is the same. But the transfiguration of the 'real' person metaphorically to emphasize the spiritualization of romance, the naming of the ideal, in poetry is an innovation and does represent a pivotal point in a literary tradition, the implications of which Christina Rossetti explores in *Monna Innominata*. In doing this, Rossetti is locating her interest at a point far back in the history of the sonnet. But this does not mean that she is overlooking the treatment of the form in the five centuries separating her own writing from that of the Italian courtly poets, merely that *Monna Innominata* expressed the desire to retrace tradition back to a particular junction, one which, in Christina Rossetti's opinion, allows the clearest perception of the inception of a patriarchal ideology which, though gently challenged by a few male sonneteers over the years, had yet to be engaged from a female perspective. In her preface to *Monna Innominata*, Rossetti's correlation of Dantean/Petrarchan poetics with those of Elizabeth Barrett Browning's *Sonnets from the Portuguese* shows her provocatively aligning the formulation of the phallocentric gender-equation within the sonnet with its unchallenged expression by a Victorian woman poet. This considered, intertextual approach to the implications of poetic tradition, undertaken from an avowedly female position allows us to regard *Monna Innominata* as a truly radical work.

III

Thus far, I have attempted to proclaim and demonstrate certain ways in which Christina Rossetti's deconstruction of literary tradition from a female perspective is both breathtaking and groundbreaking in literary and proto-feministic political terms. Hers is radical poetry, and it is and has been oft misunderstood. I have tried to explicate those things too. All of this has become somewhat of a quest for me, and I intend to continue that journey here. The polemical structure and arguments of Rossetti's poetry in general make her writing, in my humble opinion (and, I am pleased to say, in the opinion of more persons these days than was the case when I first read Rossetti some three quick decades ago), revolutionary of its epoch and challenging to readers even of today. The concentrated, methodical, summarizing sway of her masterpiece (or one of them), the *Monna Innominata* sonnet sequence, which will form the ultimate focus of my attention in this study, is a prime place to look for condensed and crystallized instances of tenets and techniques that this poet repeatedly proffered and promoted in her art over time.[18]

In her eloquent but rational study, *Christina Rossetti: the Patience of Style*, Constance Hassett observes that 'evident everywhere in the [*Monna Innominata*] poems is Rossetti's desire to write a sequence unlike any other and to combine speaker, situation, and style in ways that are consistent with her own best tendencies as a writer'.[18] This is so, but Rossetti's cycle feeds on tradition as much as it attempts to mend it. At so many levels, Rossetti's open and unambiguously stated (from the 'Preface' onwards) intertextual poetic performance in the *Monna Innominata* cycle (as well as the less obvious revisionist performances in her many other sonneteering ventures) knowingly takes place within and *without* the history of the sonnet which, as a Victorian artist, she inherits. In particular, and most relevant to my aims and purpose here, the studied critique of the male-ordered conventions of the love lyric which Rossetti's poems openly effect is itself not wholly original. In this area, Christina Rossetti can be read as not inventing but innovatively extending a subversive strain which had long sought to ironise the 'true' perspective upon the world which the sonnet, with male speaker as subject and woman as silent, passive object, had originally set out to promote and legitimise. Though, certainly prior to the Victorian age, they remain marginal to the central male-determined patterning of the sonnet form, there are examples through history of sonnets aiming to subvert the patterns passed down as stock conventions and positions form the time of Dante up to the nineteenth century.

Reading Italian courtly love poetry, we find that many of the attitudes, images and modes of address present in the lyrics of Dante and Petrarch - which also inhabit the sonnets of Ronsard, Sidney and Shakespeare - are already well established as standard conceits by the time these two poets come to employ them. Of course, there is an important, vast difference between a 'standard' conceit and a 'stale' conceit - the success or otherwise of an image turns on matters of context (an issue informing Rossetti's own frequent employment of recontextualisation of discourse in pieces such as *Monna Innominata*). If conducted in a manner that is not born of idle assimilation of ideas, the echoing of earlier images (within the same work, or intertextually through history) can expand meaning, as in John Milton's 'Lycidas' or Thomas Gray's 'Elegy', for instance, where the summoning of traditional forms serves to reinforce the elegiac need for continuity in a mortal world by conveying a sense of continuing tradition both reassuring and admonitory. This is also the case with modern as well as ancient authors - one need only think of T. S. Eliot's re-management of conventional images in *The Waste Land*. If we are able to recognise a 'cliché' as active and functioning anew, then it transcends the dead realm of 'cliché' and begs re-interpretation: it is this potential for the revitalisation of language which makes Christina Rossetti's for the revitalisation of language which makes Christina Rossetti's interest in Dantean and Petrarchan forms one worth considering carefully. Towards the end of Dante's *Vita Nuova* (a work translated by Dante Gabriel Rossetti and referred to later in more detail) a sonnet appears whose theme is set out in its opening couplet: 'For certain he hath seen all perfectness / Who among other ladies hath seen mine'.[19]

The same motif occurs in Petrarch's *Canzoniere*:

> Who seeks to see the best Nature and Heaven
> can do among us, come and gaze on her …
> … all loveliness, all regal-mannered ways
> joined in one body, tempered marvellously…[20]

Such exalted praise, visualising the female addressee in terms of divine perfection, is (unlike the naming of the woman) not a device original to these two sonnets, but, rather, a stock, repeatable stance adopted by the lyric speaker. It may be found in the work of the Sicilian court poet Cielo D'Alcamo, written before the birth of Dante or Petrarch, in his 'Dialogue: Lover and Lady', here translated by Dante Gabriel Rossetti:

> For I never did love a maid
> Of this world, as thou art,
> So much as I love thee…
>
> Yea, even to Babylon I went
> And distant Barbary:
> But not a woman found I anywhere
> Equal to thee, who art indeed most fair.[21]

The same attitude prevails in the Messinan judge, Giudo delle Colonne's 'To Love and his Lady', written before 1250 and, again, translated by Dante Gabriel Rossetti: 'O comely-favored, whose soft eyes prevail, / More fair than is another on this ground'.[22] And similes, like modes of metaphorical address, are also repeatable. Delle Colonne's poem concludes with an extended simile in which the frustrated lover sets himself within a nautical image: 'Love rocks my life with tempests on the deep, / Even as a ship round which the winds are blown'.[23] This scenario is reproduced by Petrarch in the *Canzoniere*: 'My ship full of forgetful cargo sails / through rough seas at the midnight of a winter... / ... and I despair of ever reaching port'.[24]

Many such rhetorical constructions become assimilated into the lyric poetry of the Italian renaissance as stock, repeatable devices: the personification of Love as a divine essence 'who conquers all'[25] (bringing a sense of potential order to the emotional turmoil articulated by the lyric speaker); the imaging of Death as a spectre; the comparison of the lady to the red rose; and the capturing of her essential qualities in idyllic pastoral imagery to provoke a reading of her as the universal essence of Beauty, ultimately unattainable but a metaphor for the neo-Platonic ideal, the Divine Goddess of Beauty. All these forms, and many more, can be located side by side in the thirteenth-century text, gradually being assimilated into the poetic stream to become stereotypical modes of articulation, in turn adopted by poets taking up the lyric cause in later times, until each writing of a lyric becomes a re-writing of tradition, a mixture of set patterns and sometimes innovation of the poet's own making. Indeed, the majority of these expressions are established literary vehicles long before the writings of Dante - they are present in Ovid and Catullus, certainly - and, as such, their appearance affirms the fact that, at one level anyway, Dante and Petrarch were content to write within a conventional tradition, that descended from the troubadours of twelfth-century feudal France.

Passed on through history, these standard modes of address are largely accepted by male bards as conventions by means of which the lyric poem constructs identities. Sometimes, however, the integrity of these conventions is questioned and the passiveness of response of the female addressee is vigorously qualified in certain male poets. We need look no further than Spenser, Drayton, Donne and Shakespeare for examples of the mockery of traditional idealisation and the questioning of absolutes, leading to a (re)humanisation of the sonnet and lyric mode, often through something close to jesting. At one level, the symbolic 'unknown' - the neo-Platonic function - continued in the late sixteenth and early seventeenth century sequences: the naming of Sidney's 'Stella' (the pole-star) and particularly Drayton's *Idea* would seem to indicate an attachment on the part of these poets to the traditional male-derived *idealistic* modes of lyric address. The naming of Spenser's *Amoretti* (little love pieces) certainly allows for traditional idealisation of a Stella type, as exemplified, in true Dantean fashion, in the twenty-fourth sonnet of the cycle:

> When I behold that beauties wonderment,
> And rare perfection of each goodly part:
> Of natures skill the onely complement,
> I honour and admire the maker's art.[26]

But, simultaneously, the intimate 'little love pieces' encourage a much more personal, even jesting perspective to emerge within the sonnets, by means of which the poet ironises his conventional stance as 'lover tormented' by introducing another recurrent theme, the notion of the *'theatrum mundi'*:

> Of this worlds Theatre in which we stay,
> My love lyke the Spectator ydly sits
> Beholding me that all the pageants play,
> Disguyfing diuersly my troubled wits.
> Sometimes I joy when glad occasion fits,
> And mask in myrth lyke to a Comedy:
> Soone after when my joy to sorrow flits,
> I waile and make my woes a Tragedy.
> Yet she beholding me with constant eye,
> Delights not in my merth nor rues my smart;
> But when I laugh she mocks, and when I cry
> She laughes, and hardens euermore her hart…[27]

The initial recognition in this sonnet of woman's customary passivity - 'like the Spectator' - and its emphasis upon the male-subject's

conventionally 'troubled wits' are fully in concord with the standard
gender relationship as conditioned by mediaeval lyric. However, the
conventionality of the opening quatrain immediately gives way to
the lover's knowingly ironic description of his woes, as, extending the
theatrical image of the poem's opening lines by allusion to literary
genres, the artificiality of the lover's 'mask' or conventional pose is
emphasised and mocked. The sonnet's sestet offers a further critique
of the traditional lyric love-scenario by light-heartedly picturing the
woman's active involvement in the drama: her mockery of the lover's
predicament forms an ironic commentary upon the whole artifice of
the sonnet mode.

In Michael Drayton's sonnets we encounter a fertile, inquisitive
mind intent on questioning and redirecting the absolute ideals of
image and address that the sonnet mode offered to the poet as his
raw materials. In the dedicatory sonnet to his Ides sequence, Drayton
makes clear his reluctance idly to adopt an idealistic position.

> Into these loves, who but for passion lookes,
> At this first sight, here let him lay them by,
> And seeke else-where, in turning other bookes,
> Which better may his labour satisfie.[28]

There is an overt rejection of the traditional pose of the male speaker
of love lyrics which, as this sonnet proceeds, is reinforced by a yearning
for poetry 'desiring change', denying the 'farre-fetch'd' conventions of
the mode and injecting a refreshing degree of humanity and realism
into the traditionally idealised form, 'still desiring change'.

> No farre-fetch'd sigh shall ever wound my brest,
> Love from mine eye a teare shall never wring,
> Nor in ah-mees my whying Sonnets drest,
> (A Libertine) fantastickly I sing;
> My verse is the true image of my mind,
> Ever in motion, still desiring change...

Drayton provides a direct, at times sarcastic treatment of the old lyric themes, disregarding convention in favour of a skepticism that is both invigorating and (unlike the traditional male poetic posture) self-deflating. 'They that are blind, are minstrels often made', he pointedly opines from his position of commentator upon the customary poetic etiquette.[29] For example, the speaker of the *Idea* sequence manages an attack upon the traditionally extolled figure of Cupid:

> Cupid, I hate thee, which I'de have thee know,
> A naked starveling ever may'st thou be,
> Poore rogue, goe pawne thy fascia and thy bow,
> For some few ragges, wherewith to cover thee…[30]

Drayton's unwillingness to re-employ the idealistic tone of the sonneteer gives his *Idea*, first published in 1594, a refreshing incisiveness. The determined avoidance of a stable, idyllic relationship between speaker-subject and ideal-addressee is sometimes cuttingly cynical. Though his ultimate goal is traditional in nature - 'All that I seeke, is to eternise you'[31] - Drayton's mockery of the traditionally silent, passive role of woman in the love lyric is achieved with considerable charm:

> Noting but no and I, and I and no,
> How fals it out so strangely you reply?
> I tell yee (faire) ile not be answered so,
> With this affiming no, denying I.
> I say, I love, you sleightly answere I:
> I say, you love, you peule me out a no:
> I say, I die, you eccho me with I:
> Save mee I crie, you sigh me out a no…[32]

The surfeit of punning here, whilst conveying the traditional pose of the tormented male poet-speaker, functions to introduce a measure of equality of input to the poem from subject and addressee: Drayton's loved one is far from wholly passive within the scheme of the *Idea* cycle. Drayton's sonnets manage to maintain the image of the lover in torment so essential of the female-addressee in the love-relationship, rather than from the idealistic presentation of the passive, unattainable female essence of yore.

> Since ther's no helpe, come let us kisse and part,
> Nay, I have done: you get no more of me,
> And I am glad, yea glad with all my heart,
> That thus so cleanly, I my selfe can free,
> Shake hands for ever, cancell all our vowes,
> And when we meet at any time againe,
> Be it not seene in either of our browes,
> That we one jot of former love reteyne...[33]

The lovers' relationship is still predominantly presented from the male perspective (to be questioned in the poem's sestet), but the subjectivity of the speaker is here constructed through interaction with the object of his desire, allowing the woman a degree of activity outside the restrictive codes set out by the thirteenth-century love lyric. 'Vowes' made are 'our vowes', with both parties engaged in their formulation. When Drayton's speaker desires a 'selfe' that is 'free', his female counterpart is allowed to share in the liberation: she becomes something of an equal - the 'kisse' and '(s)hake hands' represent a contract of equality - and no longer a secondary consideration.

Shakespeare's sonnets provide many similar instances of dissatisfaction with the stylised discourse of the sonneteer and implications this has concerning the gender structure of the love relationship. Specifically, Shakespeare addresses the lofty deification of the loved one, that time-honoured trademark of the love lyric:

> So it is not with me as with that Muse,
> Stirred by a painted beauty to his verse,
> Who heaven itself for ornament doth use
> And every fair with his fair doth rehearese,

Making a couplement of proud compare,
With sun and moon, with earth and sea's rich gems,
With April's first-born flowers, and all things rare
That heaven's air in this huge rondure hems.[34]

It is almost certain that the poet directly referred to here is Sir Philip
Sidney who, in praise of his heroine in *Astrophel and Stella*, calls
upon the 'proud compare' Shakespeare now rejects. But, whatever its
particular target, this sonnet locates and attacks a general trend integral
to the whole sonnet tradition, a trend seen as dispensing with relevant
particulars of information in favour of repeatable, stock images. '[L]et
me... but truly write', begs the speaker of Shakespeare's verses,[35] and
this search for a mode of articulation outside that preferred by poets
like Sidney (though Sidney too was capable of ironising his role as
poet-speaker) leads him to write an mocking satire of the idealised
portrait of the loved one which dominates the history of the love lyric:

My mistress' eyes are nothing like the sun,
Coral is far more red than her lips' red;
If snow be white, why then her breasts are dun,
If hairs be wires, black wires grow on her head.
I have seen roses damasked, red and white,
But no such roses see I in her cheeks;
And in some perfumes is there more delight
Than in the breath that from my mistress reeks.[36]

This series of parodic inversions, where the expected idealistic simile
is switched to an uninhibitedly realistic overview conveyed in plain,
predominantly monosyllabic language, forms a plainly spoken attack
upon the unreal comparisons common to the Dantean and Petrarchan
lyric. The purity of the love which Shakespeare's speaker wishes to
articulate would be 'belied by false compare', were he to adopt the
traditional, idealistic imagery of the troubadour poet. Instead, this
sonnet attempts to retrieve a degree of purity of vision by lampooning

the empty diction of traditional amatory representation. Shakespeare's sonnets are repeatedly drawn to such analysis and exposure of the ideological implication of standardized poetic conceit - 'mine eyes ... in thee a thousand errors note', we are informed us at another place in the cycle.[37] Comparing his predicament as a writer to that of an 'unperfect actor on the stage'.[38] Shakespeare's speaker shows himself supremely aware of the inherited formal structuring and codes of the medium within which his utterances will be judged. Finally, with many of the other antique conventions exposed, the passivity and silence traditionally demanded of the female addressee of the sonnet are openly questioned:

> Those lips that Love's own hand did make
> Breathed forth the sound that said 'I hate'
> To me that lanfuished for her sake.
> But when she saw my woeful state,
> Straight in her heart did mercy come,
> Chiding that tongue that ever sweet
> Was used in giving gentle doom:
> And taught it thus anew to greet,
> 'I hate' she altered with an end,
> That followed it as gentle day
> Doth follow night who, like a fiend,
> From heaven to hell is flown away.
> 'I hate' from hate away she threw,
> And saved my life, saying 'not you'.[39]

Woman is, quite literally, here allowed a voice, and her vocal activity lets her, equally literally, become the ultimate controller of the sonnet's direction and conclusion. The male speaker is totally under the command of the usually submissive female addressee; it is she, now, who actively defines the poet- speaker's identity. By metaphorically saving the life of the speaker in the closing couplet, the woman is repaying the debt of life - of a voice, and thus potential for active self expression - allowed to her by this sonnet's inversion of the standard gender placing prescribed by the traditional love lyric. Unlike Caliban, who uses his gift of language to curse the giver, Shakespeare's lady, resurrected to life by being allowed a voice chooses a less hostile attitude towards the provider: 'I hate … not you', declares the lady. Woman becomes now the guiding subjectivity of the verse, because this particular masculine 'you' is one who has temporarily stepped down from the position of male dominance traditional to the love poem, to allow the normally silenced female to speak. That this egalitarian 'you' is repaid with a coy and flirtatious reprieve (and not vitriolic curses) might be read as confirmation that the poem, though its conclusion is determined by the terms of female utterance, is ultimately ascribable to a male hand.

It can be seen, then, that the lyrics of Spenser, Drayton, and Shakespeare go some way towards achieving the realisation that women may play more than an idealised, passive role in a heterosexual relationship expressed in a sonnet. However, being male, these writers lack the oppositional sensibility of Christina Rossetti in their approach to the phallocentric ideology masquerading as truth within the terms of the love poem, and they are certainly not as consistent as she in their re-evaluation of the hitherto male-monopolised poetic equation. Nevertheless, the ironic tradition that the sonnets of these male poets graft on top of the broader literary canon of love poetry is one which partially foreshadows the central subversive concern of *Monna Innominata*. It represents a concession on behalf of the male poet-speaker, an admittance of the injustice to woman perpetrated by the traditional love lyric. No doubt Christina Rossetti would have welcomed such a concession, but, as the preface to *Monna Innominata* with its bold alignment of the mediaeval position with the Victorian ethos makes clear, it is not sufficiently radical an ideological shift entirely to placate the female consciousness and redress the balance of five centuries of inequality.

The cynic might argue that these female-friendly, markedly non-traditional sonnets of Spenser, Drayton and Shakespeare (and especially the lyrics of John Donne) merely illustrate the dominant male-subject's power occasionally to retreat from a position of superiority and allow the little woman a brief and temporary say in matters. In doing so, they do not offer a total, only a very slim, partial relinquishment (and certainly not an absolute rejection) of the patriarchal ideology inscribed in poetic tradition since the days of Dante. The version of woman and her words received by the reader remains a wholly male creation. Donne and the Metaphysical poets were well versed in this partial critique of the male perspective, but the Cavalier poets and Rochester returned in a more cynical, dogmatic way to the absolutist male perspective. An opportunity was lost, and the subversive tradition is little more than a footnote to the phallocentric canon through history. Ultimately, this is why Christina Rossetti must trace tradition back five centuries to Dantean and pre-Dantean poetics in her search for a relatively unpolluted perspective.

Dante himself gave the name 'Dolce Stil Nuovo' ('Sweet New Style' or 'Sweet New Manner') to the variety of courtly love address developed in Tuscany and favoured by the lyricists of the school with which he was associated.[40] It is a form of writing whose discourse overlaps with that of the contemporary physiology, inherited from Ancient Greece, and philosophy based upon the theories of Aristotle, as expressed in *De Anima*. Intellectual power of reason was seen as removed from the emotional. These were the vegetative, the sensitive and the rational, operating in the body through three faculties - the natural spirit in the liver, the vital spirit in the heart, and the animal spirit in the brain. In his study *Dante*, Holmes summarises the relevance of this physiology to the conventional presentation of the affected lover in the courtly lyric: 'The mechanism of love was that the impression made upon the eyes by a beautiful lady sent sprits moving to the heart, the seat of the emotions, from which other spirits informed the reasoning and memory faculties in the brain'.[41]

This operation, metaphorically realised in the love lyric, finds the poet intellectualising over the structure of the human soul, examining notions of the self and its divided nature. The extended image which speaks of love entering through the eyes, usually as darts or arrows, thence attacking the heart and thereby informing the mind, marks the conventional manifestation of this contemplation. Many of the sonnets of Guido Cavalcanti (to whom Dante dedicated the *Vita Nuova*) revolve around this notion:

> Love, who hath drawn me down
> through devious ways...
> 'Tis he who hath hurled the dart, wherefrom my pain,
> First shot's resultant! and in flanked amaze
> See how my affrighted soul recoileth from
> That sinister side wherein the heart lies slain.[42]

An early lyric of Dante, 'Deh, Violetta, che in ombra d'Amore', illustrates just how firmly he remained within the mainstream tradition, where male is agent and female is idealised, passive, and silent:

> Ah, Violetta, you who so suddenly appeared to my
> eyes in Love's shadow, pity the heart that puts its
> trust in you and is dying of desire...
>
> You, Violetta, in a more than human form, you
> kindled a fire in my mind through the heart,
> that I saw; and then by the action of a fiery spirit
> you quickened a hope that partly heals me
> when you smile at me...[43]

In the third poem of the *Canzoniere*, Petrarch recalls this recurrent image.

> I was caught, and I put up no fight,
> my lady, for your lovely eyes had bound me...
> Love found me all disarmed and found the way

was clear to reach my heart down through the eyes
which have become the halls and doors of tears.

It seems to me it did him little honour
to wound me with his arrow in my state
and to you, armed, not show his bow at all.[44]

Here are many conventions borrowed from the long tradition of
courtly love poetry: the personification of Love; the disturbing power
of the supra-human vision of beauty; the resulting turbulence of
heart and mind; and the 'spirits' transmitting effects through the
body. Both Dante and Petrarch make free usage of these inherited
forms. Centuries later, Christina Rossetti would put the same set
of ideologically-filtered schemata to very different usage, and with
potent, compelling effect. Dinah Roe has observed that 'Monna
Innominata is so successful because its network of allusions allows it
to act simultaneously as tribute and critique of both the motivations
of its speaker and the poets of the past'.[45] We will see that this is true.
Lines from a characteristically cryptic letter to her brother William
Michael, in which Christina discusses Monna Innominata, would
appear to confirm Roe's estimation: 'I rather wonder that no one (so
far as I know) ever hit upon my semi-historical argument before ... - it
seems to me so full of poetic suggestiveness'.[46]

Bearing in mind a revisionist reading of Monna Innominata's
intertextual and transtextual treatment of traditional and contemporary
ideologies and concerns, literary and social, we achieve a position
from which we may now accurately and adequately 'hit upon' that
'semi-historical' argument to which Rossetti herself suggestively and
provocatively referred almost a century and a half ago. Honouring
the past whilst necessarily rewriting it for a woman's present, Monna
Innominata confirms the author's constantly articulated urge to
redirect tradition backward and forward to purer points of origin.
Rossetti wants to lead us quietly but firmly to places that might permit
the exposure and renegotiation of patriarchal schemata that, although

sporadically challenged by certain male poets over time, remained thitherto unengaged from a widely read *female* poetic perspective. In *Monna Innominata* such places abound.

IV

It is not so difficult, then, to demonstrate thematic and strategic similarities between the lyric writings of Dante and Petrarch and the lesser-read poetry of their contemporaries. Both writers embraced the broader conventions of the form. But they also revolutionised the tradition and, consequently, there are certain crucial ways in which the sonnets of these two major Italian writers diverge from the male-ordained, male-ordered poetic tradition that they directly inherited and within which they otherwise composed. Given Christina Rossetti's pronounced and avid interest in radically rewriting tradition and exposing/subverting received phallocentric poetic conventions (an interest she most openly declares in her uncharacteristically direct 'Preface' to *Monna Innominata*), there can be no doubt that it is their *differences* from, rather than their similarities to the typical poeticizing strategies and modes of their forerunners and contemporaries which caused Christina Rossetti directly to identify Dante and Petrarch as seminal authors in a poetic canon she was keen to subvert and re-address.

In order to discover what is genuinely new (as opposed to reiteration of established poetic practice) in Dante's lyric writings, we must deconstruct his self-christened 'Dolce Stil Nuovo'. A prominent revolutionary device pioneered by Dante (most clearly of interest to Christina Rossetti when she came to write *Monna Innominata*) is his repeated insistence upon a historical referent for the 'lady' object of his poetic praise, denoting an innovative desire to anchor his ideal female form to an empirical, external 'reality' rather than construct her as a stylised spiritual ideal. Beatrice is not the only female addressee of the Dantean lyric given a proper name - others include Violetta, Matelda, Pietra, and Lisetta - but she is the ultimate symbol of his spiritual life, occupying the same position with regard to the speaker of the poetry as does Laura, also verifiable as a figure from history, in Petrarch's work. Dante's Beatrice was born a Portinari and married a Bardi (both were more distinguished families than Dante's own), and died, aged twenty-four, in 1290. Apart from these recorded facts, she exists primarily as a poetic configuration in the *Vita Nuova*, possibly the most highly attuned visualisation of a poet's spiritual self in the history of the lyric. The work was well known and highly admired by the Rossettis. Dante Gabriel made a translation of the text, which he sent to Tennyson in 1850,[47] eventually to be published in *The Early Italian Poets* in 1861.[48] Christina's eldest brother praised the *Vita Nuova* greatly as being 'so full of intricate and fantastic analogies … much more than appears on any but the closest scrutiny'. [49]

We must assume that Christina Rossetti – who referred to Dante as 'a fascinating centre of thought' and was herself severally described as 'a student of Dante' and 'deeply influenced by Dante' by her first biographer Mackenzie Bell - gave the Dantean text 'the closest scrutiny', particularly in the period of conception of *Monna Innominata*, which coincided with the publication of her brother's translation.[50] After all, the Rossetti family was steeped in knowledge of Alighieri's life and works. Christina's father, Gabriele, (who also wrote on Petrarch, which leads to the conclusion that Christina's 'knowledge of Dante, and even of Petrarch was great') had, after all, been possibly the foremost Dante scholar of his age, studying the Italian poet with an intensity which 'reached the far side of devotion'.[51] In an obituary, published in *The Spectator* after his father's death in 1854, William Michael paid tribute to Gabriele's studies, calling him 'the most daringly original of the commentators on Dante':

> [H]e engaged deeply in studies of the letter and spirit of Dante's imperishable works. Rossetti's leading idea (indicated in his work, and enforced in subsequent productions with the fervour of a discoverer, vast literary diligence, and indefatigable minuteness of criticism) is that Dante, in common with numberless other great

authors, wrote in a language of secret allegory, which
embodies, in the form now of love, now of mythology,
now of alchemy, now of freemasonry, the most daring
doctrines in metaphysics and politics.[52]

In particular support of William Michael's eulogistic claims, Gabriele
Rossetti's publication *La Beatrice di Dante* (1842) shows an overtly
philosophical interest in the implications of Alighieri's heroine. His
daughter, Christina's older sister Maria Francesca's *A Shadow of Dante*
(1871) evinces an equally intense, though less intellectual fascination
with the Italian poet.[53] Margaret Sawtell states that, specifically during
the period 1866-1870, '[Christina's] main mental preoccupation seems
to have been the study of Dante':

> Maria [Rossetti] was engaged on her book *A Shadow
> of Dante*, published about 1870; D. G. produced in the
> course of time *Dante and his Circle* which Christina
> describes as 'a monument of loving labour'; William
> Michael made a translation of *The Divine Comedy*
> which she calls 'the best we have'… and in 1867 an
> article by Christina herself, called 'Dante: an English
> Classic,' was published in the *Churchman's Shilling
> Magazine*.[54]

In *Dante and his Circle*, Dante Gabriel calls the *Vita Nuova* an
'Autopsychology'.[55] He is correct to do so since, like Christina's poetry,
the *Vita Nuova* consciously offers a sustained conception of the inner
mental (as opposed to physical, outward) growth of its speaker. In
1293, by taking thirty-one of his early poems and embedding them
in a prose narrative which maps the history of his relationship with a
lady named Beatrice, in such a fashion that the poems are offered as if
intimately inspired by stages in that love story, Dante (willing to write
within a defined sonneteering tradition) undertakes a bold literary
experiment. Like Christina Rossetti with her loaded contextualising

of *Monna Innominata*, at both surface narrative and poetic levels, Dante becomes the direct critic and interpreter of his own work, its conception and meaning. This concern with literariness and context, a concern repeatedly echoed by Christina Rossetti in her own work, is clearly announced in the opening paragraph of the *Vita Nuova*: 'In that part of the book of my memory before the which is little that can be read, there is a rubric, saying, Incipit Vita Nova. Under such rubric I find written many things; and among them the words I purpose to copy into this little book; if not all of them, at least their substance'.[56]

There is an immediate and pronounced interest here in processes of reading and writing: 'book', 'read', 'rubric', 'written'. The text openly tackles the problem of 'words' and their 'substance', thus raising the issue of signification, which intensifies into the central theme of the work. When Beatrice appears in the narrative, we are provided with precise details of her dress, age and history - she is forcefully presented as a historical entity, an actual person. But, coupled with this empirical presentation, a simultaneous idealism is established in the text. Dante speaks of Beatrice as seeming 'not to be the daughter of a mortal man, but of God', and stresses that 'her image ... was with me always'.[57] The moment when the speaker of *Vita Nuova* first sees Beatrice at the age of nine is described as that time 'when first the glorious Lady of my mind was made manifest to my eyes'.[58] So, in the terms set out here, it is clear that the figure of 'the glorious Lady' stands primarily as a mental essence, an essence allowed signification by the poet-speaker through the medium of an actual person, Beatrice Portinari on earth, consciously grounding an abstract ideal in an identifiable version of reality. Indeed, later in the narrative, the speaker admits of the object of his desire that 'no sooner do I image to myself her marvellous beauty than I an possessed with the desire to behold her, the which is of so great a strength it kills and destroys in my memory all those things which might oppose it'.[59] Plainly expressed, this stresses beyond question the speaker's unquenchable need for a concrete, visual manifestation to image to him the elemental essence which is his soul-mate or anima, traditional object of the lyric poem. For Dante,

Beatrice Portinari becomes that which actualises and signifies the spiritual yearning of the poet. The text fixes upon the actual person of Beatrice and transforms the empirical actuality into the heavenly metaphor.

Once it is established as a consistent metaphor, the *Vita Nuova* seeks to affirm the inevitability, the 'proper' nature of this innovative procedure: the naming of the ideal and seeking to verify the internal, unknowable by the external, knowable. The text repeatedly strives for stability. The pursuit of certainty becomes a governing theme of the work: the relevance and employment of Beatrice as a divine metaphor is lightly questioned upon occasion, but the issue is always resolved in favour of the inevitable correctness of the configuration of heroine and ideal, a reflection of the divinely ordered scheme of things that the *Vita Nuova* (notably in its dealings with notions of signification) continually strives to echo. The letter and spirit are reconciled, and the bridge between them is one founded upon religious certitude. Early on in the work, the speaker openly ruminates upon this desire to close the gap between the 'word' and the 'thing': 'The name of Love is so sweet in the hearing that it would not seem possible for its effects to be other than sweet; seeing that the name must needs be like unto the thing named: as it is written: *Nomina sunt consequentia rerum*'.[60] Names are the consequents of things: this thought gives the speaker 'no rest'. A concern with names and what they signify looms large in the text of *Vita Nuova*, colouring the symbolism and semantics of the narrative, and is emphatically reflected in the use of language itself. As with *Monna Innominata*, Dante's work is one (though not to such an extent as Christina Rossetti's cycle) where action takes second place to meditation. The speaker returns to contemplation of names and their consequents: 'And by ... these thoughts I was so sorely assailed that I was like unto him who doubteth which path to take, and wishing to go, goeth not. And if I bethought myself to seek out some point at the which all these paths might be found to meet, I discerned but one way'.[61] The 'one way' which the speaker strives to attain is the path of truth, the position of stability, finally resolved as total certitude in the text, proceeding from an orthodox and dogmatically held faith in a deicentric cosmos, with God, the ultimate ordering principle, accepted without challenge.

In the very first sonnet of the *Vita Nuova*, this desired state of order is optimistically invoked:

> To every heart which the sweet pain doth move,
> And unto which these words may now be brought
> For true interpretation and kind thought,
> Be greeting in our Lord's name, which is Love.[62]

The 'true interpretation' called for here is held to be a reading process directly consequent of an absolute faith in an omniscient, omnipotent deity, an idea which dominates the *Vita Nuova* and becomes a central motif in the text. Visions have 'true' discernible meanings (as do the sonnets which the poet himself decodes one by one in the work) as opposed to 'false' counterfeit readings, and mistaken interpretations of signs (of which the speaker claims to possess the 'true meaning') are gently mocked in the narrative.[63] For a poet so initially critical of absolutism as the younger Christina Rossetti, this theme of the Dantean text is one that *Monna Innominata* can not possibly ignore. Dante's poetry assumes the principle that, interpreted correctly, the material signs of this world reflect with total certainty the truth which will be perceived directly in the kingdom of God.

Subsequently, signification and interpretation do not become (as Christina Rossetti would have it) arbitrary processes - unfixed and shifting and capable of subversion by the intrusion of ideologies masquerading as truth - but rather equations with fixed, finite solutions available to the reader who knows the password. For Christina Rossetti at this stage of her poetic career, there is no password, no cipher, because there are no certainties, no absolutes (a position we witness in all but, I will argue, her later devotional writings); for Dante, the password is God and the absolute certitude that faith in God generates. Thus, for Dante, the move towards naming his Lady becomes an inevitable step - 'Names are the consequents of things' - since earthly referents must be unfailingly perceived as certain signs of heavenly essences. Making Beatrice Portinari, 'wherein alone I found that beatitude which is the goal of desire', signify a spiritual ideal is, in the Dantean scheme, a sure consolidation of that ideal, never a reduction of the divine universality of the divine essence thereby signified.[64] The sacred symbol of Beatrice is at once Beatitude and Beauty, on earth as in heaven. The naming might well be read by later poets as the first step towards subversion of the ideal - tethering the divine in some way to the 'real' - but, for Dante's speaker it is not a *subversion* at all.

Thus, notably within a church (symbolically beneath, inside, and as part of a holy structure), the *Vita Nuova* offers the reader a microcosmic image of its dogmatically adopted strategy towards representation. Beatrice is discovered at worship:

> Now it fell on a day, that this most gracious creature was sitting where words were to be heard of the Queen of Glory; and I was in a place where mine eyes could behold their beatitude; and betwixt her and me, in a direct line, there sat another lady of pleasant favour; who looked round at me many times, marvelling at my continued gaze which seemed to have her for its object. And many perceived that she thus looked; so that departing thence, I heard it whispered after me, 'Look you to what a pass such a lady hath brought him;' and in saying this they named her who had been midway between the most gentle Beatrice and mine eyes. Therefore I was reassured, and knew that for that day my secret had not become manifest. Then immediately it came to my mind that I might make use of this lady as a screen to the truth … By her means I kept my secret concealed till some years were gone over…[65]

Dante's speaker, who knows exactly to whom his gaze refers, is incredulous at, and gently mocks the error of the observers who misread the image before them. This accurately reflects the attitude of the whole work towards certainty of reference where the correlation of signifier and signified is concerned. Of the same self-congratulatory nature is the playful toying with the implied speaker of the lyric in some of the later sonnets of the series, where words are 'disguised … so as to seem to be speaking of another … in such sort that [the sonnet] might seem to be spoken by this friend of mine'.[66]

Similarly, the speaker toys with notions of the self as divisible, only in the knowledge that, within the terms of this text at least, these elements are ultimately reconcilable as components of a repeatedly proffered unitary subjectivity. The clue lies in the language. The speaker's boast that he can 'make myself into two' as a literary conceit forms a simultaneous recognition that he is wholly in control of a divisible unit, his stable self: 'In this sonnet, I make myself into two, according as my thoughts were divided one from the other. The one part I call Heart, that is appetite; the other, Soul, that is, reason; and I tell what one saith to the other'.[67] This whole operation of division stands governed by the repeated 'I' figure, forcefully guarding the claim of the unified self, which dominates the intellectually playful juxtaposition of 'Heart' and 'Soul' undertaken by the seemingly complacent poet-speaker here. These experiments with notions of representation are alluded to locally and fleetingly (knowingly, smugly even) in a work whose overall perspective negates the possibility of 'truth' ever being misread. At one point in the *Vita Nuova*, the speaker decides to use the 'screen to the truth' woman of the church as a decoy, in order that his 'true' love for Beatrice might not be discovered. But this plot backfires, and it becomes obvious that Beatrice herself is unaware of the speaker's real affections: the potential for misreading is all around the speaker, yet never within him. Distressed (at the errant interpretative powers of others) the speaker falls weeping to sleep in his chamber. Love personified shortly appears to him in a dream, also weeping, and the words addressed to the poet by this vision are crucial to the methodology of the poetry itself. 'My son, it is time for us to lay aside our counterfeiting,' advises the vision: 'I am as the centre of a circle, to the which all parts of the circumference bear an equal relation; but with thee it is not thus'.[68] The vision (of Love, which reflects the governing divine principle in the Dantean scheme) warns the speaker of the perils of 'counterfeiting' - of the danger of taking images to be truths - advising him of the importance of stability and the need for a 'centre' by which all other elements in a system may be held in governable relation. In the *Vita Nuova* as a whole, God functions as this ordering principle, rendered as such a potent device that all meaning generated by this dogmatically proffered certitude is held to be irrevocable 'truth' by the terms of the stable system that generates it.

Jacques Derrida links the principle of 'coherence' to the concept of a 'centred system' such as that generated in the Dantean text (with the radical difference that he does not call this centre God). Derrida describes the kind of interpretative centre required for such a system in functional terms that are appropriate (and it is to this important point that I wish later to refer the text of *Monna Innominata*) for describing what happens in the *absence* of such a centre:

> [I]t has always been thought that the centre, which is by definition unique, constituted that very thing within a structure which while governing the structure, escapes structurality ... The centre is at the centre of the totality, and yet, since the centre does not belong to the totality (is not part of the totality), the totality has its centre elsewhere.[69]

Dante's God fulfils these conditions. Transcending the temporal, the divine ordering principle becomes, in the Dantean text, an absolute guarantee of meaning and certitude. The pervasive spiritual presence saturates Dante's lyric poetry with a guarantee of meaning, just as the all-encompassing absences in Christina Rossetti's writings function to abnegate any condition of certainty or stability of meaning in the text. The naming of Beatrice within the terms of the *Vita Nuova* and the system of signification promoted on those terms becomes one more certitude amidst a pattern of similar guarantees of intelligibility. The text becomes tautological: the naming therein cannot be questioned and, in its comfortable conveyance of closure, represents a confirmation of the unshakable stability of the linguistic and semantic system from which it proceeds. It is this self-satisfying tendency in the language of Dantean poetry that Christina Rossetti rejects in *Monna Innominata* at a poetic level, simultaneously denying the authority of the unsubverted male poetic tradition at literal level.

In the poetry of Petrarch, a dramatic shift in sensibility from that outlined above and characterised as Dantean may be detected. This is why Christina Rossetti indicates these two poets as a starting point in her own deconstruction of poetic tradition, *Monna Innominata*. Alexander Dunlop has summarised the difference of approach:

> [W]hereas Dante had been able to sublimate his passion for his lady Beatrice in his love for God, Petrarch admits no such transcendent revolution. The love of Laura and the Love of God remain in tension and the *Rime* record the effects of that tension on the lover over time. The fundamental Petrarchan tension is ultimately that between a God-centred and a self-centred universe. The only resolution is renunciation of one of these centres...[70]

If a fundamental (if not *the* fundamental) intention of the lyric writings of Dante might be said to be the promotion of certitude and stability - be it symbolic, narrative, or linguistic - then one finds no such strategy running through the Petrarchan lyric text. Instead, one detects a distinct air of unease with language, with signifiers and their endurance: the principle of intelligibility is shaken and uncertain in Petrarch's writings. Petrarch's autobiographical *Letter to Posterity* opens timidly with a revealing reference to naming: 'You may, perhaps, have heard tell of me, though even this is doubtful, since a poor and insignificant name like mine will hardly have travelled far in space or time'.[71] This can be read as implying a lack of trust in the reliability of referents, an anxiety that pervades Petrarch's work. It is a prominent mistrust, a lack of confidence reflected in the poet's unusually fragmented employment of pronomination. This tendency may be witnessed in lines from the opening lyric of the sequence of verses for which Petrarch is best remembered, his *Canzoniere*, written, ordered, and revised between 1335 and his death in 1374:

> O you who hear within these scattered verses
> the sound of sighs with which I fed my heart
> in my first errant youthful days when I
> in part was not the man I am today...[72]

The language of the poetry, with its displacement of the 'I' pronominal reference - 'I ... was not ... I' - conveys a strong interest in the possible non-fixity of identity. In similar fashion, there are many instances elsewhere in the *Rime* where both lover and addressee are referred to (in the Italian) as first person singular subjunctive, again blurring certainty regarding identity as constructed by language. All this would seem to indicate a conception of the signifying possibilities of language far removed from that promoted in the Dantean lyric. Petrarch's awkward inscription of the name Laura (or 'Laureta') into the fifth sonnet of the *Canzoniere* in semi-anagrammatical form, setting up a sort of intellectual word game within the poetry, further marks a conscious disruption of set patterns of signification which, one feels, would have no place in the strategy of Dantean verse as I have interpreted it here.[73] Of course, this is not to say that, in Petrarch's lyrics, centres of intelligibility are deconstructed in the same manner in which (as I intend to show) they repeatedly are in *Monna Innominata*, but rather to illustrate the shifting conception of language which distinguishes Petrarch's writings from those of Dante.

Petrarch's poetry appears in part to play out one theory of language and interpretation, that enacted and elaborated in the mediaeval texts whose other conventions Petrarch evokes. The linguistic principles evinced by the *Canzoniere* function in a manner markedly dissimilar from those characterising Dantean poetics, where signs and that which they signify can be accurately related to each other with reference to the common centre, or principle of intelligibility, that is the divine meta-presence. Petrarch's poetry, I would argue, has lost the absolute confidence that the Dantean text placed in this divine presence; instead, the *Canzoniere* gently acknowledge the possibility of the *absence* of a principle of intelligibility capable of maintaining the integrity of the signifiers that construct the poetry. (It is, ultimately, this shift in sensibility - the first in a series of subversions later to be echoed in the sonnets of receptive writers like Spenser, Drayton and Shakespeare - that Christina Rossetti exploits in *Monna Innominata*.) In his paper 'Petrarch's Conception of the Dark Ages', Theodore Mommsen concludes that, whereas Dante's world conception might be epitomised by the question 'What else is history, if not the praise of God?' (the notion of a stable theocentric system), Petrarch's view could be rhetorically set out as 'What else is history, but the praise of Rome?'[74] The substitution of Roman glory for Christian redemption as the central event in history appears to govern Petrarch's inversion. It also becomes a subversion from within of the mediaeval mode of thought that it counters.

Dante's God fulfilled the Derridean conditions requisite for an all-encompassing central principle of intelligibility; Ancient Rome, on the other hand, most definitely does not meet these conditions. As evinced in the *Rime*, the Petrarchan conception of Rome sees it as only one part of the totality of history, of temporal origin and end. Because it is located entirely within the system (of temporal history) there is no transcendent reason for privileging the idea of Rome above any other element of that system: such elevation is necessarily arbitrary.[75] A distinction pertains between historical Rome (the Rome of Empire) and Rome the eternal city (Papal Rome, to which men and women made pilgrimage in the Middle Ages). As the Holy City and the seat of Imperial Power, Rome is an inherently ambiguous presence: the place of ruins and the work of time, and yet the place of Christ's Church, the place of eternity. Two oppositional ideas of Rome pertain. Used as a principle of intelligibility, an element such as Rome generates meaning, but the authority or certainty of such meaning is lost in an ambivalence. This *a priori* collapsing of stability (unlike the *a posteriori* collapsing consciously enacted in Christina Rossetti's poems) is detrimental to Petrarch's attempt to construct a coherent system of imagery and signification. In the sixteenth lyric of the *Canzoniere*, this flaw is highlighted in the brief narrative telling of an 'old … dear father' who leaves his family to search for spiritual confirmation:

> The old man takes his leave, white-haired and pale,
> of the sweet place where he filled out his age
> and leaves his little family, bewildered,
> beholding its dear father disappear;
>
> and then, dragging along his ancient limbs
> throughout the very last days of his life,
> helping himself with goodwill all he can,
> broken by years, and wearied by the road,
>
> he comes to Rome, pursuing his desire,
> to look upon the likeness of the One
> he hopes to see again up there in Heaven…[76]

The old man's pilgrimage is to the actuality of Rome, proffered by the Petrarchan lyric as a centre about which meaning may be generated. Yet the pilgrim's unfulfilled desire is to attain an order of stability through Heavenly redemption. Two conflicting principles of intelligibility - Roman glory and Christian faith - operate here, and each functions to disturb, even to negate, the authority and coherence of the other system. The old man's quest is doomed to failure and non-attainment of 'truth' (or meaning) because he is caught between two opposing views of the world, each only capable of offering certainty on its own terms, neither able to cope with the terms of the other. Thus certainty of reference evaporates, as individual components signify different ends in the opposing semantic spheres. The lyric ends on a note of despair: 'Just so, alas, sometimes I go, my lady, / searching as much as possible in others / for you true, your desirable form'.

In the Dantean lyric, the search for truth was guaranteed success at every turn; for Petrarch, absolutes are impossible as one generation of meaning intrudes upon the next, offering ambiguities where certainty is desired. Petrarch's use of Ancient Rome as the centre of his historical structure functions, in fact - despite its being the place of the quest - to decentre and destabilise the signifying system thereby established (since the nominal centre cannot possess absolute authority), resulting in a breakdown of the process of signification itself. It is the devout promotion of the process of signification itself and its collapse into the lack of absolutes in Petrarch, and their difference of implication, which makes these two writers unquestionably relevant to the poetic positioning of Christina Rossetti, certainly as manifest in *Monna Innominata* and the consciously provocative and polysemic attitude to matters of identity and signification pervading that remarkable work which I next intend to go about analysing in close detail.

7

SPOKEN FOR HERSELF: READING *MONNA INNOMINATA*

Had such a lady spoken for herself…
Christina Rossetti, 'Preface' to *Monna Innominata*

…let me beg your prayer's (*sic*) for the poor sinful Woman
who has dared to speak to Others…
Christina Rossetti, Letter to Frederic Shields, September 1894

I

Giving the traditionally silent beloved woman a voice, thereby producing sharp disturbances in the conventions of love poetry, *Monna Innominata* works more than a simple Sapphonic sexual inversion. Beyond the overt agenda of the work's 'Preface' the genuinely radical subversions of male-female polarity, the breaking of woman's silence, and the consequent re-addressing of the codes of love lyric, all function on an acutely subtle subtextual level. Everything to do with Christina Rossetti's sonnet cycle is deeper than meets the eye. It is not a simple poem by any means. It develops via subtle processes of thematic repetition and shifting of perspective, effected in a manner seemingly restrained but actually, I will demonstrate, rigorously controlled. The bold invocation of Dante and Petrarch, as we have seen, works not only to mark out the tradition in which *Monna Innominata* sits with revolutionary aspect, but also to focus attention upon the more complex semantic and linguistic issues at stake in Rossetti's tellingly subtitled 'Sonnet of Sonnets': these are sonnets *about* sonnets, sonnets self-consciously shaped by models and mechanisms established in pre-existing sonnets.

By taking as a starting point our examination of the comparative poetics of the two Italian poets, their similarities and essential differences, we can usefully examine the strategy of Christina Rossetti's cycle towards language and signification. The strategy located in this manner, it will be seen, is one coincident with that which I locate elsewhere in the work of Christina Rossetti. *Monna Innominata* is the most intellectually informed of all Rossetti's literary productions; its critical preface indicates that it is calculated in its methods (and yet it remains an impassioned plea at the plainest thematic level). Moreover, the intellectually provocative register of *Monna Innominata* makes it also the one poem in the Rossetti canon which *openly* admits and confirms the position symbolically adopted towards male tradition and ideology in other works of the same poet.

I have noted the significance of references made by Christina Rossetti to Dante and Petrarch in her prefatory remarks to *Monna Innominata*. She also refers directly, semi-humorously not giving her a name, to 'the Great Poetess of our own day and nation', Elizabeth Barrett Browning (*Poems*, II, 86). The poetical relationship between Christina Rossetti and Barrett Browning (1806-61) is a complex one worthy of more sustained study than has been attempted in the area. Harrison has made out a brief, but persuasive case for Barrett Browning being of much greater influence on the youthful Rossetti's verses than has usually been admitted, arguing that Christina Rossetti consistently 'had [Barrett] Browning in mind even at the beginning of her poetic career'.[1] It is true that Christina Rossetti was invited to make a biographical study of Mrs Browning for the popular *Eminent Women* series, edited by John Ingram. Eventually discouraged by Robert Browning's reputed refusal to endorse the venture, Christina Rossetti never wrote the life, but her initial comments upon being offered the project show the interest Barrett Browning held for her: 'I should write with enthusiasm of that great poetess and (I believe) lovable woman, whom I was never, however, so fortunate as to meet'.[2]

However, in the prefatory remarks to *Monna Innominata*, the *Sonnets from the Portuguese* - written by Elizabeth Barrett Browning during her courtship with Robert Browning (composed 1845-6) and published, after their marriage, in 1850 - are criticised for having more to do with 'fancy' than 'feeling' due to the poetess's 'happy … circumstances' (*Poems*, II, 86). What struck Christina Rossetti most about her contemporary's sonnet sequence was undoubtedly the sense of an opportunity missed. '[H]appy' circumstances or not, Barrett Browning's cycle betrays a comfortable passivity which, unlike *Monna Innominata* (published twenty years after Barrett Browning's death), does nothing to expose, confront, or address the inadequate presentation of woman in the conventional, phallocentric amatory lyric. In fact, the *Sonnets from the Portuguese*, in their stereotypical presentation of the male-female relationship, can be read as actively condoning the masculine tradition Christina Rossetti persistently sought to subvert. Barrett Browning gives woman a voice but then lets her use it only in the praise of the established male tradition which has hitherto kept her silent, passing over a vital opportunity, from a radical female position, further to expose the canon's one-sidedness in the manner of the subversive lyrics of Drayton and Shakespeare. In contrast to the authorial comments which preface *Monna Innominata* with a note directly antagonistic to the unsubverted masculine poetic tradition, Barrett Browning's sonnets open with the speaker casting herself directly in that tradition:

> I thought once how Theocritus had sung
> Of the sweet years, the dear and wished for years…
> And, as I mused it in his antique tongue,
> I saw, in gradual vision through my tears,
> The sweet, sad years, the melancholy years,
> Those of my own life…[3]

The speaker here is able to find a frame for her own experience 'in his antique tongue', that is, within the terms of an unquestioned masculine tradition. The conventions established in the male love lyric are held as adequate to articulate female emotion and thought. Nothing could be further away from the view expounded in Christina Rossetti's poetry, where male-ordered discourse is repeatedly exposed as wholly unable to offer a realistic version of female identity and experience.

The speaker of the 'Portuguese Sonnets', paradoxically, uses the voice which her sonnet cycle allows her to state that she is content, in the relationship with her lover, with being silent: 'Nay, let the silence of my womanhood / Commend my woman-love to thy belief'.[4] Such a maxim, with the submission it implies, would be anathema to Christina Rossetti, yet subjugation to the 'lordly' and 'conquering' male addressee is the dominant theme in Barrett Browning's sonnets. Rossetti's cycle attempts an attack upon and a recasting of male courtly love poetry; Barrett Browning's sequence can too often be read as a faint-hearted echo of masculine dominance.

Dorothy Mermin would have us believe otherwise. She frames a case for Barrett Browning as a feminist, seeing her as involved in 'painfully dislocating' masculine poetic conventions, whereas Christina Rossetti, Mermin states, 'does define herself within the terms set by male poets', by virtue of the fact that she uses Dantean and Petrarchan epigrams to precede the sonnets of *Monna Innominata*.[5] Mermin overlooks the possibility of recontextualisation, or subversion from within, that I have identified as a defining characteristic of Rossetti's poetry. Though her critical evaluations are, of course, as worthy as my own, I feel that Mermin's judgement reflects a tendency that has plagued criticism of Christina Rossetti's writing as much as the biographical determinism upon which I commented earlier. Heavily swayed by biography In her estimation of the 'Portuguese Sonnets', Mermin takes writing at face value and is thereby bound by an overly literal appreciation of the poetry she analyses. Writing poetry within the Victorian age, poetry published by men and, by and large, critically deciphered by men, it is not surprising that literal levels often belie that which is operating beneath the surface of Rossetti's work. Christina Rossetti was probably grateful to be able to pull the wool over the eyes of Victorian male critics when offering up such a feminist tract as *Monna Innominata* for their approval. I do not think she would be so grateful to discover, exactly a hundred years on, that a (female) sophisticated twentieth-century critic was still not able to see through the wool.

In the light of the above detailed study of Dantean and Petrarchan poetics, not forgetting the dissatisfaction evinced at the Sonnet from the Portuguese, I now propose to offer a detailed, close reading of *Monna Innominata*, firstly at a literal, thematic level and latterly in terms of the attitude towards language displayed by the poem's intertextual and symbolic subtext.

II

The first four sonnets in the 'Sonnet of Sonnets' map the cycle's opening thematic movement, an expression of the speaker's longing for conjunction with her absent lover on a decidedly physical (though never overtly sexual) level. The first sonnet laments the lover's absence in plain terms, whilst the second verse articulates the desire to rekindle memories of that 'first moment of your meeting me' (II, 2). Sonnet III, reiterating the loved one's current absence on a physical level, conveys a yearning for 'happy dreams' since now 'only in a dream are we at one', concluding the sonnet somewhat melodramatically: 'If thus to sleep is sweeter than to wake, / To die were surely sweeter than to live, / Tho' there be nothing new beneath the sun' (III, 12-14).

Notably, up until the fourth sonnet of the cycle, there is no definite indication as to whether or not (beyond the realms of the speaker's imagination and 'dreams') the relationship under discussion is one which is reciprocated. Sonnet IV clarifies the picture by giving an commentary upon the actual fortunes experienced by the lovers in the course of their romance: 'I loved you first; but afterwards your love / Outsoaring mine, sang such a loftier song / As drowned the friendly cooings of my dove' (IV, 1-3). This initially competitive exchange of affection, with love assessed in terms of 'weights and measures', is reconciled in this sonnet's sestet where unity (now on earth, not just 'In happy dreams') is achieved by the speaker and her loved one:

> With separate "I" and "thou" free love has done,
> For one is both and both are one in love:
> Rich love knows nought of "thine that is not mine;"
> Both have the strength and both the length thereof,
> Both of us, of the love which makes us one.
> (IV, 10-14)

Harrison emphasises the role which the imagination has played in achieving this plainly expressed instance of secular unity which emphatically marks the end of the first quartet of sonnets: 'Such union has been achieved, as far as the reader can tell, exclusively through the exercise of the poetic imagination, in an operation reminiscent of Keats's comparison of that faculty's workings to Adam's dream: "He awoke and found it truth"'.[6]

However, as soon as the 'truth' of this unity is achieved, it is immediately disrupted by the subjugation, in the second quartet of sonnets, V through VIII, of the lovers' secular union before God's higher presence. In the fifth sonnet, the speaker recommends that the 'noble service' of her addressee be directed not towards herself, but wholly towards the divinity. The sixth sonnet goes some way towards reinstating the notion of present unity so recently disturbed by the speaker's devotional proclamations, but it is now a notion modified by the declaration of the poet's ultimate dependence upon holy direction:

> Trust me, I have not earned your dear rebuke,
> I love, as you would have me, God the most;
> Would lose not Him, but you, must one be lost,
> Nor with Lot's wife cast back a faithless look
> Unready to forego what I forsook …
>
> … Yea, as I apprehend it, love is such
> I cannot love you if I love not Him,
> I cannot love Him if I love not you.   (VI, 1-5, 12-14)

This anaphoric dualistic denouement (a feature found so often at the end of Rossetti's lyrics: 'Remember' and 'Song (When I Am Dead My Dearest)' stand as notable examples), along with the dilemma which such an open-ended conclusion offers up for debate, seems quickly resolved by the initial implications of sonnet VII, where the speaker, seeking Christian 'comfort in his Book', presents an image of equality and unity in a heavenly afterlife.

> "Love me, for I love you" - and answer me,
> "Love me, for I love you" - so shall we stand
> As happy equals in the flowering land
> Of love, that knows not a dividing sea.   (VII, 1-4)

The eighth poem of the fourteen that make up *Monna Innominata*, thereby standing as the volta of this self-styled 'Sonnet of Sonnets', marks the crucial moment of the cycle as well as its turning point (though the geometric structuring of the sequence is far from simple or casually conceived, and is analysed in detail later in this chapter). Somewhat unexpectedly, this pivotal sonnet offers an enigmatic and sensual (on might say Keatsian) version of the biblical fable of the Jewish woman Esther, who, in a scenario prefiguring the martyrdom of Christ, used her feminine intuition (and her beauty) to outwit her husband for the good of her race. Her story is employed here to preface a plea to divinity from the speaker for heavenly blessing of her love on earth: 'If I might take my life so in my hand, / And for my love to Love put up my prayer, / And for love's sake by Love be granted it!' (VIII, 12-14)

On this note, with a deliberately devotional overview of the earthly union that was achieved by parts in the preceding verses, the octave of the sequence concludes. Immediately, as the sestet of the sequence is entered, the tone of the work shifts. Gone is the fervent optimism of the eighth sonnet; the ninth opens on an entirely different theme, recognising the tension between the opposing - secular and spiritual - versions of unity outlined in the cycle's octave.

> Thinking of you, and all that was, and all
> That might have been and now can never be,
> I feel your honoured excellence, and see
> Myself unworthy of the happier call...   (IX, 1-4)

The earlier mood of charged expectancy and the sense of immanent relief it insinuated into the text are deftly replaced by a doleful atmosphere of ascetic renunciation as the speaker now rejects the earthly communion (and thus the ideology of male sonneteers who persistently seek such a physical union) so energetically outlined in the closing lines of sonnet IV. Yet for all this seeming despondency, the female speaker still finds solace in the notion of a spiritual union to supersede that physical conjunction possible in this life. This idea is poignantly and plaintively expressed in the sestet of the tenth sonnet:[7]

> Life wanes; and when love folds his wings above
> Tired hope, and less we feel his conscious pulse,
> Let us go fall asleep, dear friend, in peace:
> A little while, and age and sorrow cease;
> A little while, and life reborn annuls
> Loss and decay and death, and all is love.   (X, 9-14)

If the *Monna Innominata* sequence were to end at this point, then the orthodox Christian moral of the work would be clear and emphatic: *vanitas mundi* is proven to be a mere shadow of the eternal peace to be enjoyed in the afterlife. But this is not to be. The cycle continues, further highlighting the speaker's tendency towards a mood of irresolution via a progressively metaphysical series of renunciations occupying the trio of sonnets XI to XIII. The 'So much for you; but what for me...?' theme of sonnet V is revisited in the eleventh poem, now with distinctly sarcastic and feminist overtones:

> Many in aftertimes will say of you
> "He loved her" - while of me what will they say?

> Not that I loved you more than just in play,
> For fashion's sake as idle women do.   (XI, 1-4)

This sonnet introduces an abrupt contradiction of the idealised, religious persuasiveness of its predecessor. Even in the afterlife, the speaker now suspects, there may be room for difference:

> …we knew
> Of love and parting in exceeding pain,
> Of parting hopeless here to meet again.
> Hopeless on earth, and heaven is out of view.   (XI, 5-8)

The pressing desire for unity, therefore certitude, that has become controller of thematic rhythms of the sonnet cycle, is again frustrated. The chance of stability, which seemed all but achieved more than once already in the sequence, is again acknowledged potentially to be 'out of view'. Once more faced with a decentred world-view, and the resultant loss of intelligibility so far as the love relationship is concerned, in sonnet XII the speaker seeks to reaffirm the speaker's recently shaken confidence in the love-bond between herself and her beloved, this time by means of a further ascetic renunciation.

> If there be any one can take my place
> And make you happy whom I grieve to grieve,
> Think not that I can grudge it, but believe
> I do commend you to that nobler grace,
> That readier wit than mine,
>   that sweeter face…   (XII, 1-5)

'Your pleasure is my pleasure', affirms the speaker. This new version of equality, reached via a sequence of reappraisals and renunciations, is the predominant theme here. Déjà vu beckons as a predictable attempt to reinforce this sense of oneness, sonnet XIII (directly echoing sonnet V) commends the lovers' relationship entirely to 'God's hand …

Whose knowledge foreknew every plan we planned'. Again, however, at the very moment that certitude seems to have been reached, a by now familiar tone of self-doubt interrupts the speaker's contentment:

> Searching my heart for all that touches you,
> I find there only love and love's goodwill
> Helpless to help and impotent to do,
> Of understanding dull, of sight most dim;
> And therefore I commend you back to Him
> Whose love your love's capacity can fill.   (XIII, 9-14)

Sonnet XIV completes the *Monna Innominata* sequence on a resigned and dolorous tone. The speaker admits the mutability of existence, as illustrated by the cycle and the terms of the love relationship outlined therein, in a manner which is resigned to instability. 'Youth gone and beauty, what remains of bliss?', the speaker asks, still retaining a sense of touching personal dignity:

> I will not bind fresh roses in my hair,
> To shame a cheek at best but little fair,-
> Leave youth his roses, who can bear a thorn,-
> I will not seek for blossoms anywhere...   (XIV, 4-7)

Repetition of negatives here - 'I will not... I will not...' – emphasises a stoical and self-conscious refusal to oppose the forces of mutability and change that have disputed and abnegated stability and certitude throughout the sonnet sequence. The cycle does end with a silent passivity, but it is a considered stance: silence becomes the most poignant statement the speaker can make. The speaker of Rossetti's sonnets, initially craving a physical union with her loved one, eventually constructs a desire for communion on a spiritual plane (revealed at first in 'happy dreams') which will, she hopes, be complete and eternal and mark the perfectibility of the self. God is proffered as a potential centre of intelligibility with the power to unite and yet to divide. As such,

His potency is emblematic of that which informs the text of *Monna Innominata*. Consequently, the speaker's embracing of mutability, accepting the inevitability of instability on earth and contrasting with this the eternally stable afterlife, is not just an admission of defeat (in terms of the cycle's quest, and that of all Rossetti's early poetry), but also a blissful refuge from the painful quest for earthly knowledge which traditionally forms the basis of any love-relationship, as expressed in lyric verse. *Monna Innominata*'s relinquishment of profane indulgence is, I hope to show, simultaneous with Rossetti's own withdrawal, as a writer, into the sphere of exclusively devotional work.

I hope that the summary of *Monna Innominata* that I have given is enough to alert us to the fact that there is much more going on in the poem than meets the eye. Many times in the cycle the poetry reflects upon 'song', to the extent that the poetry becomes a critique of itself. The intellectual journey taken by the speaker of Rossetti's sequence is one which involves areas of meaning beyond the surface literal level of the poem. In its symbolic analysis of language, ideology and meaning, the work enacts some highly sophisticated intertextual, semantic and linguistic manoeuvres which it is now my purpose to examine in detail.

III

Christina Rossetti's 'Sonnet of Sonnets' addresses matters of signifying potential and writing within a tradition of other writing. Notions of context are questioned and the frames of reference these rely upon for the production of meaning are shown to be shifting and unstable. Because of this, the text forbids itself any easy closure, and *Monna Innominata* is not a straightforward poem to read or to interpret. The sequence operates not around, but *within* systems of difference, establishing so-called 'certitudes' only to challenge them in terms of contradictions that become apparent via recontextualisation. In short, like Goblin Market and The Prince's Progress, the text continually interrogates and deconstructs its own premises. The work's motto could be the line from another Christina Rossetti poem ('An Old-World

Thicket' (*Poems*, II, 123-8)) that I have cited throughout this study: 'For all that was but showed what all was not', and the sequence finally exhausts itself in a silence both ambiguous and provocative, which forewarns of the relatively passive embrace of orthodox Christian piety to which Rossetti turned in her later writings.

It is worth reiterating here, this time in full, a passage from Derrida referred to earlier:

> it has always been thought that the centre, which is by definition unique, constituted that very thing within a structure which while governing the structure, escapes structurality ... The centre is at the centre of the totality, and yet, since the centre does not belong to the totality (is not part of the totality), the totality has its centre elsewhere. The centre is not the centre. The concept of a centred structure - although it represents coherence itself, the condition of the episteme as philosophy or science - is contradictorily coherent.[8]

More than any other single work of Christina Rossetti, *Monna Innominata* addresses the literary inter-relationships inscribed in all poetic texts between a notion of the self and its history or story, raising certain issues concerning narrative representation. The resultant questioning of all that tradition has bequeathed as the 'norm' and held to be stable, highlighting the pluralistic signifying potential of language (and structures which obtains between subjects and predicates, selves and narratives) accentuates the peculiarly non-narrative element which is always operative whenever Christina Rossetti tries to narrate a story.

I have outlined the similarities and differences between the linguistic principles constructing some of the Dantean and Petrarchan texts alluded to by Christina Rossetti in her prefatory remarks to *Monna Innominata*. As previously stated, I believe that the Rossetti sequence reveals an insistence upon the priority of poetic relationships in its production of significance, and hence in its presentation (or rather its investigation) of poetic tradition and literary history. In an avowed attempt to write as a woman - to explore a manner of discourse outwith the phallocentric 'masculine' register of the poetic tradition she aims to subvert yet extend - Rossetti is forced to consider the signifying possibilities of male-ordered discourse, particularly that in the writings of Dante and Petrarch, which underpins the traditional courtly love lyric. Consequently, I read Christina Rossetti's poetry, and *Monna Innominata* in particular, in response to, as well as to arrive at an understanding of, certain formal and stylistic features which seem to me motivated by a recognition (or decision) that the signifying possibilities of the male mode of discourse are no longer imaginatively available for a woman wishing to write from a woman's point of view. *Monna Innominata* plays out various notions of the signifying capacities of discourse, displaying a sophisticated degree of awareness of the nature of centring principles of intelligibility, their power and treatment in texts written by men.

The first sonnet of *Monna Innominata* regenerates the Petrarchan anima/animus model and introduces a main theme of the sequence with its attention to the issues of 'love' and 'song' and their psychological relationship. The poem's opening quatrain, wistfully and plainly phrased, is a familiar device in the poetry of Christina Rossetti. On one level a love's lament over the absence of a loved one, the lines may also steer attention towards another absence - the absence of the poetic voice heralding (as it did at the beginning of *The Prince's Progress*) the desire for artistic fruition:

> Come back to me, who wait and watch for you:-
> Or come not yet, for it is over then,
> And long it is before you come again,
> So far between my pleasures are and few.   (I, 1-4)

A lament for a lover becomes a summons to a song that will crystallise and preserve the lament. As with 'Echo' and many other of

Christina Rossetti's lyric pieces, rhythmic intoning and progression of monosyllables create a sense of charged invocation. These opening lines function, in a post-Romantic internalised sense, as a modified self-reflexive summons to the traditional poetic 'muse'. Part of the success of this device, then, relies upon the intended fusion of poetic inspiration/object, where the addressee of the verse becomes the source of energy behind the song, the raison d'être of the lyric both narratively and metaphorically. In striving to find a discourse that is free from the patriarchal ideology traditional to the love sonnet, a main objective of the poetry must be to come to terms with the female psyche, somehow to estimate and define female identity. The traditional poetic muse, - that of masculine literature - even when acknowledged as metaphor for an internalised operation, is always read as being a female form. This 'anima' figure qualifies as a concentration of the spiritual and creative capacity within every man's self. In a forthright attempt to write from a feminine stance, Christina Rossetti must here disturb such sexual role-allocation and, still in the service of an invocatory summons, the nature and essence of her desire as manifest in this poetic form is revealed: 'For one man is my world of all the men / This wide world holds; O love, my world is you' (I, 7-8).

Inverting the conventional notion of the energy source governing all courtly love poetry, the speaker offers a concise and clear statement concerning the idealised conception - the 'idea' - she has of the object of her desire. The sense of strain in the text here is significant: due to social constraints established by a patriarchal society, it is difficult, on every level, for female sexuality freely to be acted out. The poet-speaker's 'hope', her yearning for fruition of the creative impulse, is said to hang 'waning, waxing, like a moon / Between the heavenly days on which we meet' (I, 12-13).

It is highly appropriate, if we read this opening sonnet as a subtle musaic invocation, that the image of the waning and waxing 'moon', a symbol (also used in *The Prince's Progress*) of fecundity and creativity (but also mutability), is associated with the desire for a conjunction of poetic voice and inspiration. The 'days on which we meet' - when a conjunction is achieved, a union effected - are seen as 'heavenly', not of earthly concord but of a divinely inspired, spiritual plane. Later in the sequence, the addressed lover figure is described as 'my heart's heart, and you who are to me / More than myself myself' (V, 1-2). This unusual and deliberately awkward grammatical construction conveys the speaker's sense of strain whilst deftly reinforcing the notion of an internalised conception of the absent 'loved one'. A similar reinforcement of this idea lies in the avoidance throughout *Monna Innominata* of the traditional descriptive element essential to the courtly love poem, the exaltation of the lady's beauty which was seen as a direct reflection of divine goodness. Typically for Christina Rossetti, the unnamed male addressed in these verses is never afforded any degree of external delineation. No hint is given of the man's appearance. In this manner, all the negotiations and interchanges effected in the course of the cycle are operating on a psychological level. For Rossetti, visualisation of the lover, a necessity in the poetry of Dante and Petrarch, is only possible on a dream level, and even this seems traumatic: 'In happy dreams I hold you full in sight, / I blush again who waking look so wan' (III, 5-6).

The notion of exposure to the visual manifestation of the abstract mental ideal is important within the broader strategy of *Monna Innominata*. The playful and ironic 'wan'/'one' pun imports the idea (just how relevantly will be clear from the detailed reading of the third sonnet) that the speaker's awakening from dreams marks a fall from a desired state of unity. Such light-hearted punning, with its hint of sarcastic understatement, is very uncharacteristic of Christina Rossetti in a lyric such as this - although many such devices can be found in her ballads and children's writing - but it works well here, emphasising the poet's ear for the fecundities of language. In contrast to the lyrics of Dante and Petrarch, nowhere in the collection of sonnets does the speaker feel the need to look for or to posit from fancy an image in the likeness of her loved one. As the poetry becomes the written enshrinement of the impulse to create, the 'vision' of the text is turned inward and we are soon aware that a different pattern of signification is at work than that of Dantean and Petrarchan texts.

Early in this opening sonnet, the speaker admits that 'when you come not, what I do I do / Thinking "Now when he comes," [is] my sweetest "when"' (I, 5-6). The now/when construction is repeated in the closing couplet of the sonnet and is interesting in its own sake as a means of grasping the methodology of this work so far as the approach to signification is concerned. In this first instance, the 'now' - traditionally used in philosophy as the ultimate example of an unreliable signifier, since that time which it purports to denote is over before the signification can be received - of 'when he comes' is said to be 'my sweetest "when"'. This peculiarly experimental lifting of a linguistic semantic unit - 'my sweetest "when"' - from immediate context, yet still kept within the broader poetic framework, represents an overt interest in the capacity of language momentarily to signify and thence hold connotation as retrospective value. Simply put, this is temporal blurring of the subtlest form. Time, for the speaker, refuses absolute guarantee of certainty, an idea developed in sonnet II.

The Dantean epigraph to this opening sonnet, another example of a recontextualised unit of meaning, is translated by William Michael Rossetti as '[t]he day that they have said adieu to their sweet friends' (*Works*, 462).[9] But in Christina's exposition the 'friends' are words themselves and, as so often with her lyrics, this signals an immediate awareness of the poetry's own stance as such, as poetry. A recent commentator has, I think rightly, proposed of this Rossetti sequence that 'sweetness gets attached to the words that are talismans of the lover's presence', going on to note that 'her desire has made them substitutes for the presence that is their true signified'.[10]

The last couplet of Sonnet 1 (recalling Keats's demand 'Where are the songs of spring?' in 'To Autumn') is crucial to an understanding of the strategy of the whole sequence to follow, so far as matters of literariness and signification are concerned: 'Ah me, but where are now the songs I sang / When life was sweet because you called them sweet?' (I, 13-14).[11] The repeated now/when construction again interests itself in questions of language and reference, here 'the songs I sang'. Like the loved one, the 'songs' are absent here, and still in the service of a invocation to a muse, these lines simultaneously exhibit a theory of signification and context. Life was 'sweet' not because it was called 'sweet' by direct nomination (the Dantean notion of certitude of reference as displayed in the poetics of the *Vita Nuova*) but because the songs sung were 'called...sweet'. In this way a chain of signification is established:

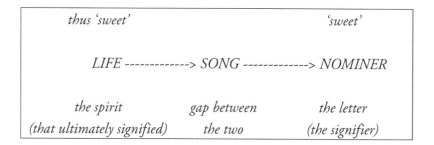

Whilst asserting the primacy of the creative process as a means of defining love and the self, this conundrum raise questions regarding the relationship of 'truth' to (poetic) subjectivity. 'Song' generates the vision of transcendent 'love', whatever that vision may become. All importantly, the 'gap' between that signified and its signifier is the song which the text itself invokes. The song stands as testimony to the fruition of this invocation. Hence, this 'song', *Monna Innominata*, explores that gap between letter and spirit both literally and on a subtle symbolic level. Poetry again becomes its own subject as Rossetti endeavours to construct a manner of poetry radically opposed to that traditionally found in the lyric, informed with a sophisticated consciousness of the implications of the very tradition it subverts.

The second sonnet of the *Monna Innominata* sequence upturns another convention of the male courtly love tradition. It provides an almost parodic exposition of Petrarch's *Canzoniere* LXI, which, with the speaker seeking explicitly to pinpoint the exact moment of meeting, has the opening quatrain:

Oh blessed be the day, the month, the year,
the season and the time, the hour, the instant,
the gracious countryside, the place where I
was struck by those two lovely eyes that bound me...[12]

The speaker goes on to discuss, in poetry, 'the poetry / I scattered, calling out my lady's name', going on to bless 'all the paper upon which / I earn her fame'. Rossetti's second sonnet likewise deals with a first meeting and the recording of the impression made by the loved one, but the approach is different. Following on from the opening sonnet more by way of tone than any narrative, causal progression, the subject matter of this woman's verse is still conceived of at an internalised, spiritual level. It is appropriate, then, that sonnet II opens on a theme of temporal blurring, in direct contrast to the Petrarchan precedent.

I wish I could remember that first day,
First hour, first moment of your meeting me,
If bright or dim the season, it might be
Summer or Winter for aught I can say...   (II, 1-4)

This familiar loss of certainty as to external reference reinforces the notion that the text is to be read as self-reflexive, not as a straightforward narrative tract, but rather a psychological exploration of the poet-speaker's frame of mind. This quatrain alerts us to the fact that the experience the speaker is narrating here is agonisingly ephemeral. The sonnet's insistence upon the absence of memory (compounding the absence of the loved one) is disturbingly un-Romantic and extremely effective. The use of verb tenses is especially significant. To qualify the instance of the 'first moment of your meeting me' as one single event from the past, the following tag clause would have to be 'it might have been / Summer or Winter...'. The usage of the present tense, 'it might be / Summer...' implies an ongoing issue, that this 'first moment' qualifies as a repeatable occurrence, one that has happened and may well happen again. If we accept a reading of this sequence which sees it in terms of an internalised exploration of processes of discourse formation, the development of a 'feminine' style of writing, then it is indeed appropriate that the 'first moment' of conception of the creative impulse is presented symbolically in this ambivalent manner - always an original urge, but one that may return. As the impulse is described in this quatrain, the quatrain itself forms monumental testimony to the association it describes. The rest of the sonnet is taken up with a investigation into ideas of writing, as the speaker attempts imaginatively to reconstruct an event which is absent from her memory and, hence, founded on uncertainties.

> So unrecorded did it slip away,
> So blind was I to see and to foresee,
> So dull to mark the budding of my tree
> That would not blossom yet for many a May.
> If only I could recollect it, such
> A day of days! I let it come and go
> As traceless as a thaw of bygone snow...   (II, 5-11)

There is a pained desire in these lines to record the creative impulse, a desire seen as natural and cast in images of a blossoming tree and melted snow, themselves from the natural world. 'Unrecorded' a tree bud will grow into blossom whereas snow will simply thaw to a 'traceless' condition - furthering the dichotomic presentation at symbolic level, the conflicting images drawn from the same source - nature - emphasise the potential of the artistic impulse to progress to differing degrees of substantiality. And around all this recognition of the non-fixity, temporally and qualitatively, of the 'meeting' at a psychological level, a broader theme of the sonnet is the actual passing of time and the uncertainty of identity with this passage. The urge to 'see and to foresee' is noted, whilst the speaker seeks to remember a 'moment' and later a 'touch', both insubstantial instances and, in the same vein, this sonnet seems to promote a vision of the individual identity as a concept rooted on insubstantiality. The Petrarchan epigram, which William Michael translates as 'I recur to the time when I first saw thee' (*Works*, 462), is an illustration of this tendency in the verse. The conditional clause demands a split in the subject of the whole sentence at grammatical level and this division must also be recognised in terms of semantic continuity. The 'I' seeks to 'recur' to a previous time occupied by a previous 'I' who is and yet is not the same presence as the 'I' who remembers. This division echoes the instability of personal pronouns in a text such as the Rossetti sonnet which deals with the recollection of former incidents. The alternation of 'I's in the Rossetti text is of a very sophisticated nature, especially when coupled with the temporal blurring I have already noted. For example, still with the second sonnet: 'If only I could recollect it, such / A day of days! I let it come and go / As traceless as a thaw of bygone snow' (II, 9-11).

The modal construction 'If only I could recollect' functions (as did the opening statement of the sonnet beginning, 'I wish I could remember') to deny certainty as to the temporality it describes. (I noted earlier that the actuality of the lovers' relationship is wholly unestablished at this stage.) The 'day of days' might be of time past or of an ongoing future sense. The deliberate choice of verb in 'I let it come and go', which could be past or present tense, confirms the desire to leave uncertain the temporal dimensions delineated. The enforced lack of correlation between the first person singular pronouns of this section make a stable poetic subjectivity impossible to deduce with any degree of reliability, even though, overriding all of this is the fact that the 'I' signifier is itself a constant. Such complexity behind the alternation of pronominal signifiers in their context highlights, in a very sophisticated manner, the unreliability of pronominal reference which is a marker illustrating the instability of personal identity through time. The shifting signification ultimately leaves direct referents 'unrecorded' in the terms of the fiction of the text: external 'truths' become indeed 'as traceless as a thaw of bygone snow'.

'It seemed to mean to little, meant so much' (II, 12). Thus the speaker describes what is now an absence, an uncertainty, but this comment, with its pronouncement upon the unreliability of the status of any 'fixed' interpretation, could also be applied to the *Monna Innominata* cycle itself thus far, as it continues, acknowledging the uncertainty of its own particular linguistic strategies and the open possibility of a pluralistic reading. But, as was noted earlier, there is a keen desire within this text to move towards certainty and understanding at literal and psychological level, confirmed sharply by the exclamatory final couplet of this sonnet: 'If only now I could recall that touch, / First touch of hand in hand - Did one but know!' (II, 13-14).

The speaker, as fractured as the conception of her own identity has become, nonetheless feels the drive towards a state of conjunction. It is notable that the state of harmony sought here, the 'touch of hand in hand' is a conjunction which itself may be performed alone by the single individual in the act of prayer, hence another 'heavenly' meeting, and as notable is the choice of personal pronoun - 'one' here and not 'I' - used directly after the imaging of the conjunction. The sonnet has focused itself upon an illustration of the instability of reference of the 'I' signifier and it closes with the desire for a state of being nominated by the pronoun 'one', denoting some kind of concord and unity to give reassurance to the text after the exhibition of uncertainty which has gone before. There are seven 'I's in the fourteen lines of Sonnet II, but the unit 'one' is, indeed, used only once. The striving for 'one'-ness, for unity, comes to occupy much of the mid section of *Monna Innominata* bringing with it the related desire to find an adequate system of signification which will reflect the stability and likewise be able successfully to interpret it.

As an actual figure in the terms of the altogether vague narrative fiction offered by *Monna Innominata*, the male addressee, like the forgotten 'first moment of … meeting', is never present: his immediate function is as an absence and all that this entails. Yet, as the source of the poetry, both dramatically and mentally, this non-presence is the element which gives inspiration and, at one level, a degree of inner coherence and birth to the poetry itself. The poem cannot exist outside of the idea of the unnamed male and vice versa, the absent lover could not possibly exist outside the terms of the sonnet sequence. We have already noted the entire lack of visual description afforded to the addressee of these sonnets; he stands wholly as an idea (and an ideal) and thus the third sonnet considers a psychological framework which may subvert notions of 'actuality' and narrative causal connection - the 'dream' sphere. The speaker longs to remain in the realm of 'happy dreams', since the radiant presence (a kind of meta-presence in terms of the immediate narrative of the sequence) of this soul-mate there 'makes day of night'.

> I dream of you, to wake: would that I might
> Dream of you and not wake but slumber on;
> Nor find with dreams the dear companion gone,
> As Summer ended Summer birds take flight.
> In happy dreams I hold you full in sight,
> I blush again who waking look so wan;
> Brighter than sunniest day that ever shone,
> In happy dreams your smile makes day of night.
> Thus only in a dream are we at one...   (III, 1-9)

Unity, promoted thus far in the cycle as necessary prerequisite for stability of reference, is the desired state here, and it may be found in the non-empirical world of the dream. And yet 'only in a dream' already betrays an admittance that the unity in that context is not the stable entity it may seem when viewed within a different context, from the point which, in describing the dream and the conjunction achieved therein, must itself be outwith that dream. 'I dream of you to wake', says the speaker, and this is an essential point - the waking is necessary to an assessment of the dream from a position that is not of the dream itself. Thus the speaker desires to 'not wake but slumber on', but cannot, and in describing the dream process sets herself outside it, finding the unity only a fleeting image, 'the dear companion gone'. This admitted, the sonnet has negotiated the search for a centring principle only to find an image of stability full of contradictions. The desire to escape temporality by entering the dream sphere ironically culminates in a picture of harmony which is indeed ex-temporal but only in an unworkable sense since, viewed from the position of poet-subject established in this and the other sonnets, the dream can be only a fleeting, thus a temporal interlude. As a system of signification, the dream satisfies its own terms but cannot connect with those of the broader context demanded by the terms of the ongoing central narrative of *Monna Innominata*: thus, the sonnet presents a microcosmic image of the problematical process of recontextualisation investigated repeatedly by the intertextual nature of the whole cycle. A self-satisfying image, with solid internal balance, semantically and grammatically, and yet meaningless in any broader sense, confirms the failure of the speaker in the search for overall intelligibility: 'Thus only in a dream we give and take / The faith that maketh rich who take or give' (III, 10-11).

The strategy of this sonnet, then, has collapsed into the realisation that an ordering principle, to be useful, must be able to pass the test of recontextualisation. A fall into pessimism. 'To die were surely sweeter than to live', reinforces the tone of dissatisfaction with the progress of the argument felt by the speaker, and the closing line - 'Tho' there be nothing new beneath the sun' (III, 14) - seems particularly despairing and unenthusiastic. This line is itself a recontextualisation of a biblical phrase and is worth quoting in its original context, by way of further illustrating the point reached at its placing in the Rossetti text. It is taken from the first chapter of Ecclesiastes, the section of the *Old Testament* most frequently alluded to in the poetry of Christina Rossetti.

> 8. All things are full of labour; man cannot utter it: the eye is not satisfied with seeing, nor the ear filled with hearing.
> 9. That thing that hath been, it is that which shall be; and that which is done is that which shall be done: and there is no new thing under the sun.

10. Is there any thing whereof it may be said, See, this is new? it hath been already of old time, which was before us.
11. There is no remembrance of former things; neither shall there be any remembrance of things that are to come with those that shall come after. (Ecclesiastes 1, 9-11)

'[M]an cannot utter it'. Similarly, the Rossetti text has been unable, thus far, to find a mode of utterance suited to the expression of a woman's way of 'seeing', a wholly 'feminine' discourse 'whereof it may be said, See, this is new?' Unsuccessful in its attempt to find a principle of intelligibility around which to posit the term of a 'feminine' register, *Monna Innominata* cannot yet make order of the chaos it seeks to commit to signification and is thus caught up in a centreless state of indeterminacy where, indeed, 'that which is done is that which shall be done: and there is no new thing under the sun. 'Another strategy must be tried, and it is by this trial and error methodology (rather than by any predictable narrative continuity) that the Rossetti sequence moves forward in this, its early stages.

It will be useful at this point to identify some subtle supra-textual structuring principles behind the ordering of the fourteen sonnets that make up *Monna Innominata*. On the evidence of a first reading, it might not be unfair to propose that these sonnets are set down in random succession. I have already noted the distinct lack, or rather avoidance of direct causal narrative linking: *Monna Innominata* is built around debate rather than plot. The speaker muses and sings her songs whilst the addressee stays absent throughout - this is the sum total of the 'action' of the sequence read as a dramatic narrative. This lack of external directives means that at this level any one of the sonnets could be removed from the sequence and replaced at an alternative stage in the text with no disruption felt to the drama in progress. Whilst this is so, it must be acknowledged that the text comes to us in its set order, and, subtle as they may be, there will be reasons for the position of each sonnet in the cycle. Christina Rossetti addresses this issue herself in two letters. One is to Macmillan, dated 24 November 1886, and refers specifically to *Monna Innominata*: 'I ... make a point of refusing extracts, even in the case of my Sonnet of Sonnets some of which would fairly stand alone'.[13] Three years previously Christina had been even clearer as to her position with regard to the notion of a general structure, replying to an enthusiastic American anthology editor and, again, mentioning her 'Sonnet of Sonnets':

> I do not mind which piece you select subject only to your taking any piece in question in its entirety; and my wish includes your not choosing an independent poem which forms part of a series or group, - not (for instance)... one Sonnet of '*Monna Innominata*'. Such compound work often has a connection (very often) which is of interest to the author and which [the reader] an editor gains nothing by discarding.[14]

Christina's father had delved deeply into the numerological implications of the structuring of Dante's writing (in particular, the *Vita Nuova*), and it is clear from the above statements that she had inherited this concern.[15]

Monna Innominata is pointedly subtitled a 'Sonnet of Sonnets' with all the formal implications that this description entails: fourteen constituent units, an octave leading to a meaningful volta, and a concluding sestet. Given that the sequence is labelled as structured deliberately in this knowingly literary form, an awareness of the poetry as poetry, as writing, is clearly at work. Moreover, much of the symbolic resonance of *Monna Innominata* concerns itself with matters of signification and their relevance to a (reclaimed, potentially) 'feminine' poetic discourse. I believe that the overall shaping of the sequence is carefully, holistically designed to parallel, reflect, and reinforce important narrative or symbolic patternings occurring within or across the fourteen poems themselves. Such numerological symbolism, for lack of a better term, is directly appropriate to a form, the sonnet sequence, whose internal balance (or lack of it) relies upon the juxtaposition of defined internal units, octave and sestet. Fowler has shown the possible structural metaphor implicit in the pyramidal formation of Shakespeare's sonnets, and made a detailed and revealing numerological study of Sidney's *Astrophel and Stella*.[16] Fuller, reads these structurally emblematic overviews as 'one way of imposing a meaningful structure on a possibly open ended form'.[17]

In *Monna Innominata*, one might argue, the structuring of the sequence, taken as metaphor, is managed in such a way as to emphasise, not redress, the open ended nature of the whole work's argument, emblematically embodying an ironic image of the notion of centrality/stability which is repeatedly assumed and then dismissed, at literal and symbolic levels, in the sequence. The eighth sonnet of the *Monna Innominata* series taken as a whole (that dealing with the story of Esther) marks the moment of the volta in the Rossetti cycle, and thus functions as an interpretative centre around which, and from the import of which the other poems take their place in the debate. This geocentric patterning works by coupled inversions thus:

Sonnet:	1	2	3	4	5	6	7	8	9	10	11	12	13	14
	{	{	{	{	{	{	*	*	}	}	}	}	}	}
Sonnet:	14	13	12	11	10	9	8	7	6	5	4	3	2	1

In the terms of this geometrically metaphoric structuring, sonnets IV and V lie in the same relations to the central principle of the debate as sonnets X and XI and this positional bearing is a guarantee of the register upon which the coupled sonnets figure to operate, their weight and import in the face of the totality of the argument. (There is no need to elaborate upon specific instances of this at present: its relevance will become apparent when I come to discuss the later sonnets in terms of those which have gone before.) The first sonnet of the series becomes the complementary partner to the last, and all exhibit themselves as stemming from the centre of the text as a whole.

But there are, of course, other ordering energies at work within the sequence. The actual placing in sequence of the verses as we have them, actively reinforced by their specified enumeration, cannot help but suggest a progressive statement, read as a continuous narrative, which the subtextual workings of the poetry attempt to subvert. And the 'Sonnet of Sonnets' directive dictates that within the text we recognise a separate octave and sestet, with the rise and fall in poetic energies that tradition had brought such structuring to entail. Hence, even where the subtle but elaborate patterning of the sonnets into their seemingly loose ordering is concerned, one detects the awareness of conflicting modes of structuring which juxtapose one another in a perpetual exercise of 'deconstruction'. The legitimacy of one system is defined by its own terms and yet is deftly laid bare by a recontextualisation which allows it to be read on other premises. The pertinence of this general reading will become clear as a fuller interpretation of the whole methodology of *Monna Innominata* unfolds.

To return to analysis of the poems, the fourth sonnet of *Monna Innominata* is rather different in tone from the third. The language is still direct and plain but the despondency is forgotten as the text prepares to make another attempt at ordering the disorder and expressing a woman's view of a world traditionally structured to her disadvantage. The anti-Petrarchan portrayal of a balance (as opposed to the mediaeval imbalance) of love-power between speaker and addressee which opens the sonnet is, appropriately, imaged in terms of the articulation of song, from which point the speaker proceeds to question notions of (in)equality and (dis)unity in love and in language:

> I loved you first; but afterwards your love
> Outsoaring mine, sang such a loftier song
> As drowned the friendly cooings of my dove.
> Which owes the other most? my love was long,
> And yours one moment seemed to wax more strong;
> I loved and guessed at you, you construed me
> And loved me for what might or might not be -

Nay, weights and measures do us both a wrong.
For verily love knows not "mine" or "thine;"
With separate "I" and "thou" free love has done,
For one is both and both are one in love:
Rich love knows nought of "thine that is not mine;"
Both have the strength and both the length thereof,
Both of us, of the love which makes us one. (IV, 1-14)

Taken on its own, this sonnet might be read as representing a lightly sarcastic historical analysis of woman's gradually relegated position - and the unfairness of that relegation - in the inherited tradition of amatory literature. It begins with an abrupt assertion of female identity - 'I loved you first...' - before outlining woman's enforced passivity in love matters and the resultant male monopoly in areas of poetic expression, finally focusing attention upon language itself. The interest in the interaction of opposite, complementary elements of a system of integration indicates that this sonnet, like the third, will move around and towards notions of unity and stability, of 'the love which makes us one'. The progressive displacement and reorganisation of energies here, might be seen as manoeuvring the text somewhat towards the negotiation and construction of a stable poetic subject.

As noted before, the exposition of a radically feminine perspective necessarily involves a primary investigation of the female self and its constituent psychological make-up. One possibility, then, open to *Monna Innominata* would be the provision of a integral, stable poet-subject as symptomatic of the achievement of the ordering centre of which Derrida speaks, by which principle of intelligibility all other subsidiary elements of the proposed system may be deduced and thus comprehended. As is so often the case with the poetry of Christina Rossetti, the terms in which the balance is proposed, the actual language used, soon alert us to the sub-textual implications at work here: 'I loved and guessed at you, you construed me / And loved me for what might or might not be' (IV, 6-7). These lines are significant and reveal the complexity behind what, superficially, may a seem very straightforward use of language. The speaker 'loved' first and then 'guessed at' the loved one. The drive preceded (or was coincident with) the estimation of the qualitative nature of the oppositional party. Similarly 'you construed me': the speaker exists as 'construed' (interpreted, analysed, *constructed* grammatically) in words by the addressee of the poetry, 'loved for what might or might not be'. There is, then, a definite move towards giving an assessment, a definition even, of the nature of the poetic subject here, yet the admission of the uncontainability, unpredictability, and uncertainty of identity is still a prominent feature of the text. The related interest in the instability of pronouns in the face of a desired order is then pursued, as the speaker once more turns away from empirical evidence:

> Nay, weights and measures do us both a wrong.
> For verily love knows not "mine" or "thine;"
> With separate "I" and "thou" free love has done,
> For one is both and both are one in love… (IV, 8-11)

These lines provide another direct example of the poetry's very proto-modernist (perhaps proto-structuralist) concern with language itself, as the poetry openly queries the signifiers that constitute its discourse. Transcending the rejected world of 'weights and measures', the power of 'love' - here a secular, very human 'love' with lower-case initialling - may possess potential to provide a sure principle of intelligibility. This, in turn, by becoming a guarantee of meaning over and above the fickleness of unstable pronominal signification, injects certitude into the philosophy of the text. The 'faith that maketh rich' was discussed previously in terms of the unworkable dream ideal of harmony and stability, the desire for belief in an ordering concept to make smooth the chaos of unsure identities. It has now evolved into a more appropriate centre: '[r]ich love'. In knowing 'nought of "thine that is not mine"', this ideal may dissolve the uncertain referential potential of signifiers to leave a harmoniously functioning system. Balanced elements can have certain identity and place within that system, allowing the construction of a stable poetic subject: 'Both have the strength and both the length thereof, / Both of us, of the love that makes us one' (IV, 13-14).

The epigram from Petrarch which precedes the fifth sonnet, translated as 'Love led me into such joyous hope' (*Works*, 462), functions in this recontextualised position to reflect and reinforce a 'joyous' tone in the poetry. In direct juxtaposition is Dante's ominous reminder that all elements of a centred system must submit to the government of the ordering principle: 'Love, who exempts no loved one from loving' (*Works*, 462). The dichotomy evident here is thematically echoed in the sonnet itself. We witness joy at spiritual certitude tempered with despair at earthly division, as the 'love' in question is directed toward God for divine sanction. The octave opens with an affirmation of the sense of unity described in the previous verse. The poetic subject is momentarily stable, embracing this unity as a means of reinforcing the internalised conception of the poetic impulse: 'O my heart's heart, and you who are to me / More than myself myself' (V, 1-2). This fusion of signifiers - 'heart's heart... myself myself' - with consequent semantic concentration effected, offers a stabilising effect appropriate to the idea that a competent discourse has been established in which to frame remaining verses. However, in the very moment we have been led to feel comfortable with the terms of one discourse, once more a fierce intrusion upon the flow of the text may be perceived. As the secular passion is offered up for divine approval (essentially a request for absolute stability, for 'perfection' of the issue) a new and different language register is suddenly introduced: 'God be with you, / Keep you in strong obedience leal and true / To Him whose noble service setteth free' (V, 2-4).

This liturgical pronouncement is bred of orthodox Christian biblical discourse and heralds the way for the complete embrace of piety the speaker (and Rossetti) is eventually to perform. This language type had been alluded to before (notably at the end of Sonnet III) but was always recontextualised, the remanagement of adopted registers being a prominent feature of *Monna Innominata*, to promote the idea of a fledgling system of meaning assimilating influence from other established registers, in consequence reworking and extending the potential semantic range of the borrowed input. This functions, as Kathryn Burlinson rightly observes in an excellent 1998 study, not to 'dilute', but to 'complicate' the text.[18] The usage of Dantean and Petrarchan motifs to head poems written six centuries later is a device with similar implications with regard to the pluralistic generation of meaning. The entrance of 'God' and His attendant system of theology into proceedings at the opening of this fifth sonnet represents an intrusion into the argument of the cycle up to that point. It is an entrance brought about by the speaker's stringent desire for utmost stability but, in the terms set out thus far by the poem, it represents an intrusion, and not a stabilising factor in the argument. As soon as a harmonious, centred system appeared to have been discovered (as at the close of Sonnet IV) a radically new principle of intelligibility is cast into the face of this framework. 'God' is introduced as an oppositional centre, an orthodox principle as used in the Dantean text, within and yet outside the system, and here the centrality of this organising factor is immediately stressed in its ability to keep the significatory nominers (specifically 'you') 'in strong obedience leal and true'. Additionally, the upper case initialling in 'Him… He…' traditionally demands that the whole discourse proffered from the central 'God' principle be seen as a reflection of divine power as governing that whole system. Keeping all the subsidiary elements of the system 'leal and true' in a 'service' which paradoxically liberates, the Christian deity stands at the head of a mode of discourse heavily at odds with the terms of the philosophy of earthly union argued and resolved in the previous sonnet. In desiring to

> Give you all good we see or can foresee,
> Make your joys many and your sorrows few,
> Bless you in what you bear and what you do,
> Yea, perfect you as He would have you be…. (V, 5-8)

the divine meta-presence demands, and is allowed (since His influence extends beyond that which 'we see or can foresee') overwhelming authority over the condition of the ministrant elements of the network at the head of which 'He' is placed. Structurally, this whole sonnet collects as a unit around the word 'He' which is the central word of the central couplet (in line 8) of the poem, emblematically but also semantically a pivotal point since it establishes the volta of the sonnet which ends the octave. This geometrically central positioning of the word 'He' is a direct indication of the centrality the sign demands over the discourse fashioned thereby. After this bold intrusion of one self-perpetuating doctrine upon what had just been proffered as a balanced frame of discourse, the speaker, now once more deconstructed (or possibly un-constructed) by the language of the text as a whole, can only sardonically interject: 'So much for you; but what for me, dear friend?' (V, 9).

This blunt, somewhat pathetic interrogation emphasises the renewed desperation of the speaker in the face of sudden collapse of the theory of identity and signification that the early verses of *Monna Innominata* had deliberately made it their business to construct. The speaker's forthright question also neatly and directly contradicts the terms of the unity stemming from the system proposed in Sonnet IV: 'With separate "I" and "thou" free love has done, / For one is both and both are one in love' (IV, 10-11).

The promotion of 'the love that makes us one' as a central ordering principle to give stability to the relationship between speaker and addressee outlined in the cycle thus far - encouraging the linguistic stability which made relevant the 'heart's heart' and 'myself myself' constructions which opened the fifth sonnet - would render wholly irrelevant a question such as 'So much for you; but what for me, dear friend?' proposed some seven lines later. The point to be taken from this provocative shifting from register to register, from certitude back to irresolution, is that a self-contained system with its own established governing principle (say, the 'faith' in secular 'love') stands adequately as a law unto itself - as a grand tautological exercise, such as that made manifest in the poetics of Dante. However, if the finely balanced constituent elements of this system are allowed to be recontextualised around a new, albeit equally feasible ordering principle, here the orthodox Christian deity, they take upon themselves a whole new measure of signification and thus can no longer be relied upon for their former stability and referential certainty. Given knowledge of this fall from certainty which comes with even the most marginal recontextualisation, it is hardly surprising that Sonnet V more or less peters out in a despairing, unquestioning cliché of woman's status and purpose (coloured also by the belief that the biblical and Victorian amatory ideology recognised at this point is one which fails adequately to appreciate the desires of 'woman … made for man'):

> So much for you; but what for me, dear friend?
> To love you without stint and all I can
> Today, to-morrow, world without an end;
> To love you much and yet to love you more,
> As Jordan at his flood sweeps either shore;
> Since woman is the helpmeet made for man. (V, 9-14)

To her position of ardent investigation into the possibility of a radically 'feminine' discourse, the female speaker must now reconcile the submissiveness demanded with the admission that 'woman is the helpmeet made for man'. The reconciliation is an impossible one. The effect, in context, of this bland assertion of biblical dogma is painfully ironic - an irony which is deliberately an uncomfortable disruption of expectation, as the sentiments of the text become increasingly at odds with the register explored in the earlier sonnets. This citation of pious dogma in a purportedly confident manner as the conclusion to a fervent inner debate which precludes such complacent summary is characteristic of Rossetti's earlier devotional lyrics, and is discussed in detail in the following chapter. The speaker wants to believe the biblical doctrine, but doubt will out. At this point, *Monna Innominata* begins to inhabit that state, defined with regard to Wordsworth's 'Intimations of Immortality' by F. W. Bateson, where 'the contradiction between what the [poem] is meant to say and what it actually says is acute ... the tone of voice in which the claim is advanced at once throws doubt upon its validity. Can what is so clearly felt to be only a second best be considered a success at all?'[19]

'My heart's a coward though my words are brave' (VII, 9), the speaker of the sonnets gravely admits. Rossetti's sonnet cycle begins to live a lie: its attempts at the justification of divine writ are conducted in a manner which shouts 'Compromise!' when it wishes quietly to disavow the struggle that has gone before. Preparing the way for her late, dogmatically pious works, Rossetti attempts vainly to turn the failure of her quest for stability into an announcement of religious conviction - a sad strategy we will find prevalent in her exegetical tracts when we examine them shortly.

Yet, taken as a whole work, *Monna Innominata* still maintains a compelling tension due to the debate with itself seen in action already thus far, which continues by degrees as the cycle continues. The poem can never wholly assume the dimension of religious propaganda because the speaker can never wholly escape from the secular, intellectual tension erected in the early sonnets of the sequence. But the sense of two sets of values working together, desired at this mid-section of the work, is not to be. Sonnet X, where the tone has become one of resignation and 'tired hope' and yet the lyric 'still finds breath to pray and sing', again argues faith in 'love ahead of all' as a central principle of intelligibility, concluding that 'life reborn annuls / Loss and decay and death, and all is love' (X, 13-14).

But, again, the sentiments here are suspect: the lulling repetition of 'and...' suggests a rhetoric disguising lack of substance. This over-emphatically proffered attempt at closure and certitude, ultimately positioned in the sonnet as was the unifying notion of 'the love which makes us one' in Sonnet IV, again stems from the interaction of two opposing absolutes (here, 'life' and 'death') and is gradually subjected to the test of recontextualisation witnessed earlier in the sequence. Notions of unity are cast into the balance in terms which recall the abruptness of the 'So much for you; but what for me, dear friend?' charge of the fifth sonnet: 'Many in aftertimes will say of you / "He loved her" - while of me what will they say?' (XI, 1-2). This potentially disruptive tone is temporarily averted by the end of the verse by the re-assertion of 'love' as an all consuming absolute, indeed by an insistence finally that this 'love' is a system in itself ('life') and not simply a sign of such ('breath', a 'sign' of 'life'). This assurance attempts to bring a settled sense of harmony to the next sonnet, again expressed in language very similar to that of Sonnet V:

> O my heart's heart, and you who are to me
> More than myself myself...   (V, 1-2)

> ...the heart is yours that was mine own,
> Your pleasure is my pleasure, right my right,
> Your honourable freedom makes me free,
> And you companioned I am not alone.   (XII, 11-14)

But this newfound conviction is immediately redirected at a different set of premises with the (re-)introduction of the Christian deity, named as the 'Primal Love' (*Works*, 463) in the Dantean epigram to the piece, marking an assertion of 'God' again as an absolute centre of a system of generation of meaning, in the face of which the unity newly proffered by the speaker no longer holds the same order of signification: 'If I could trust mine own self with your fate, / Shall I not rather trust it in God's hand?' (XIII, 1-2).

Notably, in a text so deeply concerned with matters of language and literariness, the return of 'God' as image of the absolute principle of intelligibility is marked by an image evoking the idea of *writing* - 'in God's hand' - as the text proposes to rewrite its own parameters. The poetry once more pulls apart its own argument, highlighting issues of discourse recontextualisation. The speaker of *Monna Innominata*, one feels, turns to God in lieu of the affirmation sought thus far, as much as for commendation of that faith. Self-assertion gives way to adoption of a socially approved stance of religious conviction as the sequence anticipates the explicit, conventionally pious tone of Rossetti's later poetry. The embrace of divine ordinance is not a convincing one, and remains unconvincing throughout the work.

The sixth sonnet of the sequence continues the switch into orthodox biblical symbolism.

> Trust me, I have not earned your dear rebuke,
> I love, as you would have me, God the most;
> Would lose not Him, but you, must one be lost,
> Nor with Lot's wife cast back a faithless look
> Unready to forego what I forsook...   (VI, 1-5)

The plaintive and soothing tones of this sonnet's opening line superficially mark a return to hope, or at least a turning away from resignation and despair, on the part of the speaker. And yet the words ring hollow. In the terms of the meta-fiction I have identified as operating in the text, the line is still addressed, on one level of meaning, inwardly. In this manner, the opening of this verse heralds a self-reflective consolidation: this can be another new beginning. The balancing of syntactic structures which runs through the argument of this sonnet reflects a desire, born of the confusion of the preceding verse, to achieve some kind of synthesis of the two systems of intelligibility - that founded upon earthly values, and that based on Christian theological principles – to which the sequence has alluded thus far. The two are incompatible when seen as opposites simply cast together: such a reading demands that one centre assume absolute authority at the expense of the other. This kind of fusion, attempting a conjunction by means of the overlap in the boundaries of the two discourse types, is a potentially reductive step: 'I love, as you would have me, God the most; / Would lose not Him, but you, must one be lost' (VI, 2-3).

The worldly-versus-spiritual dilemma, in terms of the surface narrative of these lines, is one that Christina Rossetti knew well from her own experience, with the proposals of marriage from Collinson and Cayley. In her poetry, the irreconcilable nature of the two modes of philosophy, secular passion and holy devotion, must move towards some manner of successful integration in order that the flow of the sequence continue. One detects a rather uneasy air surrounding the compatibility of the two modes of discourse, the one governed by secular desire, the other by divine omnipresence. The speaker seems to think that by mechanically repeating her devotion, 'Trust me... I love... God... I love my God... I love Him more', she will convince herself (and the reader) that it brooks no contradictions. The dilemma of the speaker here is cast in two images lifted from biblical tradition: the tale of 'Lot's wife' and the image of Christ the shepherd. This represents another attempt at integrating the new devotional discourse into the terms of the poetic text as a whole. Like the lovers' relationship at a literal level, the desire for 'meeting' of sign and referent is now translated into a new translated into a new context, a move towards a manageable synthesis of the two systems at work here, with their given differing centres of intelligibility. A revolutionary ordering principle must be found which can govern the totality of the fully integrated structure, its influence pervading that totality to engender stability in the whole synthesised system of discourse and thus to the pattern of signification generated thereby. The earthly and the heavenly, the letter and the spirit, must correlate.

> I love Him more, so let me love you too;
> Yea, as I apprehend it, love is such
> I cannot love you if I love not Him,
> I cannot love Him if I love not you.   (VI, 11-14)

This plainly expressed conclusion confirms the strain felt by the speaker over the disruptive influence that the quest for a singular centre of meaning is exerting upon *Monna Innominata* at this juncture. Turning on a deliberate syntactic and semantic balance, the desire for a mode of speaking which will encompass yet allow expression to each of the two separate doctrines becomes a major energy within the text.

It is a positive energy from which the speaker does not seek to escape, as confirmed in the terms of the Petrarchan epigram: 'I do not choose that Love should release me from such a tie' (*Works*, 462).

Subjected to this inspiring energy, the 'quality of the love' outlined in the text of *Monna Innominata* may thus be heightened, since the assimilation of the two modes of thought will doubly reinforce the depth of import of the new unity under construction. The simple syntactic and rhythmic balance of the sonnet's closing couplet harmoniously frames the sentiments (ironically couched in terms of negativity born of the chaos from which order proceeds) which represent the speaker's self-justifying enactment of the desired interaction. 'Him' and 'you' are quite literally - and lexically - absolutely balanced: 'I cannot love you if I love not Him, / I cannot love Him if I love not you' (VI, 13-14).

Sonnet VII's opening couplet attempts, again self-consciously, to echo the staged mood of balance, harmony and stability that ended the previous piece. The 'faith that maketh rich who take or give' sought fruitlessly from the extemporal but unsatisfying world of 'happy dreams', wherein the desire to achieve a stable ordering principle was first exercised, is envisioned in the more manageable principle of intelligibility that is spiritual 'love'. As in the 1849 lyric 'An End' (*Poems*, I, 38), this considered and heightened form of love is proffered as an absolute idea, to be understood in terms of absolutes: it is 'strong as death'.

The couplet is carefully, crucially balanced: '"Love me, for I love you" - and answer me, / "Love me, for I love you" - so shall we stand' (VII, 1-2). With the linguistic proposition received and echoed directly as an 'answer' – this, ironically, relies upon the direct interchangeability, and thus the referential unreliability of pronouns - speaker and addressee (thus symbolically in terms of this text signifier and signified, as we have no reference outside the speaker's own terms and conception of the world and the word) 'stand / As happy equals in the flowering land / Of love, that knows not a dividing sea' (VII, 2-4). Firm foundation 'on rock and not on sand' is established when the 'dividing sea', the gap in interpretative potential, the area between sign and referent, is no more. But the very 'song' of *Monna Innominata* has already been imaged as an emblematic sign denoting the gap between letter and spirit. Here we receive the first indication of the dilemma which, given the premises set forth so far, will inevitably occupy *Monna Innominata* as it moves to reach a conclusion (a conclusion the poem has warned itself against reaching by its own repeated assertions and illustrations of the perils of attempting any form of closure or immutability). The 'song' seeks, on one important level, to bridge the gap between sign and signifier, to achieve a principle of intelligibility which is radical in that it stands aloof from those played out in the phallocentric tradition of poetry Christina Rossetti sought to oppose and subvert, ignoring the presuppositions thereby entailed and thus constructing a new mode of writing capable of addressing the issue of female identity in neutral and unloaded terms.

The song, then, attempts a return to innocence, the desire (akin to that symbolically fantasised in *Goblin Market*) for a unified state on all levels. It becomes emblem, in writing, of the 'dividing sea' between sign and referent, the gap that allows the possibility of the misreading of signifiers. We saw this in the chain of signification established in Sonnet I, and, as the song plays out its own motives, it seeks to resolve the gap between letter and spirit. But the 'song' is an emblem of the 'gap' it seeks on one level to abolish. Thus it is clear that the poem is irretrievably at odds with its own envisioned terms and demands. It is as if the 'song' gives itself a death wish: a wish that must be fulfilled if a return to innocence is symbolically to be achieved. The ultimate deconstruction performed by *Monna Innominata* is of itself as a text tested under its own terms. It knows itself to be a contradiction.

As the volta of the sequence is approached, this disabling and disruptive intelligence starts to become truly apparent. It underlies Sonnet VII, and it is an awareness triggered by the progression of the argument of the sequence up to this point and reflected in the casting of images. Initially, there was no reconciliation of devotional iconography and secular situation: one was merely an intrusion upon terms of the other. Latterly, the speaker's dilemma was translated into and imaged in terms of authoritarian Old Testament imagery, in the 'Lot's wife' image in Sonnet VI). Now desired stability stemming from an achievement of a synthesis of discourses is itself pictured in orthodox Christian imagery, in a scene from the Gospels of Matthew (7, 24-27) and Luke (6, 48): 'Love builds the house on rock and not on sand, / Love laughs what while the winds rave desperately' (VII, 5-6).

Resolution of what appeared earlier to be irreconcilable modes of address might ideally engender stability in the form of equality, where speaker and addressee become 'happy equals'. From this harmonious state might stem great abundance (the sonnet's Dantean epigram translates as 'Here always Spring and every fruit' (*Works*, 462)) imaged in elysian terms of 'the flowering land / Of love, that knows not a dividing sea' (VII, 3-4). However, this consciously wrought, conventionally imposed rejection of division has other, less welcome implications. In Sonnet I of *Monna Innominata* this 'song', the poetic text itself, was set up symbolically as interlocutor between signifier and signified. And, in the early poems of the cycle, any lack of concordance between signs and referents was reflected in the disharmonious state of the speaker's utterances, striving ever towards a condition of unity and stability Now, though the exercise of repeated recontextualisation has taught the speaker that no single dogmatically proffered ordering principle is enough, conventional pious faith is offered as a panacea to bridge the 'dividing sea' between letter and spirit. But this release from struggle condemns the speaker's song to 'death'. Now an emblem of that which it sought to negate (that is, ideology unchallenged), the 'song' itself has abnegated the basis of its own methodology, verifying that previously cited condition upholding Rossetti's finest work.

> ...all that was but showed what all was not,
> But gave clear proof of what might never be;
> Making more destitute my poverty,
> And yet more blank my lot...   (*Poems*, II, 125)

This painful anxiety that stability, by definition, argues the possibility of instability, persistently informs the text of *Monna Innominata*. This sense of strain comes to a head in sonnet VII with two ambiguously rhetorical questions. 'And who hath…?' is followed by a frustrated admission: 'My heart's a coward tho' my words are brave - / We meet so seldom, yet we surely part / So often; there's a problem for your art.' (VII, 9-11)

A poignant acknowledgement of compromise, this statement might be taken as a crystallisation of the interests at work in the *Monna Innominata* cycle. The speaker's 'heart' and 'words', the spirit and the letter, 'meet so seldom, yet… part / So often'. This is a plain acknowledgement of the danger of disregarding the possibility of instability once a manner of stability has been achieved in a discourse. It also forms an admittance that the text *needs* its 'dividing sea' in order to continue. Once the poem's discourse 'knows not a dividing sea' then its raison d'être, made clear right from the outset, is removed. That signs and referents 'surely part / So often' is indeed 'a problem for your art', for it is the problem that this art strives to resolve, only to find that closure of the 'dividing' gap in significatory procedure ultimately means removal of forward-reaching energies from the poetic text. In a similar way, as I will try to demonstrate in chapters to follow, the adoption of an unswervingly devotional perspective can be said to remove from Rossetti's writing those vital, analytic energies which I have identified as integral to the enduring appeal and effect of her best work. As the central point of the sequence approaches, a summary of motives of the cycle is attempted in the light of recent developments. Turning for guidance to a self-contained literary text (the Bible, 'his Book'), which stands as a doctrine with its own clearly drawn codes of signification, the speaker seems content, in a way that would previously have been inconceivable, with a set of absolutes: 'Still I find comfort in his Book, who saith, / Tho' jealousy be cruel as the grave, / And death be strong, yet love is strong as death' (VII, 12-14). Progressively, it seems, 'comfort' is sought unquestioningly from the philosophy represented by 'his Book', and yet seeds of doubt, or regret at having made this compromise, remain.

Sonnet VIII, central by the geocentric structuring mentioned earlier and also heralding the volta of the sequence, re-narrates and recontextualises the biblical story of Esther. As Cynthia Scheinberg observes, it occupies an 'important position' in the sequence, but 'has been either ignored or named "puzzling" and "perplexing" by even the most adept of Rossetti's critics'.[20] The Esther sonnet stands as a dramatic interlude at the heart of a text with little drama elsewhere and is to be read as a fable, illustrative of the interests of *Monna Innominata* as a complete text. It is a wonderfully compact yet evocative poem, and worth quoting in full here.

> "I, if perish, perish" - Esther spake:
> And bride of life or death she made her fair
> In all the lustre of her perfumed hair
> And smiles that kindle longing but to slake.
> She put on pomp of loveliness, to take
> Her husband thro' his eyes at unaware;
> She spread abroad her beauty for a snare,
> Harmless as doves and subtle as a snake.
> She trapped him with one mesh of silken hair,
> She vanquished him by wisdom of her wit,
> And built her people's house that it should stand; -
> If I might take my life so in my hand,
> And for my love to Love put up my prayer,
> And for love's sake by Love be granted it! (VIII, 1-14)

The story of Esther, as told in Christina Rossetti's words, is a woman's story. It is the story of a woman understanding and coming to terms with a male viewpoint in a world totally ordered by masculine principles, and, by means of feminine 'wit', the tale of woman attempting to manipulate the male codes to her advantage, thereby re-shaping existence to her own ends and desires. In doing this, Esther is trying to rewrite tradition and subvert received ideology in a manner akin to that attempted by Christina Rossetti's sonnet cycle. But like the speaker of *Monna Innominata*, Esther can only resolve her quest in compromise - to achieve her desired goal, Esther too must adopt an ultimately conventional role, the role of temptress and Eve figure. It is notable that Esther is described as 'Harmless as doves and subtle as a snake', in a quite deliberate, recontextualised echo of Christ's ambiguous instructions to his apostles in Matthew 10, 15-16: '15. Behold, I send you forth as sheep in the midst of wolves: be ye therefore wise as serpents, and harmless as doves. 16. But beware of men'. Christ's words image the notion of innocence going abroad amongst those who seek, and have sought to usurp it, 'as sheep in the midst of wolves'; to overcome, it is implied, it may be necessary to be opposites, to accept a contradiction, 'serpents, and… doves', rather than to attempt a reconciliation. Esther is forced into a similar compromise, so far as Rossetti reads her plight, becoming part-courtesan, part-feminist in attempting to control her own destiny and resurrect gender-equality. The Old Testament Book of Esther is only ten chapters in length, and the actual 'deception', or rather the manipulation of the desires of King Ahasuerus, a discussion of which forms the main preoccupation of the Rossetti sonnet, is described briefly in only three verses:

> 1. Now it came to pass on the third day, that Esther put on her royal apparel, and stood in the inner court of the king's house, over against the king's house; and the king sat upon his royal throne in the royal house, over against the gate of the house.
> 2. And it was so, when the king saw Esther the queen standing in the court, that she obtained favour in his sight; and the king held out to Ester the golden sceptre that was in his hand. So Esther drew near, and touched the top of the sceptre.
> 3. Then said the king unto her, What wilt thou, queen Esther? and what is thy request? it shall be even given thee to the half of the kingdom.   (Esther 5, 1-3)

It can be seen from this that Rossetti's retelling of Esther's experience uses considerable poetic license and, moreover, evinces a relocation of interest in the story. The biblical text places the authority, the ultimate control over the proceedings, in the hands of the king, with Esther very much submitted (and submissive) to the monarch's will. Notably, *Monna Innominata* shifts the power balance so that Esther becomes the would-be director of the drama. In Rossetti's eleven line version Esther is the governing subject of every verb as the passivity of the Bible's 'she obtained favour' is redrawn by Rossetti's active constructions 'She trapped him … She vanquished him'. Emphasis is place wholly upon the manner in which the woman manages to manipulate the motivations of the male. Within a male-dominated sphere, Esther used her feminine intuitiveness - the 'wisdom of her wit' - to control by subversion what she deduces to be predictable codes of masculine conduct.

And how is this subversion brought about? Purely by Esther's understanding of signs and how they will be (mis)read 'through his eyes' by the male interpreter. Refusing to submit to the governing influence of any one absolute - she is 'bride of life or death' - Esther 'put[s] on pomp of loveliness' as a 'snare' - she places to her advantage neutral signifiers which she knows Ahasuerus will read as loaded signals in order to provoke a response which, through experience of a phallocentric logos, Esther can accurately predict. But the triumph is a precarious one. In articulating an active identity, Esther has simultaneously inhabited the traditional image of female deviousness. Her victory, like that experienced by the speaker of *Monna Innominata*, is ambiguously established and has the hollow ring of compromise about it. The tale is introduced by that which *Monna Innominata* has sought to promote in its entirety - female utterance, as Esther voices her own power over her own fate. Her words, as reconstructed and rendered by Rossetti, are of supreme importance: "'I, if I perish, perish" - Esther spake' (VIII, 1).

Esther's speech is tautological. The gap, literally, between the subject and predicate, 'I … perish', is taken up with a direct reinforcement of the import of the main clause: 'if I perish'. The intermediate 'dividing' clause merely serves to add absolute certainty to the signification of the main force of the utterance. And yet, on the same level of reading, this makes the linking clause nothing more than a redundant item, by consummately closing the gap of (mis) interpretation it renders itself useless as a semantic conveyance. This device works as a brilliant microcosmic representation of a dilemma around which, as we have seen, the poetics of the whole text of *Monna Innominata* revolve. Esther's story continues:

> …she made her fair
> In all the lustre of her perfumed hair
> And smiles that kindle longing but to slake.
> She put on pomp of loveliness, to take
> Her husband thro' his eyes at unaware;
> She spread abroad her beauty for a snare,
> Harmless as doves and subtle as a snake. (VIII, 2-8)

This is a fable of the coming to terms with outward signs, a description of the deliberate management of signifiers around a centre that is woman, the 'feminine' principle, and which must yet acknowledge the influence of other absolutes, 'life' and 'death', and the masculine orientated society into which the female registering will be born. Esther knows that man will read and interpret the signals she will 'spread abroad' in a manner established by a tradition of masculinity. Thus to subvert this tradition, as she does, she must herself understand its premises and acknowledge its position as an inscribed structure. Like the Rossetti text, Esther is adept at this intellectual juggling but, again like Rossetti's poetry, she must ultimately employ a conventional stance. By evading one objectionable ideological pose, Esther is seen to inhabit one that is (considering her goal) equally insidious: desiring to usurp male authority, she turns herself into the archetypal seductress 'subtle as a snake'. By these means, Esther is victorious and, in an image directly recalling the cycle's own yearning for stability in the previous sonnet, builds 'her people's house that it should stand'. Using the 'in… hand' image negotiable in terms of the writing process, the speaker confesses: 'If I might take my life so in my hand, / And for my love to Love put up my prayer, / And for love's sake by Love be granted it!' (VIII, 12-14)

This 'prayer' encapsulates (literally) a central energy behind *Monna Innominata*. From a woman's perspective, Christina Rossetti's sonnet cycle demonstrates the urge to readdress the phallocentrically biased balance of power as expressed in the traditional love lyric, written by men according to values constructed by men. Like Esther, Rossetti is engaged in an attempt to reclaim symbols and signifiers from the patriarchal ideology-laden realm they have occupied for so long, making them imaginatively bereft of meaning where the construction of a realistically feminine viewpoint is concerned. Esther's quest is shown to be partially successful, a compromise: Rossetti's, thus far, is of the same order. The whole strategy of the octave of sonnets of *Monna Innominata* stands to prove this plaintive wish an untenable desire, the yearning to establish an uncontroversial centre of intelligibility (here 'Love') about which to build a stable mode of truly 'feminine' discourse. Caught in the progressive re-evaluation of its own premises, *Monna Innominata* continually abandons its speaker 'not hopeless quite nor faithless quite, / Because not loveless' (IX, 9-10) and yet perpetually 'turning to the wall' (IX, 8) of language which refuses to be held in fixed signification around a workable centre. The continual procedures of recontextualisation and deconstruction performed by the text upon its own arguments always focus attention onto language in its search for a 'feminine' poetical perspective, only to illustrate that it is language itself that ultimately denies the possibility of the stability and unity towards which the speaker (in language and, thus, in life) continually strives. Conventional piety offers that stability.

The recontextualised story of Esther, then, in the terms of the whole octave of *Monna Innominata* as interpreted above, stands as an (ironic) ideal - a vision of 'all that was, and all / That might have been and now can never be' (IX, 1-2). In the stylised sphere inhabited by

Rossetti's recontextualised Esther, woman may usurp the male-ordered social and semantic codes and reorder signifiers to her own ends, never minding that, by doing so, she betrays her sex in other ways, inhabiting another male-revered stereotype and corrupting the purity of beauty with a consciously provocative sexuality. In Christina Rossetti's world, such an act is socially impossible and yet, symbolically, her poetry has performed it: however they may subvert the terms of the patriarchal tradition, the poetics of *Monna Innominata* are still irreparably the product of that tradition's polarised values. The whole Rossetti cycle itself is, in an important way, a recontextualisation of tradition - in its openly intertextual nature it relies for effect upon the reader's knowledge of the codes and ideological implications of the literary and social forms (mediaeval, Dantean, Petrarchan and Victorian) it both echoes and repudiates. Consequently, the last six sonnets of *Monna Innominata* again relocate the focus of the work where the search for a feminine subjectivity is concerned and bring the series around to a conception not of how things 'might have been and now can never be', but of how things are.

Progressively embracing God's will, the tone of the macro-sestet of the cycle is not one of optimism, but one of resignation. The first eight sonnets have convinced the speaker of the untenability of a stable perspective, except in terms of a conventionally pious, ideal vision, and now the sestet seeks to salvage some kind of intelligence from the resulting sense of compromise.

> Thinking of you, and all that was, and all
> That might have been and now can never be,
> I feel your honoured excellence, and see
> Myself unworthy of the happier call:
> For woe is me who walk so apt to fall,
> So apt to shrink afraid, so apt to flee,
> Apt to lie down and die (ah, woe is me!)
> Faithless and hopeless turning to the wall.
> And yet not hopeless quite nor faithless quite,
> Because not loveless...   (IX, 1-10)

The shift in tone at the volta of this sonnet is crucial. The speaker 'so apt to fall' is the eternal Eve, on the one hand, admitting defeat here, 'hopeless, turning to the wall' of battle lost which has repeatedly stood in the way of the cycle's progress towards purity of expression. Yet this acceptance of mutability, 'Apt to lie down and die', brings with it the ultimate possibility of salvation in the afterlife 'out of view', thus the potential for eternal harmony. With the solemn resignation to the impossibility of earthly fulfilment comes the symbolic acceptance by the speaker that the hitherto fruitless quest for a stable principle of meaning - for an ultimate absolute - must be relinquished. The speaker's 'song' has by now generated firstly a transcendent vision (or version) of unity with respect to the lovers' relationship and, secondly - in the octave of sonnets culminating in the re-signified Esther myth - an ironic, fantasy portrait of a female- ordered, compromised existence. The promotion of 'God' in the first eight sonnets, opposing the secular conjunction simultaneously desired, has functioned in a disruptively ambivalent fashion; the divine centre has presented to the speaker a guarantee of transcendent stability. Now Rossetti prepares utterly to subsume her identity in the face of devotional ordination. The speaker 'yet not hopeless', attempting not just a spiritual salvation but also a salvation of meaning, emphasises this new recognition in the tenth sonnet.

> Time flies, hope flags, life plies a wearied wing;
> Death following hard on life gains ground apace;
> Faith runs with each and rears an eager face,
> Outruns the rest, makes light of everything,
> Spurns earth, and still finds breath to pray and sing...
> (X, 1-5)

Armed with the knowledge afforded to her by the outcome of *Monna Innominata*'s octave, the speaker shows herself here coming to terms with the irresolution experienced earlier. There is a marked shift of emphasis here from absolutes - 'Time... hope... life... Death...' - now proven to be mutable (and thus imaged in terms of fatigue) towards an all encompassing relativity in the higher 'Faith' that 'runs with each' and, thus, 'makes light' of the reductive struggle towards the establishment of one absolute above the other.

> ...when love folds his wings above
> Tired hope, and less we feel his conscious pulse,
> Let us go fall asleep, dear friend, in peace:
> A little while, and age and sorrow cease;
> A little while, and life reborn annuls
> Loss and decay and death, and all is love. (X, 9-16)

This embracing of divine 'love' (portrayed in conventional and sentimental form), and the consequent rejection of any oppositional, secular passions, offers the one remaining possibility of 'life reborn' for the speaker and 'breath to pray and sing' for the sonnet cycle. And yet, in its affirmation of earthly mutability, the divine 'life reborn' heralds the (positive) acceptance of submission to 'silence' on the speaker's part. Moving towards the sudden and absolute submission of the devotional work of her final years, Rossetti has the speaker attempt to rationalise the newly embraced divine centre in terms of the intellectual debate conducted earlier. The 'conscious pulse' must be renounced, and, eschewing the struggle for stability on earth (and thereby rejecting the literary tradition which advocates that such stability be sought after), the speaker will gladly 'fall asleep … in peace'. Having spent half of her poetic career evading the snares of tradition, Rossetti finally settles on the convention that says that all is resolved in heaven, if only we have 'Faith' and refrain from questioning it. The prospect of divine salvation, for so long a source of tension and inner debate in Christina Rossetti's writing, is now looked upon as a self-justifying certitude.

As the language of the first eight sonnets progressed from one register attempting to articulate a secular passion to offer its resolve towards an omnipotent deity for the sanctioning of the speaker's re-allocated desire. Thus the earlier vision of earthly union is surrendered by measures in sonnets XI to XIII, thereby marking a thorough rejection of the previously interrogated ideology of male sonneteers who strive to construct such a secular conjunction. The speaker deferentially retains the 'nobler' vision of union and stability in the afterlife 'out of view' - a vision which, ironically, previously was introduced as harbinger to the consummation of secular unity, only to become the precluder of that stability.

Sonnet XI - in a manner initially echoing but finally opposing the import of its geometric counterpart, sonnet IV - witnesses the speaker renouncing (the first of a series of renunciations in the service of divine sanction) the premises of the masculine lyric tradition whose ideology the whole cycle has interrupted and found to be duplicitous towards woman.

> Many in aftertimes will say of you
> "He loved her" - while of me what will they say?
> Not that I loved you more than just in play,
> For fashion's sake as idle women do.
> Even let them prate; who know not what we knew
> Of love and parting in exceeding pain,
> Of parting hopeless here to meet again,
> Hopeless on earth, and heaven is out of view. (XI, 1-8)

The speaker's avowed ideal in *Monna Innominata* - to purify the lyric mode to a degree where the expression of an active female identity in language was a possibility - has failed by reason of the irreparable nature of the culture of the love poem, so long contaminated by earthly, patriarchal values. Were equality within the lyric attainable through the relocation of ideological bias, the shift in accepted significatory patterns attempted by the language of the early verses of the cycle, the poem would still operate within the parameters of the tradition it reinvents, (as Esther, to overcome, had to become seductress) and would thus be misread as writing 'just in play' and 'for fashion's sake'. An implicit reference back to the prefatory indictment of Elizabeth

Barrett Browning, the 'happy' poetess representative of 'idle women' with no knowledge of 'parting in exceeding pain', deftly contemporises the historical critique. Countering the comparatively naive argument of sonnet IV, that 'Both [participants] have the strength' to demonstrate the condition of love, the sestet of sonnet XI acknowledges that, at the symbolic 'Judgement', it is the male version of events which will satisfy the (male-determined) conditions of poetic expression. Men have made he rules of the love game, ensuring that the rules deny the possibility of non-male advancement (unless, like Barrett Browning, they surrogately adopt the male position or, like Esther, they inhabit the role of seductress and satisfy another male expectation). As it stands, then, this literary tradition cannot be made innocent of ideology from within - 'Hopeless on earth', that quest must, then, be renounced before the higher, purer possibility of love's holy sanction in 'heaven … out of view'. Retiring wearily from the phallocentricity of the literary canon, as written and as read, Sonnet XIII furthers the withdrawal from the profane artistic arena by disavowing singular attachment to the lover on earth himself, thus refusing to participate in the specified terms of the love relationship prescribed by the lyric mode.

> If there be any one can take my place
> And make you happy whom I grieve to grieve,
> Think not that I can grudge it, but believe
> I do commend you to that nobler grace,
> That readier wit than mine, that sweeter face...
> (XIII, 1-4)

The speaker's simply expressed disavowal of the profane principles of courtship here is specifically anti-Petrarchan and generally directed against the male-formed, secular platitudes of the courtly love poem. Renouncing the one's affection on earth, the speaker further removes herself from the values of the traditional love poem by allowing her lover the freedom to from attachments with whatsoever paramour he may choose. By revealing the transferable nature of the supposedly singular,

heartfelt emotions expressed through the tormented outpourings of
the conventional phallocentric love lyric, Rossetti's speaker exposes
the duplicity of that tradition. Her own seeming altruism serves to
disassociate the speaker firstly from the lover's undivided attention
and secondly from the type of poetry that lover would write, all in
the service of a purer, unpolluted form of 'love' which transcends the
earthly love games played by male poets, a better 'freedom' awaiting
in the afterlife.

> For if I did not love you, it might be
> That I should grudge you some one dear delight;
> But since the heart is yours that was mine own,
> Your pleasure is my pleasure, right my right,
> Your honourable freedom makes me free,
> And you companioned I am not alone. (XII, 9-14)

The 'heart is your that was mine own', admits the speaker of woman's
resting place in the male version of the love relationship, and so only
by a compete repudiation of the emotionally monopolising values
of that tradition can an active female identity be expressed. Actively
granted by the female party, and thus a positive expression of her
identity, the lover's 'freedom' to dally on earth as and where he may
please, does indeed make Rossetti's speaker 'free' - 'free' from the
constraints imposed upon her by the subjugating affections of the
male definition of womanhood and therefore at liberty to choose now
her own fate. Now deliberately divorced from the codes of patriarchal
poetic ideology, and consequently exempt from the struggle to reinvent
the language of the male courtly lyric form that occupied earlier stages
of *Monna Innominata*, the speaker composes her own denouement.
Earthly passions, and the conventions they rely upon for their poetic
communication, have been wholly renounced; a transcendent union
with God (now not at odds with, but rather a refuge from secular
desires) is now gratefully accepted. The higher patriarchy is now

warmly embraced - with God the father as the ultimate provider of salvation from the struggle.

> If I could trust mine own self with your fate,
> Shall I not rather it in God's hand?
> Without Whose Will one lily doth not stand.
> Nor sparrow fall at his appointed date... (XIII, 1-4)

This sonnet reinforces the tone of abdication from tradition felt in the previous two verses by further expressing the speaker's retreat from the vigorous questioning which occupied the octave of *Monna Innominata* and its painful quest for amatory and linguistic stability. All things of this world are renounced now, as the speaker requests sanction from God,

> Who numbereth the innumerable sand,
> Who weighs the wind and water with a weight,
> To Whom the world is neither small nor great,
> Whose knowledge foreknew every plan we planned...
> (XIII, 5-8)

There are crucial sentiments. Earthly and divine love do not contradict now, but complement each other here so long as God is in control. The divinity can transcend the 'weights and measures [which] do us ... a wrong' alluded to in sonnet IV since God's providence is a radical principle (akin to the Derridean centre) which pervades a system and yet remains aloof from it. Now not competing with oppositional secular drives, God may re-assimilate an untarnished intelligibility. His 'knowledge foreknew every plan we planned' - by accepting the holy ordinance over and above the earthly 'plans' laid down by the phallocentric literary tradition, Rossetti's speaker negotiates a return to a priori principles, a retreat into a state wholly governed by set, religious principles where she may escape the passivity imposed upon her by the male ethos and reinstate her own identity outside profane poetic tradition. In this orthodox, ecclesiastical scheme, this purification of the love-impulse will be beneficial scheme, this purification of the love-impulse will be beneficial not just to woman, but to artistic expression in general and thus, heralding her own adoption of strictly religious forms as a writer in later life, Rossetti's speaker advocates pious discipline for her lover on earth. The recommendation is, symbolically, offered at profane poetic tradition and the (male) creators of that tradition.

> Searching my heart for all that touches you,
> I find there only love and love's goodwill
> Helpless to help and impotent to do,
> Of understanding dull, of sight most dim;
> And therefore I commend you back to Him
> Whose love your love's capacity can fill. (XIII, 9-14)

Poetic tradition, as conditioned by the masculine authority, has so corrupted the love relationship with its insidious ideologies of power that the venture undertaken by Rossetti's speaker in the cycle, the expression of love from the female perspective, has failed. A pure articulation of female desire is rendered 'Helpless ... and impotent' by the codes of patriarchal poetic language structuring. Ideology masquerading as 'truth' has resulted in an anti-feminine, blinkered portrayal of the world, 'Of understanding dull, of sight most dim', and only by a recessive departure from the world thus constructed and a return to a state of innocence in God, can the duplicity be shown as such and the balance redressed. The speaker knows, by now, the impossibility of positive action within the codes of the male canon; the beautifully elegiac fourteenth and final sonnet, therefore, presents inaction (chosen and not prescribed) as the only strategy left for woman.

> Youth gone, and beauty gone if ever there
> Dwelt beauty in so poor a face as this;

Youth gone and beauty, what remains of bliss?
I will not bind fresh roses in my hair,
To shame a cheek at best but little fair,-
Leave youth his roses, who can bear a thorn,-
I will not seek for blossoms anywhere,
Except such common flowers as blow with corn.
Youth gone and beauty gone, what doth remain?
The longing of a heart pent up forlorn,
A silent heart whose silence loves and longs;
The silence of a heart which sang its songs
While youth and beauty made a summer morn,
Silence of love that cannot sing again.   (XIV, 1-14)

Thus Christina Rossetti concludes what began as a reproach to the conventional love lyric with a dignified but painful confession of her inability to inhabit the terms of such a literary form. In this regard, Matthew Arnold's critical comments, made in his 1853 'Preface' to his own *Poems*, upon 'situations, from the representation of which… no poetical enjoyment can be derived', may be recalled: '[These situations] are those in which the suffering finds no vent in action; in which a continuous state of mental distress is prolonged, unrelieved by incident, hope, or resistance; in which there is everything to be endured, nothing to be done'.[21]

Rossetti's speaker inhabits such a situation in the last poem of *Monna Innominata*. She is, indeed, as Diane D'Amico observes, she is left 'unnamed … alone in sorrowful silence'.[22] But, for Rossetti's speaker, this state is somewhat relieved by self-imposed hope in divine resurrection. The final sonnet wistfully recalls the enthusiastic tones of the opening movement of the cycle, where the 'budding' of the love relationship was held to be worth cherishing and its 'blossom' was anticipated; now the speaker actively represses such desires and, pointedly, 'will not seek for blossoms anywhere'. The sequence began with a fervent yearning, on the speaker's part, to revisit 'the songs I sang / When life was sweet' (I, 13-4). The octave of *Monna Innominata* witnessed the attempt to sing those 'songs' in a manner untethered by the restrictions of the male poetic tradition; the attempt was unsuccessful because the culture too corrupted. On a linguistic level, also, the speaker has found no success in her attempt to reinvent patterns of signification and free them from their earthbound, phallocentric bias. The speaker's final resolve, then, progressively enacted by the sestet of the cycle, is inevitably one of abdication from the worldly poetic arena, eschewing secular artistic passion and resigning herself to a life of ascetic humility whilst awaiting holy salvation, her final refuge now welcomed and no longer called to justification of its terms. Hers is a 'love' (and therefore an identity) which 'cannot sing again' in a world constructed by and interpreted by men. Desire is still present - the 'silence loves and longs' - but, since the female desire has found no possible outlet in the profane patriarchal poetic structures, it must readdress itself to the divine eternal. This last sonnet is specifically about loss. Arnold makes a distinction between 'painful' and 'tragic' representations of mental distress such as that finally conveyed in Sonnet XIV, but Rossetti's speaker's sentiments are both. It is the most moving Rossetti's own withdrawal from the secular poetic arena - the doleful expression of her inability to continue with inner debate, prefacing the retreat into pious, exegetical verse and prose which she doggedly produced in the 1880s and up until her death in 1894. It is highly significant that, in a work marking the utter, unquestioning final embrace of piety by the Rossetti text, the closing sentiments are those of regret and self-imposed resignation to 'silence'.

I have shown that the sonnets which make up *Monna Innominata* move from a position of initial playfulness to one of considerable torment whose culmination lies in a self-imposed exile from the potent joys (and tribulations) of earthly love in deference to an equally self-imposed faith in spiritual resurrection. The speaker's ultimate acceptance of a 'silent heart whose silence loves and longs' is both acknowledgement of compromise and a sign of triumph, indicating as it does that the struggle against earthly values, against powerful desire and its expression, has been simultaneously lost and yet, in the

Christian sense, conquered (since only by accepting mutability can the spiritual afterlife be achieved). The female identity constructed by the sequence, which allows woman now to be the speaker of the amatory lyric, is, in traditional form, initially a product of the identity of the man by whom she is loved or desires to be loved. But the male-object of Christina Rossetti's work is an absence throughout the cycle - even the notion of his potential presence only serves to emphasise his actual non-attendance:

> ...come not yet, for it is over then,
> And long it is before you come again...
>
> Howbeit, to meet you grows almost a pang
> Because the pang of parting comes so soon...
> (I, 2-3, 9-10)

The speaker of *Monna Innominata* quickly realises that to be defined by absence is to be absence and, thus, a radically different manner of interaction with the love tradition is required if female identity is fully to be asserted as an active presence. Thus, from the unique perspective of the woman poet, abdication from the jurisdiction of phallocentric ideology is called for - the subversion of pre-Dantean tradition which Elizabeth Barrett Browning had completely failed to undertake and which only a handful of male poets had vaguely acknowledged as a possibility through history. The withdrawal for Rossetti is total - away from questioning to a place of divinely ordered certitude where 'silence' signals faith unshaken. Harrison has commented upon the theme of 'silence' which runs through most of Rossetti's verse: '[W]e feel close to the source of Rossetti's strength as a woman and poet, and that strength, in opposition to Elizabeth Barrett Browning's, lies, not in assertive outspokenness, but rather in a baffling and defiant, sometimes ostensibly self-contradictory, sometimes masochistic, and sometimes riddling, silence'.[23]

This is indeed so. At the end of the cycle, Rossetti's speaker seems a sad, worn and beaten figure, but one still with an instinct for some kind of self-preservation. She has been frustrated into acceptance of a God she would, it appears, be more comfortable questioning - she is willing herself to accept Him totally, unflinchingly, completely. This acceptance itself is a form of resurrection; it has to be, because it is all that remains for the broken speaker at the end of the fourteen sonnets. Rossetti's final placing of the female active poetic consciousness in the realm of silence, beyond worldly constructs, is an affirmation of power regained (or at least innocence resurrected) since it dramatically marks the final recognition of the inability of the female self to play the love-lyric game on male terms (whether as passive passenger or as fallen seductress). This refusal is doubly reinforced by its implicit stemming from both the subjectivity of Christina Rossetti as a Victorian woman (at odds with patriarchal Victorian codes and values and the poets, like Barrett Browning, who are prepared unflinchingly to regurgitate them) and also, importantly, from the equally polarised subjectivity of the 'donna innominate', the woman (and all womankind) from history called by men to engage passively in a literary tradition which holds them trapped as second class citizens. The abnegation of the authority of traditional phallocentric ideology is, then, both effected in retrospect - thus the attention to pre-mediaeval platitudes - and simultaneously contemporised to the Victorian present. As such, it is a timely, and a timeless critique.

At a literal level, as I have attempted to demonstrate, *Monna Innominata* advances its argument by a process of thematic repetition, where notions of permanence or stability, hence certitude, once established as such, are immediately recontextualised to reveal their inherent contradictory elements. Those energies that motivated the challenging tones of *Goblin Market* and *The Prince's Progress* are clearly present in the first stages of the cycle and its resistance of complacency. At this level, the cycle is as frustrating an experience for the reader as it appears to be for the speaker, as complacency is persistently denied us - happy peace is repeatedly the harbinger of doubt and despair. This sense of rhythm, from order to chaos to order reviewed, renders the ending of the cycle not an absolute conclusion, but merely an arbitrary cut-off point where the flux has finally exhausted itself. The cycle decrees its own resting place in 'silence', on one level the same silence which the fourteen sonnets of the sequence have so radically broken by offering a voice to the 'donna innominate', herself silenced so long by tradition, yet on another level a new 'silence' since it is now a silence chosen and not prescribed by others. There is an implied circularity in this strategy, but it is a circularity whose centre has been disturbed by the process of revolution.

In another, linked sense, *Monna Innominata* is a revolutionary text because it quite self-consciously tries to subvert the courtly love conventions to generate a psychological and aesthetic polemic that raises questions concerning language and signification. The avowed intertextuality of the piece - its determined collusion of biblical, Dantean, Petrarchan and nineteenth-century discourses - denotes a deeper desire to play off against one another various self-contained modes of intelligibility, each balanced and centred in its own right but flawed when encroached upon by another, equally inherently coherent system of thought. Literary and religious notions are stretched and placed into conflict with one another in the continuous promotion of relativity until, finally, the holy writ overcomes. As the female poet-speaker repeatedly asserts her desired union with her lover, only immediately to upset this potential stability by suddenly couching it in an alternative set of circumstances, so the text continually seeks to deconstruct (indeed to destroy) illusions of certitude or 'truth' as constructed by ideological patterns. This rejection of stability stems, as it does elsewhere in the works Christina Rossetti, from the desire radically to question literary tradition and the position generally (with some exception which we have acknowledged) allocated to women within that phallocentric canon.

The position taken by the speaker of *Monna Innominata* also has a sociological relevance to the Victorian age; it challenges nineteenth-century notions of 'proper' conduct in matters amatory by readdressing the gender relationship preferred by the Victorians, as reflected in the lyric poetry of the period. At every level, Rossetti's sonnet cycle abjures absolutes and illustrates how easily ideology, if unchallenged, may pass for truth. *Monna Innominata* undertakes a process of purification - of gender-balance, of poetic practice and, essentially, of language itself - in its desire to purge poetry of the anti-female bias that has characterised the subjectivity of the post-mediaeval love lyric. Its difference, in this, from the position adopted at the end of *The Prince's Progress*, lies in its acceptance of orthodox Christian faith as a way out from the struggle. Christina Rossetti was to close her career in sustained celebration of that consciously developed acceptance.

Monna Innominata is a marvellously rich and allusive poem. It is the most difficult of Christina Rossetti's long poems to pin down, consistently refusing to be reduced to any one, assimilable plane until the devout belief in the divinity arrives to offer refuge. It is true to say, however, that the sequence depicts, at more than one level, an artistic resurrection for the female poet - and yet the redemption is achieved indirectly, through a series of re-evaluations and not by the route initially set out upon by the speaker. *Monna Innominata* begins by attempting a polarised inversion of the value-laden codes of conventionally expressed male sonneteering only to realise that inversion of that tradition necessitates falsely inhabiting the parameters and directives upon which it has thrived through history. Consequently, Rossetti's heroine reassesses her quest and offers herself up to holy affirmation, thereby seeking a resurrection of innocent grace through another channel. To achieve this end, earthly passion must be wholly renounced, and Rossetti's renunciation of secular desires is projected as a repudiation of the post-mediaeval lyric tradition which drove her to the quest in the first place. Abnegating a corrupt literary and intellectual form which has presented patriarchally realised ideology as the norm, *Monna Innominata* seeks refuge in a conventionally religious prognosis. The God of whom Rossetti tries to convince herself in the course of *Monna Innominata* is embraced at the last with the simmering placidity of a conquered will - no self-satisfying reflection of certitude's on earth (as Dante's God functions) but a condition of secular instabilities. The strain felt by the cycle's speaker as the sonnets write this argument is a tension experienced in turn by the reader of the sonnets faced with a work which repeatedly denies complacency at all levels only to be forced into conventionality at the last breath; it is the culmination of a sense of strain - the tension between earthly fulfilment and devotional asceticism - running through the greater part of Rossetti's poetic output. In fact, *Monna Innominata* stands as the most important work in Christina Rossetti's oeuvre because it provides a tremendously accurate, microcosmic image of the direction taken by Rossetti's philosophy of love and self, as recorded in her total written output through time. At a literal level, the sequence illustrates the recurring struggle between physical passion and spiritual deferment which occupies much of the poet's lyric verse. At symbolic level, its concerns mirror the close scrutiny of inherited ideologies and their transmission through loaded patterns of signification which colours the subversive poetry of works like *Goblin Market* and *The Prince's Progress*. By its repeated processes of recontextualisation, *Monna Innominata* seeks, like all Christina Rossetti's writing, to reveal the unreliability of given 'truths' and the inevitably unstable nature, when deconstructed, of what literary (and social) tradition has offered up as certitude's. Initially tentative in tone, the cycle grows into a complex and thorough semantic investigation, offering relativity as preferable to corrupt absolutism. The sequence finally resigns itself to a considered, pregnant 'silence' affirmed, with a Christian God as the speaker's remaining immutable guarantee of intelligibility.

Like the speaker of *Monna Innominata*, Christina Rossetti was ultimately to turn her passions and desires towards the sanction of a divine omnipotence, concluding her career as a poet with the fervent production of Tractarian devotional literature. *Monna Innominata* provides a detailed context and a background against which the withdrawal into piety may be measured, (perhaps excused?) and, at best, understood. Again like the speaker of the fourteen sonnets, the intellectual decisions Rossetti ultimately made concerning her spiritual life stemmed not from 'happy circumstances' but from a pained evaluation of the various options available to a Victorian woman artist.

The whole-hearted and dogmatic turning to God in her later years, along with the renunciation of earthly pleasures (of which one was love poetry itself) marks the disappearance from Rossetti's art of that active, engaging tension we have detected to be the life-force of her writing in this study thus far. It would be unfair, in an investigation of this nature, simply to ignore the later devotional work of Christina Rossetti, disappointing though it is when set beside her more inventive earlier art. If the exegetical pieces possess an unchallenging flatness and narrowness of vision which might remind us of the challenging breadth of inquisition we have found in Rossetti's earlier poetry, then an examination of them, with reference to the life they lack, is not unrewarding.

8

THE FIRE HAS DIED OUT: THE EARLIER DEVOTIONAL POETRY

No: at least I will not profane Holy Things; I will not add this to all the rest.
I have gone over and over again, thinking I should come right in time,
and I do not come right. I will go no more...
Christina Rossetti, *Maude*

It is sometimes proposed that the intellectual route plotted by the speaker of Christina Rossetti's momentous sonnet cycle *Monna Innominata*, the questioning of profane and holy issues eventually reconciled in a compromise-laden faith, emblematises the direction taken by Christina Rossetti's poetic output as a whole. William Michael Rossetti, in plain and provocative terms, sums up this broad thematic shift through time:

> Over-scrupulosity made Christina Rossetti shut up her mind to almost all things save the Bible, and the admonitions and ministrations of priests. To ponder for herself whether a thing was true or not ceased to be a part of her intellect. The only question was whether or not it conformed to the Bible, as viewed by Anglo-Catholicism. Her temperament and character, naturally warm and free, became 'a fountain sealed'.
> (*Works*, lxviii)

'Impulse and élan were checked, both in act and in writing', her brother continues, and his chosen image (appropriately biblical) of 'a fountain sealed', conveying the inertia self-imposed upon a free-flowing poetic mind now subjugated to religious instruction, recalls a maxim formulated by Christina Rossetti herself in the prose devotional calendar, *Time Flies* (1885): 'Only one process there is which renders water stable in itself; the process of freezing. To freeze suggests discipline'.[1]

This self-conscious 'freezing' into a 'fountain sealed' of the energies fuelling the best of her earlier, 'secular' work enabled Christina Rossetti to close her poetic career with the intense and sole production of verse and prose devotional commentaries. At the last, the poet was able to express a stable, settled world-view to replace the insecurity and doubt that form the subtext to her 'secular' poetry. Yet there is something discomforting in all this. Presented with the orthodox, religious dogma Christina Rossetti brought prolifically forth in the last quarter of her life, readers might well wonder how the interrogation and subversion of received patterns of thought motivating former work could so abruptly give way to the pious repetitions of a sensibility which had ceased 'to ponder for herself whether a thing was true or not'. Contrasting the poet's youthful writings with the reams of liturgical exposition Rossetti published in the last twenty years of her life, it is tempting simply to concur with the poet's own verdict, expressed in a letter of 1874 to her publisher Alexander Macmillan, that her 'fire' has 'died out': 'The fire has died out, it seems; and I know of no bellows potent to revive dead coals. I wish I did.'[2] Four years earlier, Christina had used the same metaphor in another letter to her brother Dante Gabriel: 'it becomes scarcely optional when one is a person of one idea. It is impossible to go on singing out-loud to one's one-stringed lyre. It is not in me ... If ever the fire rekindles availably, tanto meglio per me'.[3]

But is the above too simplistic a reading? Whilst agreeing that it is, roughly, the correct overall view, I think it is one has been too simplistically argued and thus needs qualification and clarification. It is, certainly, a perspective worth evaluating in terms of poetic strategy, rather than one that should pass unchallenged. In the past, critics have tended to ignore (or brush underneath the carpet for convenience's sake) Christina Rossetti's devotional writing - a rather unreasonable approach, since the religious prose and poetry taken together forms most of her total published output. Those commentators who have taken the time actively to condemn the religious writing have generally treated it as a uniform ideological mass, declining to give attention to individual works within that bulk and failing to observe any development or alteration of method or tone from the earlier to the later devotional pieces. Of course, this is a tempting trap to fall into where any writer's overtly religious productions are concerned. J. J. McGann begins an essay entitled 'The Religious Poetry of Christina Rossetti' with an observation of this tendency, noting that 'One of the difficulties which explicitly Christian poetry or art presents for criticism is its appearance of thematic uniformity'.[4]

When we turn, shortly, to specific analysis of various devotional pieces from the Rossetti oeuvre we will detect not just the 'appearance of thematic uniformity' but the gradual movement towards a steadfast adherence to this stable code in the work of a writer who has previously, actively resisted such a complacent adoption of stability. As I have demonstrated in previous chapters, Christina's earlier 'secular' poems repeatedly warned of the dangers of blinkered acceptance of ideology masquerading as truth or certitude. *Monna Innominata*, in attempting, dramatically, the construction of a new, radical centre of intelligibility ends in a compromised nod towards religious belief as a guiding principle hinted at throughout the Rossetti canon but never comfortably assimilated into the overall philosophical scheme. The later, religious writings of Christina Rossetti, I hope to show, demonstrate a sustained, last gasp attempt at resolution. It is the argument of this essay that not just the devotional work *per se*, but the implications behind that work - the final rejection of doubt and the gradual development of Rossetti's art inexorably towards this position - further define and reinforce (by default) the poetic strategy which characterises Rossetti's earlier non-devotional work.

Religion was always the prominent guiding factor in Christina Rossetti's life. In 1968, the critic J. A. Kohl uncovered a statement handwritten by the one-time Rossetti family physician, Dr. Hare, affirming that Christina was diagnosed as suffering from 'a kind of religious mania' when she was in her middle teens.[5] The two offers of marriage she received, in 1848 and 1866 respectively, were both declined on pious grounds, and at one point we know that she considered taking orders, as had her sister Maria, to become an Anglican nun.[6] In the final fifteen years of her life, Christina's Anglican beliefs so increasingly dominated her inner and outer existence that the latter part of her literary career is occupied with the near exclusive production of unswervingly exegetical verse and prose. The casting of the self and its motives before divine sanction, alluded to as a possibility in the earlier lyric poems and (pain)fully dramatised in *Monna Innominata*, with its simultaneous repudiation of worldly pleasures, accurately prefigures the ultimate path chosen by the author herself.

The acknowledgement of Christian faith, and the refuge it offered to the troubled soul, was always a visible element in Rossetti's poetry, as it was in her life. Religion held a fascination for Christina; she repeatedly returned to Christian doctrine as affirmatory, a granter of certitude (improvable, but equally undeniable) in a world of mutability and contradictions of which she felt painfully aware. Often in an openly Adventist manner, her early eschatological lyrics self-consciously achieve a position of temporary resolve by performing a conflagration of the earthly and the divine by means of what Wheeler has termed the folding of 'present renunciation into future judgement, future heaven into present vision'.[7] But the reconciliation of the two areas is not effected with such ease as Wheeler seems to suggest; the profane and the sacred are incompatible in many ways and this lack of correlation colours much of the poet's 'religious' musings. This agonising dichotomy of sensitivity is patently at the heart of many of Christina Rossetti's finest poems: that she was conscious of this governing tension in her life is evident in part of a moving letter written to her ailing brother, Dante Gabriel, in 1881 (the year *Monna Innominata* was published), four months before his untimely death.

> I want to assure you that, however harassed by memory or anxiety you may be, I have (more or less) heretofore gone through the same ordeal. I have borne myself till I became unbearable by myself, and then I have found help in confession and absolution and spiritual counsel, and relief inexpressible. Twice in my life I tried to suffice myself with measures short of this, but nothing would do; the first time was of course in my youth before my general confession, the second time was when circumstances had led me (rightly or wrongly) to break off the practice. But now for years past I have resumed the habit, and hope not to continue it profitlessly… I ease my own heart by telling you all this…[8]

The marriage proposals of Collinson and Caley are the instances directly referred to in the letter, but the overall importance of the orthodox Christian outlet on a life otherwise trapped in flux and uncertainties is apparent in the resigned yet firm tone of the missive. Five hundred (about half in total) of the published poems of Christina Rossetti deal explicitly with religious matters and, as we have seen, many of the verses normally classified as 'secular' ('An Old-World Thicket' (*Poems*, II, 123-8), and *Monna Innominata*, for example) have an overtly devotional, frequently eschatological undertow.[9] As I have shown, it is possible to read Rossetti's early poetry as progressively mediating between religious (Tractarian) and artistic (Romantic and Pre-Raphaelite) values in a kind of pantheistic synthesis of nature as analogous of God's power, eventually settling on the side of religion as divine truth for its own sake. The general movement is taken as being from the vision of God through the sacramentally symbolic veil of nature, as expressed in the writings of Keble and Newman, to discarding the veil and focusing sole attention onto the form of the divinity Himself. 'Earth and Heaven' (*Poems*, III, 85-6), written on 28 December 1844 when Christina was just fourteen years of age, is one of the simplest expressions of this sacramental treatise. The short poem begins with a naturalistic listing of God's beautiful works and culminates in the plainer admission of the 'unchanging... undying' divine Love which made the earthly works.

> Water calmly flowing,
> Sun-light deeply glowing,
> Swans some river riding,
> That is gently gliding
> By the fresh green rushes;
> The sweet rose that blushes,
> Hyacinths whose dow'r
> Is both scent and flow'r,
> Skylark's soaring motion...
> ...All these are beautiful,
> Of beauty Earth is full: -
> Say, to our promised Heaven
> Can greater charms be given?
> Yes; for aye in Heav'n doth dwell
> Glowing, indestructible,
> What here below finds tainted birth
> In the corrupted sons of Earth:
> For, filling there and satisfying
> Man's soul unchanging and undying,
> Earth's fleeting joys and beauties far above,
> In Heaven is Love.

This neat poem foreshadows the tone of Hopkins in pieces such as 'Pied Beauty' and sets a blueprint for many of Christina Rossetti's supposedly 'secular' poems. All the characteristic elements are there; the sensual opening, languid and enjoying earthly riches, the volta marked by the open, rhetorical questioning of the value of the preceding images, and, finally, the denouement wherein divine principles and their everlasting virtue are extolled over and above their temporal, earthly reflections. 'Glowing, indestructible' heavenly spirit finds only 'tainted birth' in its earthly manifestation and thus the speaker advocates a return to first principles in the final lines, preferring immutability in the afterlife to fleeting existence on earth.

A microcosmic version of the Rossetti philosophy? Only speaking in the broadest terms could one really concur with this proposition. This lyric (like, we will argue, the later 'devotional' writing) contains none of the tension, the discomfort and sense of strain, which pervades the poetry Rossetti wrote between the time of 'Earth and Heaven' (1844) and the mid-1870s, (after which, exegetical literature dominates) epitomised in the agonising compromise reached by the speaker of *Monna Innominata*. The intense measure of suffering and sense of mutability which pervade lyrics such as 'An End' (*Poems*, I, 38), 'After Death' (*Poems*, I, 37), 'Remember' (*Poems*, I, 37), and 'Autumn' (*Poems*, III, 301) mark a regression from certitude, consistently re-enacted in Rossetti's poetry right up to the religious works of the 1880s, where the dissatisfaction with absolutes and the mood of disquiet are transmuted to a feeling of relief, the paradisal ideal unflinchingly accepted and embraced in a resurrected vision of eternal heavenly bliss. The eclectic, provocative intertextuality of *Goblin Market*, *The Prince's Progress* and *Monna Innominata*, symptomatic of a centreless, pluralistic approach to meaning, gives way to singular, dogmatic textual duplications of biblical pronouncements. Longing becomes fulfilment and doubt becomes faith; but is this at the expense of interesting poetry?

Ifor Evans, discussing Christina Rossetti in *English Poetry in the Later Nineteenth Century* (1933), recognises the beneficial effect, so far as the immediate appeal of the poetry is concerned, of the dichotomy between earthly and spiritual impulses inscribed in the early lyrics. The tension between 'sensuous acceptance of life' and fearful endurance of sin is seen as a positive factor giving energy to the verse: 'Her early poetry dwells in a latent conflict between these two motives. They resolve themselves, a little sadly, in a faith in Christianity which is at once passionate and sombre. This devout other-worldliness leaves Christina Rossetti with a deep, somewhat baffled antagonism to life'.[10] And one year earlier, R. D. Waller had been even more to the point with his terse observation that 'Very little of [Christina Rossetti's] best verse is directly inspired by her religion'.[11]

Such estimations are not without grounds. The poems in which Christina Rossetti directly, wholly makes the Christian doctrine her subject do, indeed, seem flat and uninspiring. This is particularly evident when her exegetical pieces are set beside those lyrics where devotional principles indirectly colour an argument, or longer works such as *Goblin Market* or 'The Convent Threshold' (*Poems*, I, 61-5), where religious faith lurks enigmatically in the background offering itself as one possible (but not the only) centre of interpretation, never as an absolute truth. The prose short story, *Maude: A Story For Girls*, written as early as 1850 but not published until 1897, after Christina's death, is instructive here.[12] In an alarmingly accurate (and acutely self-conscious) manner, the tale prefigures the tensions, and their reconciliation, which form the context influencing Christina Rossetti's eventual gravitation towards purely exegetical work. Competently, though never masterfully written, the novella tells of a year in the life of Maude Foster, fifteen years old at the start of the story, who enjoys nothing more than composing little verses, often playful, occasionally introspective, but feels acutely uncomfortable with the minor celebrity status her poems have brought her in her family's immediate social circle. The perils of undertaking a poetic career when one's convictions are predominantly ascetic and pious are conveyed by the rather rudimentary plot; of more interest is Maude's mounting psychological turmoil - her dilemma becomes a melodramatic version of that contemplated by the speaker of *Monna Innominata*, the attempted reconciliation of worldly luxuries and pious humility. Haunted by the belief that her profane indulgences make her unworthy of receiving Holy Communion, and after much heartache, Maude makes a painful, never wholly credible decision to renounce her poetic excursions, and therefore her vanity, in favour of a life devoted to the church. Only with her death in a coach accident is the work's ongoing moral crisis brought to a definite conclusion. The narrative is obviously semi-autobiographical (hence, perhaps, the non-publication of *Maude* during its author's lifetime). At one point, the description given of Maude could quite easily pass, word for word, for a portrait of the youthful Christina Rossetti herself:

> Small, though not positively short, she might easily be overlooked but would not easily be forgotten. Her figure was slight and well made, but appeared almost high-shouldered through a habitual shrugging stoop. Her features were regular and pleasing; as a child she had been very pretty; and might have continued so but for a fixed paleness, and expression, not exactly of pain, but languid and preoccupied to a painful degree. Yet even now, if at any time she become thoroughly aroused and interested, her sleepy eyes would light up with wonderful brilliancy, her cheeks glow with warm colour, her manner become animated, and drawing herself up to her full height she would look more beautiful than ever she did as a child. So Mrs. Foster said, and so unhappily Maude knew. She also knew that people thought her clever, and that her little copies of verses were handed about and admired. Touching these same verses, it was the amazement of everyone what could make her so broken hearted as was mostly the case. Some pronounced that she wrote very foolishly about things she could not possibly understand; some wondered if she really had any secret source of uneasiness; while some simply set her down as affected. Perhaps there was a degree of truth in all these opinions.[13]

Observations such as this show an authorial awareness of the way in which artistic productions will be (mis)read, and are in accordance with Christina Rossetti's own intimations in favour of pluralistic interpretation - whether they be set out in letters concerning *The Prince's Progress* or symbolically framed in the poetry itself. Like Christina Rossetti, the heroine presented in the above passage, be means of multiple perspectives, is quite definitely an enigma. In his 'Prefatory Note' to the story, William Michael Rossetti is quick to address the similarities between Miss Foster and her author:

> ... my sister's main object in delineating Maude was
> to exhibit what she regarded as defects in her own
> character, and in her attitude towards her social circle
> and her religious obligations... If some readers opine
> that all this shows Christina Rossetti's mind to have
> been at that date over burdened with conscientious
> scruples, of an extreme and even a wire drawn kind,
> I share their opinion.[14]

But in the short story, as in Rossetti's poetry, it is the 'wire drawn' tension, the intellectual balancing of pride and humility, *carpe diem* and pious deferral of sensuality that gives life to the writing. Maude is described early in the tale as 'one who, without telling lies, was determined not to tell the truth'; her struggle is an inner one, the 'To be or not to be' dilemma when to 'be' is to be 'exposed' to life's profane pleasures.[15] Like her creator, Miss Foster is painfully aware of all that which she is *not*: 'How I envy you,' she continued in a low voice, as if speaking rather to herself than to her hearers, 'you who live in the country, and are exactly what you appear, and never wish for what you do not possess. I am sick of display, and poetry, and acting'.[16] Told, midway through the narrative, that a friend has 'entered in her noviciate in the Sisterhood of Mercy', Maude dolefully confesses her own partially realised devotional outlook: 'Maude half-sighed; and then answered; 'You cannot imagine me either fit or inclined for such a life; still I can perceive that those who are so are very happy'.[17]

In *Maude*, Rossetti's transparent version of her self suffers immense mental trauma through the self-imposed division of her existence into what Charlotte Brontë called 'propensities' and 'principles'.[18] The crisis is one of vocation; her pious convictions can never be fully realised so long as she participates in the oppositional, secular pleasures of the world, pleasures wholly enacted through imaginative poetic excursion - this being Victorian England, and Foster/Rossetti being of the female sex. This cataclysmic inner debate is deftly conveyed in one of the sonnets Maude (or, rather, Rossetti) copies into her 'writing-book':

> Yes, I too could face death and never shrink:
> But it is harder to bear hated life;
> To strive with hands and knees weary of strife;
> To drag the heavy chains whose every link
> Galls to the bone; to stand upon the brink
> Of the deep grave, nor drowse, though it be rife
> With sleep; to hold with steady hand the knife
> Nor strike home; this is courage as I think.
> Surely to suffer is more than to do:
> To do is quickly done: to suffer is
> Longer and fuller of heart-sicknesses...[19]

The laboured repetitions of the infinitive construction here - 'to bear... to strive... to drag' create an accumulative sense of strain in the text, leading to the pained admission, bred of devout asceticism, 'Surely to suffer is more than to do'. The speaker's literal discomfort, relayed in the octave is, by association, felt with the conclusion reached in the poem. The plaintive expression of earthly hardship - the hardship self - imposed through repudiation of worldly things - is, in itself, a challenge to the pious conclusion reached: slowly, awkwardly, the religious maxim 'to suffer is more than to do' is forced to justify itself.

Notably, this ambiguously rhetorical 'surely' begins a sestet that is all
one sentence, concluding in an all-encompassing question mark:

> Surely to suffer is more than to do:
> To do is quickly done; to suffer is
> Longer and fuller of heart-sicknesses:
> Each day's experience testifies of this:
> Good deeds are many, but good lives are few;
> Thousands taste the full cup; who drains the less?

Though the whole sonnet attempts an affirmation of its central
motif, its elements - the false bravado of the opening 'Yes...', the lame
assertions '...as I think', and 'Surely...', and the ominous final question
mark - conspire to contradict the confident opening and leave only
an ominous sense of doubt. The phrase 'to the lees', appropriately,
puts one in mind of Tennyson's 'Ulysses' (published 1842) and the
assertive 'I will drink / Life to the lees' of that poem - another work
full of ambivalences and superficial gestures towards certainty that
the text itself serves to undermine.[20] The speaker of Rossetti's sonnet
seems to have a bitter taste in her mouth. Trying to convince herself
of the appropriateness to her life of religious dogma, she fails, as does
the sonnet, to convince the reader. But the very attempt at justification
is what makes the poem interesting. The pious sentiments are not
simply offered up pat, but are put to the test of contextualisation
(a characteristic Rossetti technique), making the poetry more than
propaganda, more than dogma. This is the manner of 'devotional'
poetry that we would wish to salvage for the Rossetti canon.

The best of Rossetti's religious lyrics (predominantly the earlier
verses) exhibit this inquisitive approach to matters of holy writ and
reveal a restless mind undergoing the same intellectual strain and inner
torment as that outwardly expressed by Maude Foster. 'A Portrait'
(*Poems*, I, 122) utilises a bipartite structure in order to offer varying
perspectives on the same religious principle. The first of the two sonnets
is the later of the couple, written on 21 November 1850, whereas its

partner is dated 24 February 1847, when Christina Rossetti was only sixteen years old. The first stanza outlines a pattern of renunciation akin to that chosen by the heroine of Maude.

> She gave up beauty in her tender youth,
> Gave all her hope and joy and pleasant ways;
> She covered up her eyes lest they should gaze
> On vanity, and chose the bitter truth.
> Harsh towards herself, towards others full of ruth,
> Servant of servants, little known to praise,
> Long prayers and fasts
>   trenched on her nights and days;
> She schooled herself to sights and sounds uncouth...

Besides foreshadowing to a great extent the road taken by Rossetti's own life, these descriptive lines demonstrate, without passing judgment, the process of withdrawal, of retreat from life undertaken by the woman described, again by stolid repetition of forms - 'She gave up... Gave up... She covered up... She schooled herself'. The tone of the sonnet is one of absolute detachment; the ascetic life of the heroine is neither praised nor condemned. The ambiguous phrase 'little known to praise' conveys this unspecified relation - is she 'little known to praise others' or 'little acquainted with praise by others of herself'? And yet, because of this rigidly objective (and therefore open to plural interpretation) presentation of the symptoms of her piousness, the motives behind the renunciatory process outlined are left painfully undisclosed. The heroine hides her eyes 'lest they should gaze / On vanity', but her reason for eschewing this vanity is withheld. Equally, the preferable 'truth' is a 'bitter' option - but bitter to whom, and why? Of course, it could be said that the frugal existence pursued by the heroine is reinforced by an equally austere poetic presentation. But, if this is the case, then the poem's catalogue of unpleasant terms - 'bitter... Harsh... trenched... uncouth... stricken... hurt and loss... hated' - grows to dominate the tone of the piece so that the pervasive atmosphere is one of unease and discomfort. The images of rote discipline are also unsettling - 'She schooled… learned… counting' - implying that the asperitic life is not one found through natural, but through conditioned impulse. This uncertain, odd atmosphere is one that the final lines of the sonnet must go some way towards justifying:

> …her own self learned she to forsake,
> Counting all earthly gain but hurt and loss.
> So with calm will she chose and bore the cross
> And hated all for love of Jesus Christ.

We have been given so few tangible indicators as to interpretation that the tone of detached observation here verges on the ironic. It is certainly neither dogmatic nor confident; the heroine's motives, pointedly unevaluated by the speaker, are open to question. Consequently, we look to the second sonnet of the pair for instruction and, hopefully, enlightenment; what we stumble upon is an awkwardly conventional, trite deathbed scene:

> They knelt in silent anguish by her bed,
> And could not weep; but calmly there she lay;
> All pain had left her; and the sun's last ray
> Shone through upon her, warming into red
> The shady curtains. In her heart she said;
> "Heaven opens; I leave these and go away;
> The Bridegroom calls, - shall the Bride seek to stay?"
> Then low upon her breast she bowed her head.
> O lily flower, O gem of priceless worth,
> O dove with patient voice and patient eyes,
> O fruitful vine amid a land of dearth,
> O maid replete with loving purities,
> Thou bowest down thy head with friends on earth
> To raise it with the saints in Paradise.

The drifting, in the sestet, into the realms of conventional, sub-biblical metaphor effectively marks a retreat from actual justification of the preceding terms of the poem. (Although the attempted heightening of language through the lofty imaging is a lame attempt at self-justification, trying to make us feel better about the denouement perhaps.) The pat offering of devotional cliché, especially in the final couplet, assumes no energy other than the deceptive strength of dogmatic conviction. But this affirmatory sonnet was written three and a half years before its partner. With the production of the prefatory sonnet, as in writing the narrative section of *The Prince's Progress*, Rossetti adopts the position of critic and interpreter of her own poetry. Notably, the resulting critique, the first poem of the pair, forms an overture not of harmonious justification, but of ambivalently presented premises. 'A Portrait', taken as a whole, uses deceptive linguistic placings and an overtly dualistic structure to undermine what, superficially, seems a coherent Christian creed. Another bipartite, two sonnet work, 'Two Thoughts of Death' (*Poems*, III, 183-4), written in 1850, manages the same gentle mood of inherent dissent. With debts to Romanticism, in its emphasis on memory, and the Metaphysicals, in its Marvellian burial image, 'Two Thoughts of Death' interpolates the provocative detachment of 'A Portrait' with a tone of curious bitterness. The speaker contemplates the death of a sister figure, now in her grave:

> Her heart that loved me once is rottenness
> Now and corruption; and her life is dead
> That was to have been one with mine, she said...
> ... Foul worms fill up her mouth so sweet and red;
> Foul worms are underneath her graceful head.
> Yet these, being born of her from nothingness
> These worms are certainly flesh of her flesh.

The speaker (whose persona is rendered tantalisingly indistinct by the puzzling statement 'her life ... / That was to have been one with mine') shows him/herself painfully aware of mutability on earth, resignedly observing of the grass and flowers 'brave and fresh' which cover the loved one's grave that 'Even as her beauty hath passed quite away / Theirs too shall be as tho' it had not been'.

The mood of this first sonnet is predominantly resentful and acerbic, interrupting, right from its petulant opening line 'Her heart that loved me once is rottenness', traditionally elegiac expectations by means of a deliberate confusion of physical and metaphysical images of 'rottenness… and corruption'. The second sonnet immediately recontextualises the speaker's bitterness by placing it in past time: 'So I said underneath the dusky trees'. The subsequent vision of a 'sunlighted' moth 'that rapidly / Rose toward the sun' relieves the speaker's abject sense of flux and change as (s)he watches its flight up 'From earth … into the light', symbolically insinuating the appropriateness of belief in the resurrection of the dead to assuage the speaker's troubled mind (and yet, also presenting a picture of vulnerability and self-destruction - the moth flying into the flame): 'Then my heart answered me: Thou fool to say / That she is dead whose night is turned to day, / And whose day shall no more turn back to night'.

As in 'A Portrait', the moral offered is an orthodox Christian code and the speaker's conviction in offering the moral rings strangely hollow. The 'moth' image, in its own way, is as trite as the archaic, lofty diction of 'A Portrait' and, again, the overwhelming atmosphere of the poem taken as a whole is one of unease; the disquiet of the first sonnet is not fully appeased by the somewhat twee assertion of piousness in the second. Superficially 'proving' the theocentric philosophy which colours the denouement of the two 'Thoughts', the speaker only manages to cast doubt upon its relevance in the work taken as a complete exposition. There is no sense of overall unity; the centre cannot hold because the speaker's faith in it is by no means absolute. There is a disturbing air of tension about these works and their insidious, calculated detachment that exemplifies the unease with which Christian (and in 'A Portrait', specifically Biblical) dogma is relayed in Rossetti's earlier devotional poetry. As Rossetti warns elsewhere, 'For all that was but showed what all was not' (*Poems*, II,

125), thus God as a centre of intelligible thought is only one option thus far. It is as if the speaker is not herself convinced of her words' authority, yet, frightened of declaring her outright scepticism, she couches her lack of conviction in the most subtle and ambiguous of terms. Many critics have, rightly, commented upon Christina Rossetti's remarkably acute control of language and vocabulary; it is from awareness of this fine line between doubt and (blasphemous) objection that the need for such rigorous control arises.

However, sometimes, in the earlier devotional pieces, the tension felt at accepting the divine ordination is so strong that it cannot be kept at a subtextual level. One of the most harrowing and moving of Christina Rossetti's short poems is 'A Chilly Night' (*Poems*, III, 247-9), dealing with the speaker's 'dead of night' search for 'my Mother's ghost'. The piece was written on 11 February 1856, thirty years before the death of Frances Polidori in London, and therefore clearly resists autobiographical reading, but a simultaneous resistance of an orthodox Christian perspective also pervades the text. The speaker presents a nocturnal vision, a quest to discover the maternal spirit in the hope of obtaining affirmatory knowledge of the heavenly afterlife. Initially, the speaker assumes an affinity with the spectres:

> My friends had failed one by one,
> Middle-aged, young, and old,
> Till the ghosts were warmer to me
> Than my friends that had grown cold.

The simple, plainly expressed sentiments themselves exude a manner of half-realised eeriness in the 'ghostly' narrative as the quester attempts communion with the deceased Mother figure:

> I looked and I saw the ghosts
> Dotting plain and mound:
> They stood in the blank moonlight
> But no shadow lay on the ground;

> They spoke without a voice
> And they leapt without a sound,
>
> I called; "O my Mother dear," -
> I sobbed; "O my Mother kind,
> Make a lonely bed for me
> And shelter it from the wind…"

In this remanaged Dantean setting, Rossetti's speaker fails to obtain the solace and affirmation she anxiously, desperately seeks. The shadowless ghosts 'without a voice… without a sound' have nothing of certitude to communicate, and the discovery of the Mother figure is particularly heart-rending for this reason. Literally, the spectre and the living being cannot relate to each other:

> My Mother raised her eyes,
> They were blank and could not see;
> Yet they held me with their stare
> While they seemed to look at me.
>
> She opened her mouth and spoke;
> I could not hear a word
> While my flesh crept on my bones
> And every hair was stirred.
>
> She knew that I could not hear
> The message that she told
> Whether I had long to wait
> Or soon should sleep in the mould:
> I saw her toss her shadowless hair
> And wring her hands in the cold.
>
> I strained to catch her words
> And she strained to make me hear,

But never a sound of words
Fell on my straining ear.

Desiring confirmation (or at least clarification) of her devotional
expectations, the speaker is left 'in pain' of irresolution as the attempted
communication fails. The ghosts have no answers, and the tension of
the poetry stems from its own, similarly uncertain position. Like its
speaker, the text seeks revelation of certitude; like its speaker, the text
fails to find it. Absolute dejection follows, as the speaker (and thus
the poem) is left with a sense of utter isolation from the prospective
comfort offered by belief in the heavenly eternal:

> From midnight to the cockcrow
> I watched till all were gone,
> Some to sleep in the shifting sea
> And some under turf and stone:
> Living had failed and dead had failed
> And I was indeed alone.

'A Chilly Night' dramatically enacts the strain of irresolution that
colours Christina Rossetti's most readable theological musings. It also
epitomises the poems in which, to use William Michael Rossetti's
description,

> an aspiration for rest after the turmoil of this mundane
> life is more marked than the yearning for heavenly
> bliss. As to these cognate topics, it may be remarked
> in general that Christina's poems contemplate (in
> accordance with a dominant form of Christian belief)
> an 'intermediate state' of perfect rest and inchoate
> beatific vision before the day of judgement and the
> resurrection of the body and sanctification in heaven.
> (*Works*, ix)

This 'intermediate state' inhabited by Rossetti's earlier religious writings is also an *indeterminate* state - a limbo realm which offers rest from debate and frustrated attempts at affirmation and yet allows no development of certainty concerning the heavenly afterlife it claims to prefigure. This sense of vacillation is most explicitly presented in 'The Poor Ghost' (*Poems*, I, 120-1), written on 25 July 1863. The first speaker again finds herself faced with a spectre from the afterlife, only this time the meeting is instigated by the ghost, a former lover, who, unlike the phantoms of 'A Chilly Night', communicates visually and verbally with the shocked living party.

> "Oh whence do you come, my dear friend, to me.
> With your golden hair all fallen below your knee,
> And your face as while as snowdrops on the lea,
> And your voice as hollow as the hollow sea?"
>
> "From the other world I come back to you,
> My locks are uncurled with dripping drenching dew.
> You know the old, whilst I know the new:
> But tomorrow you shall know this too."
>
> "Oh not tomorrow into the dark, I pray;
> Oh not tomorrow, too soon to go away:
> Here I feel warm and well-content and gay:
> Give me another year, another day."

The whole poem is set out as a pattern of alternating dialogue - quatrain by quatrain for the first four stanzas, a pair of quatrains for the earthbound speaker, then a final twelve lines to the ghost. This carefully executed structural imbalance conveys a sense of awkwardness and upset to the piece reflected in the content of the spoken exchanges. The living speaker regards the ghost as something of an intrusion and desires not to 'know the new' of the 'other world'. The sad appearance of the spectre as described - a bedraggled, pallid wretch, and certainly no angel - only confirms the living lover's sense of the mutability of things, and supports her fear that to die will be to pass 'into the dark' as 'death mars all, which we cannot mend'. The quaint but sinister poem closes with the ghost's bitterness at finding this lapse in the living partner's faith, which seemed so strong in former days. The result is an incompatibility of the two philosophies, profane and Christian, as stressed as it was in 'A Chilly Night'.

> "... Never doubt I will leave you alone
> And not wake you ratting bone with bone.
>
> "I go home alone to my bed,
> Dug deep at the foot and deep at the head,
> Roofed in with a load of lead,
> Warm enough for the forgotten dead,
>
> "But why did your tears soak thro' the clay,
> And why did your sobs wake me where I lay?
> I was away, far enough away:
> Let me sleep now till the Judgement Day."

As the inhabitants of these poems look to the 'Judgement Day' for affirmation or otherwise of faith, the Rossetti text itself enacts a deferment of judgement, conveyed in the overwhelming sense of irresolution, which pervades these eschatological inquiries. Like the limbo-held spectre and perplexed speaker of 'The Poor Ghost' ('poor' on whose terms?) the early devotional poetry is prone to existence in a realm of uncertainty, as much as is Rossetti's 'secular' work - even when the attempt at devout pronouncement is a purely exegetical one. The opening section of 'Alas my Lord' (*Poems*, III, 44-5) (later retitled 'Wrestling' by W. M. Rossetti (*Works*, 247-8)), a liturgical prayer which has the repeated refrain 'Lord give us strength', openly admits the sense of incomplete faith and strain integral to Rossetti's inner debate:

> Alas my Lord,
> How should I wrestle all the livelong night
> With Thee my God, my Strength and my Delight?
>
> How can it need
> So agonized an effort and a strain
> To make Thy Face of Mercy shine again?
>
> How can it need
> Such wringing out of breathless prayer to move
> Thee to Thy wonted Love, when art Love?

The pained image of wrestling which opens this piece acknowledges the dynamic, questioning perspective Rossetti brings to devotional matters in her best religious verse. Her presentation of holy letter is informed with 'agonized an effort and a strain' coincident with that refusal idly to accept any ideology (phallocentric, patriarchal…) which characterises all her writing. The 'wringing out of breathless prayer', as opposed to an unquestioning regurgitation of pious dogma, makes the devotional poetry Rossetti wrote before 1875 often as challenging and as exciting as pieces such as *Goblin Market* in its refusal of complacency, and prepares the ground for the masterpiece of sustained uncertainty, *Monna Innominata*. Like the speaker of the 'Sonnet of Sonnets', Rossetti fails to discover a settled perspective, a stable centre, as the notion of a theocentric existence is set forth only to be contradicted and recontextualised in these formative religious works. Hence two sonnets, written only six months apart, may address the same eschatological issue and arrive at completely antithetical conclusions. 'A Pause' (*Poems*, III, 215-6) relates the affirmed, pious perspective of a recently deceased speaker whose soul awaits judgement. The dramatic conclusion is one of traditional Christian iconography:

> … first my spirit seemed to scent the air
> Of Paradise; then first the tardy sand

Of time ran golden; and I felt my hair
Put on a glory, and my soul expand.

Notably, whenever Rossetti seeks to confirm the litany, she does so
by the adoption of self-justifying Christian imagery. In 'Dead before
Death' (*Poems*, I, 59), the same premises as in 'A Pause' are explored
and yet the conclusion is markedly oppositional to that offered in the
earlier, yet roughly contemporary sonnet:

> All lost the present and the future time,
> All lost, all lost, the lapse that went before:
> So lost till death shut-to the opened door,
> So lost from chime to everlasting chime,
> So cold and lost for ever evermore.

Here, the language remains plain and deliberately stolid, as the speaker
drives home the notion of mutability and the finality of death. Taken
separately, these two sonnets offer self-contained statements of belief,
oppositional but, respectively, coherently phrased. Taken together, the
poems generate a controversy in their polarised visions, and it is the
resulting tension between contradictory ideological stances, which
finds its way into Christina Rossetti's best devotional work. These
poems, by subtly (or sometimes openly) deconstructing their own
propositions, reveal the sensibility of a poet-mind, as Packer has put it,
'hardly ready for the religious dedication to which she aspired'.[21] As we
have seen, argument and debate are always preferable to complacency
in this poet's writing, and Rossetti's work thrives upon the consequent
sense of strain; nowhere in the devotional poetry is that struggle
more evident than in the remarkably affecting piece 'The Convent
Threshold' (*Poems*, I, 61-5). In the next and final chapter of this study
I will examine this important poem, assess its place in the Rossetti
oeuvre and, finally, go on to consider the exegetical devotional writing
with which Rossetti chose to conclude her poetic career.

9

WEARIED OF SELF, I TURN, MY GOD, TO THEE: THE LATER DEVOTIONAL POETRY

Wearied of self, I turn, my God, to Thee…
Thou the Beginning, Thou ere my beginning
Didst see and didst foresee
Me miserable, me sinful, ruined me,--
I plead Thyself with Thee.
Christina Rossetti, 'For Thine own Sake, O my God'

'The Convent Threshold' (*Poems*, I, 61-5), written on 9 July 1858, is a poem pregnant with fearful doubt, swerving between a desire passively to embrace holy writ and the need actively to question its authority. Its main theme, like that of *Monna Innominata*, is one of pained renunciation, enacted through a process of telling juxtapositions; of pious and profane ideologies, of guilt and repentance, and, latterly, of dramatically relayed dream visions. The work's title provides an effective placing of Rossetti's conscience, as conveyed in her earlier religious works, on the 'threshold' of conventual (also *conventional*) belief and yet finding the crossing into unquestioning faith a problematic procedure. In the first three lines of the poem, a bold statement that echoes the plot of Shakespeare's Romeo And Juliet immediately engenders a tone of prohibition and painful separation: 'There's blood between us, love, my love, / There's father's blood, there's brother's blood; / And blood's a bar I cannot pass'.

Immediately, the power of earthly (notably patriarchal) ideology is acknowledged by the speaker in the 'blood' image descriptive of a desired, bonded state of unity. However, this striking familial overture is not pursued in the elusive narrative that follows, but proffered as a symbolic standard by which the rest of the work's attempts at unification may be gauged. The speaker immediately appeals to the symbolic realm as her profane guilt and the desire to purge it are expressed in a welter of orthodox, scriptural imagery:

> I choose the stairs that mount above,
> Stair after golden skyward stair,
> To city and to sea of glass.
> My lily feet are soiled with mud,
> With scarlet mud which tells a tale
> Of hope that was, of guilt that was,
> Of love that shall not yet avail;
> Alas, my heart, if I could bare
> My heart, this selfsame stain is there:
> I seek the sea of glass and fire
> To wash the spot, to burn the snare;
> Lo, stairs are meant to lift us higher:
> Mount with me, mount the kindled stair.

This plaintive, sermonic tone, employing deliberately placed gospel imagery, is the first manner of address inhabited, as the dramatic monologue maps out the dynamic, complex interplay of 'hope that was' and 'guilt that was' felt by the avowedly repentant speaker, as she addresses her unrepentant lover still enjoying a sensuous life on earth. 'Your eyes look earthward, mine look up', notes the speaker, as the text conveys a split, fractured sense of existence whose internal tensions effectively dismiss absolute certitude from the poem's debate. Thus the subtle disturbance of certainty in the speaker's exclamatory 'Lo, stairs are meant to lift us higher' — 'meant to', rather than an affirmatory *will* — casts a telling mantle of qualification about the purportedly positive statement, as the speaker tries to convince the addressee of the sanctity of the divine writ she calculatedly invokes here. A heavenly vision of 'the far-off city grand... where the righteous sup' is constructed, directly followed by a luscious picture of the earthly life of 'Young men and women', imaged in wanton, sensuous terms that recall the descriptive passages of *Goblin Market*:

> Milk-white, wine-flushed among the vines,
> Up and down leaping, to and fro,
> Most glad, most full, made strong with wines,
> Blooming as peaches pearled with dew,
> Their golden windy hair afloat,
> Love-music warbling in their throat,
> Young men and women come and go.

This is the vision the speaker aspires to reject and yet, within the fiction of the poem, must partly retain for its direct associations with the loved one who still inhabits this Bacchanalian province. The goblins of *Goblin Market* were vendors of language: similarly, in 'The Convent Threshold' the speaker tries symbolically to 'sell' religious faith to her dallying lover, and yet the powerful tensions established in the text's exploration of bonds (lovers on earth) painfully severed (separation of belief) lead, in the work's middle section, to the speaker's unease with the faith in which she herself has invested. First, she begs with her loved one to follow the same path as herself:

> Repent with me, for I repent,
> Woe's me the lore I must unlearn!
> Woe's me that easy way we went,
> So rugged when I would return!
> How long until my sleep begin,
> How long shall stretch these nights and days?

The unrepentant loved one addressed is urged to 'Flee for your life... / Kneel, wrestle, knock, do violence, pray' whilst there is still time left for renunciation. This atmosphere of violently ascetic repudiation of luxury colours the speaker's own words with a measure of unease emphasised by the solipsistic nature of the admonishments. Beginning with a demand that her lover repent, the speaker proceeds to describe her *own* troubled state of purgatorial suffering. The repetitions of 'Woe's me... Woe's me' and 'O weary... O weary' do little to assert the speaker's confidence in the ultimate worth of the path she advocates. The wistful reconstruction of the 'joy that went before' interacts with the antithetical 'weary Lent' informing the speaker's present state to disturb any sense of harmony as regards the poem's attempted embrace of Christian redemption. The speaker's tone is more one of sheer panic at her own predicament than the expected one of reassurance that the proper road to salvation has now been taken. There is a cutting irony in the phrase 'Surely... she prays': the would-be repentant speaker's prayers are those of despair rather than certitude. Even the promised paradisal vision cannot now escape the atmosphere of disquiet the speaker has herself instilled in the text thus far:

> How should I rest in Paradise,
> Or sit on steps of heaven alone?
> If Saints and Angels spoke of love,
> Should I not answer from my throne:
> Have pity upon me, ye my friends,
> For I have heard the sound thereof:
> Should I not turn with yearning eyes,
> Turn earthwards with a pitiful pang?
> Oh save me from a pang in heaven...

Even in heaven, the speaker's knowledge of profane indulgence colours her estimation of divine permanence. This is the problem central to 'The Convent Threshold' and characteristic of the majority of Rossetti's early devotional poetry. It is, as ever, the problem of how to establish a coherent, centred world-view when elements of the perspective deconstruct the principles upon which that coherence relies, the field of inquiry explored by so much of Rossetti's poetry. The insidious pervasiveness (reaching even to the divine beyond) of the extra-religious experiences that the speaker of 'The Convent Threshold' describes stands in opposition to the divine permanence the poem sets out to assert and justify. Through her pious meditations, Rossetti seeks to renounce the world and its ways, but only ends up despairingly acknowledging the potency of earthly passions. By this point in 'The Convent Threshold', the speaker is trying to convince *herself* of the validity of that which she is proposing, as much as any absent lover superficially addressed.

The two dream visions that follow in the poem further impress upon the narrative the unhinged state of the speaker's resolve and magnify her own feeling of isolation from certitude. The foray into the sphere of dreams is notable in itself in its indication of the need for relativity of interpretation of the matters at hand, simultaneously an escape from the causal debate elsewhere in the poem yet an advance into a new frame of reference with which to express the argument. In themselves, the dream interludes are attempts to develop symbolically the theme of guilt and repentance that the speaker pursued at the start of the monologue; however, taken in context of the tense, unresolved debate that directly precedes them, the dreams take on a fresh, less comfortably assimilated resonance. The first vision casts together a Miltonic atmosphere with a dramatic script redolent of parts of Keats's *Hyperion* to create an oddly wooden, stagy vignette:

> I tell you what I dreamed last night:
> A spirit with transfigured face
> Fire-footed clomb an infinite space.
> I heard his hundred pinions clang,
> Heaven-bells rejoicing rang and rang,
> Heaven-air was thrilled with subtle scents,

Worlds spun upon their rushing cars:
He mounted shrieking: "Give me light."
Still light was poured on him, more light;
Angels, Archangels he outstripped
Exultant in exceeding might,
And trod the skirts of Cherubim.
Still "Give me light," he shrieked; and dipped
His thirsty face, and drank a sea,
Athirst with thirst it could not slake.
I saw him, drunk with knowledge, take
From aching brows the aureole crown —
His locks writhed like a cloven snake —
He left his throne to grovel down
And lick the dust of Seraphs' feet...

This dream tells of a selfishly motivated figure's Faustian progress from unquenchable desire for knowledge, through surfeit of that knowledge, to the humble realisation of the error of his materialistic ways.[1] The epistemological quest, in the dream vision, is presented as a blustering, melodramatic process in imagery rather overblown and contrived, making Rossetti's concluding moral somewhat inappropriate to the terms of the dramatic preface:

For what is knowledge duly weighed?
Knowledge is strong, but love is sweet;
Yea all the progress he had made
Was but to learn that all is small
Save love, for love is all in all.

These *sententiae*, like the concluding lines of *Goblin Market*, have an oddly unsatisfying air about them. The charge does not quite hold. For a start, the whole scenario is presented (in a poem thus far unresolved) without debate; in a self-contained, unchallenged lesson the ecclesiastical, pat maxims are illustrated (rather than 'duly weighed') in self-justificatory, pseudo-Christian terms, hardly, therefore, a stretching of meaningful parameters. In fact, the whole vision and moral might be taken as a neat parody of Christina Rossetti's stipulated aim in 'The Convent Threshold', to justify from experience the path of repentance as a route to spiritual recovery. The speaker is patently on shaky ground, needing to resort to a predictable hellfire sermon in the hope of redeeming the argument she herself had emotionally deconstructed some few lines earlier.

As if to apologise for the hectoring, neoscriptural doctrine of the first dream vision, the speaker checks herself and returns to the exact same phrase — 'I tell you what I dreamed last night' — which began that unconvincing sermon. A new dream is narrated, and its more sincere, personal tone admits of the vulnerability that the episode of the fire-footed spirit pretended to overcome. The setting is the speaker's grave and the language of the poem — firstly biblical, secondly sermonic — becomes immediately subdued and simple, wistful and plain. The tone shifts from the hollow ceremonial to the sincerely confessional:

> I tell you what I dreamed last night:
> It was not dark, it was not light,
> Cold dews had drenched my plenteous hair
> Thro' clay; you came to seek me there.
> And "Do you dream of me?" you said.
> My heart was dust that used to leap
> To you; I answered half asleep:
> "My pillow is damp, my sheets are red,
> There's a leaden tester to my bed:
> Find you a warmer playfellow,
> A warmer pillow for your head,
> A kinder love to love than mine."
> You wrung your hands; while I like lead
> Crushed downwards thro' the sodden earth:
> You smote your hands but not in mirth,
> And reeled but were not drunk with wine.

This eschatological vision candidly accommodates the dichotomy, earthly and divine, which the major debate of 'The Convent Threshold' had found so unsettling and which the previous dream vision had attempted (unsuccessfully) to negate. The essential, projected unity sought by the speaker of the poem in the afterlife cannot, in the work's specified terms of current separation, but be a qualified, partial state, therefore a non-unified order.

In a manner akin to that evinced by *Monna Innominata*, 'The Convent Threshold', again via intertextual processes, has promoted potential order only to disqualify the notion in retrospect. This sense of partial realisation of the divinely inspired goal prevails by reason of the inevitable placement of the holy vision in the secular context of the speaker's qualifying earthly experience. Knowledge of divine permanence is drawn from, but also deconstructed by experience of earthly mutability. The speaker finally confesses to that which the work's argument has strongly prefigured; she is a self-sentenced outsider in terms of the heavenly vision of harmony offered at the start of the poem. Symbolically, the poem is uneasy with the religious platitudes it began by attempting to substantiate. The 'you', representing unrepentant, profane values, has become the integral element without which the speaker cannot decipher the world. Stripped of the desire to preach religious doctrine, the broken subject is left with a moving, vulnerable sense of her own state of trapped irresolution:

> For all night long I dreamed of you:
> I woke and prayed against my will,
> Then slept to dream of you again.
> At length I rose and knelt and prayed:
> I cannot write the words I said,
> My words were slow, my tears were few;
> But thro' the dark my silence spoke
> Like thunder.

These simple dualisms — 'woke/slept', 'rose/knelt', 'silence/thunder' — acutely enact the wavering sensibility and lack of firm belief at the heart of the poetry. 'I… prayed against my will', 'I cannot write the words I said…': like the shorter devotional lyrics examined earlier, 'The Convent Threshold' repeatedly, painfully exhibits a failure to resolve its constituent ideologies. The 'silence' that speaks 'like thunder' is the woefully extracted admittance that the religious faith the work set out to articulate has not been comfortably accepted by the speaker.

The tension in Rossetti's best devotional poetry arises from its internal questioning of the devotion it purports to advertise. Superficially embracing pious conventions, poems such as 'The Convent Threshold' display the active interrogation of inherited ideology present in the poet's 'secular' writings. As with *Monna Innominata*, the early religious pieces only achieve stability and a place of (spiritually affirmed) harmony when the questioning stops, in 'silence'. The speaker of 'The Convent Threshold', by means of her own mistrust of dogma, has manoeuvred herself, literally and symbolically, into a pose of acceptance: 'frozen… stifling in my struggle I lay'. This position reached, tension concludes and the paradisal vision may reassert itself uninterrupted by recontextualisation or scepticism:

> If now you saw me you would say:
> Where is the face I used to love?
> And I would answer: Gone before;
> It tarries veiled in paradise.
> When once the morning star shall rise,
> When earth with shadow flees away
> And we stand safe within the door,
> Then you shall lift the veil thereof.
> Look up, rise up: for far above
> Our palms are grown, our place is set;
> There we shall meet as once we met
> And love with old familiar love.

Wearied of argument and the ceaselessly unstable state it generates, the speaker, and the poetry, has reached a position of self-imposed passivity, 'safe within the door', a retreat from the flux and tension of debate, which facilitates acceptance of the holy writ and (at a textual, literary level) explains the unflinching production of exegetical religious writing by Christina Rossetti in her final years.

For the agnostic heroine of Rossetti's prose story, *Maude*, stable resolution could only come with death; for Christina Rossetti, it comes with the death of the questioning impulse. Maude Foster shrank from committing the sin of blasphemy: 'No: at least I will not profane Holy Things; I will not add this to all the rest. I have gone over and over again, thinking I should come right in time, and I do not come right. I will go no more'.[2] Amend the final phrase to 'I will *question* no more', and the above statement could adequately preface Christina Rossetti's excursion into purely exegetical writing during the latter stages of her career. The self-conscious assuaging of the formerly avid desire to recontextualise or deconstruct instances of holy ordination underpins Rossetti's late writings with stolid consistency. The Bible is no longer one of several ideological codes to be investigated; it becomes, literally, gospel truth. With the movement into unflinchingly pious exposition, no longer skirted nor prefaced by the unsettling tensions we have seen in earlier pieces, Rossetti finally attains that singularity of conviction she had so openly envied in formative pieces such as 'After This the Judgement' (*Poems*, I, 184-6), written in 1856:

> As eager homebound traveller to the goal,
> Or steadfast seeker on an unsearched main,
> Or martyr panting for an aureole,
> My fellow-pilgrims pass me, and attain
> That hidden mansion of perpetual peace
> Where keen desire and hope dwell free from pain…

Though, as we have seen, it is always the ultimate goal sought by the speakers of Christina Rossetti's early devotional poetry, divine salvation, conventionally imaged here as that cherished 'hidden mansion of perpetual peace', is never an absolute certainty. In the religious writings composed prior to the mid-1870s, doubt inhabits the verse like an unwelcome but magnetic guest at a solemn prayer meeting. Poems such as 'The Convent Threshold' and 'A Chilly Night' show that Rossetti is as prone as any Victorian writer to the disappearance of God; her fertile intellect repeatedly leaves the 'steadfast seeker' unsure and questioning, whilst 'fellow pilgrims pass' by on the route to certitude.

In the late writings, however, all this changes. By a self-imposed blinkering process, Rossetti makes sure that the divine presence never leaves her line of vision; by a chastened resistance of the questioning impulse, the later exegetical productions allow no recontextualisation nor interrogation of the biblical dogma they closely re-narrate. In place of the exciting disruption of certitude of yore, Rossetti's mature pious writing exhibits a smug complacency in its regurgitative embrace of Christian cliché which is, at best, predictable and, at worst, dull. The poet who spent the first three quarters of her career articulating the dynamics of a decentred logos occupies her final years in praise of the newly centred vision she has finally adopted. The later Christina Rossetti self-consciously inhabits the pose she had envied herself (whilst still 'panting for an aureole') in the sonnet 'In Progress' (*Poems*, III, 285):

> Ten years ago it seemed impossible
> That she should ever grow so calm as this,
> With self-remembrance in her warmest kiss
> And dim dried eyes like an exhausted well.
> Slow speaking when she has some fact to tell,
> Silent with long-unbroken silences,
> Centred in self yet not unpleased to please,
> Gravely monotonous like a passing bell…
> … Sometimes I fancy we may one day see
> Her head shoot forth seven stars from where they lurk
> And her eyes lightnings and her shoulders wings.

This poem captures excellently the feeling one has when reading Christina Rossetti's liturgical pronouncements of the 1880s and after, and comparing their lazy platitudes with the pained tensions of her earlier works. The late work consistently reveals (or rather, boasts) a mind firmly 'Centred in self' and 'not unpleased' with that state; unfortunately, the literature that this state encourages is, indeed, 'Gravely monotonous like a passing bell'. The late, pious writings come across as tired and stolid simply because they offer scriptural policy pat and unprefaced by question. Orthodox Christian assumptions are not checked and made to justify themselves any more and, as a result, the poetry and prose assume the hollow dryness of an 'exhausted well'. The timbre of the latter-day exegetical writing is such that, lyric to lyric, sentiment and style are interchangeable; it is instructive, however, to examine a couple of pieces which illustrate the general approach, before turning to a late prose work which openly expresses the orthodox philosophy, oppositional to that inscribed in all her previous works, upon which Christina Rossetti settled in the final years of her life.

The Bible has rightly been recognised as 'the principal textual influence' upon Christina Rossetti's generically eclectic and intertextually realised poetry.[3] In her later poetry and prose, the Bible becomes the exclusive influential source, no longer recontextualised alongside mediaeval, Petrarchan, Dantean, and Victorian ideologies but offered as a sole authority without question. William Michael Rossetti comments on this regurgitative tendency in the heavily devotional poetry:

> The reader of Christina Rossetti's poems will be apt to say that there is an unceasing use of biblical diction. This is a fact; and to some minds it may appear to detract seriously from her claims to originality, or to personal merit of execution. Without pre-judging this question, I will only remark that the Bible was so much her rule of life and of faith that it had almost become a part of herself, and she uttered herself accordingly.[4]

In an uncharacteristically light-hearted vein, William Michael goes on to propose that, if all the passages 'dependent upon what can be found in the Bible' were excised from his sister's writings, then her collected works would be 'reduced to something approaching a vacuum'. This would not be true of Christina Rossetti's earlier verse — the post-Romantic questioning of theological absolutes would remain — but the notion would pertain if the later poetry were the subject of the experiment. Elsewhere, William Michael refers to Christina's pious belief as relayed in the poems as an 'ardent absorbing devotion', a remark which neatly captures the sense of utter suppression of self-expression into the structures of holy, biblical writ which one repeatedly encounters in Christina Rossetti's later writing.[5] In the prefatory 'Key to my Book' pages of the prose exegetical tract, *Called to be Saints*, turned down by Macmillan in 1876 and finally published by the Society for Promoting Christian Knowledge in 1881 Rossetti boldly and officially relinquishes any claim to artistic spontaneity declaring that 'No graver slur could attach to my book than would be a reputation for prevalent originality'.[6] Similarly, in a late poem typical of this pious subjugation of inspirational energies, 'For Thine own Sake, O my God' (*Poems*, II, 150-1), the poet turns her back on the past and openly confesses her chosen path, a route strictly adhered to by her later writings: 'Wearied of sinning, wearied of repentance, / Wearied of self, I turn, my God, to Thee'.

'Wearied I loathe myself', admits the speaker of this short confessional piece, before wholly surrendering her will to the divine omnipresence, 'Thee who art my maker'. In the sixty-nine consecutive poems that make up the 'Some Feasts and Fasts' series (*Poems*, II, 211-47), mostly composed between 1877 and 1893, Rossetti recites the holy days in poetry remarkable for its lack of energy and forced tones of reverence. Many of these pieces are prefaced by epigrammatical biblical quotations that the poem proceeds to echo, more often than not in a fashion, which adds little to the import of the actual biblical phrase and which, certainly, does not question the scripture nor interpret it in any productive manner. Unlike the recontextualised Dantean and Petrarchan epigrams employed in the course of the *Monna Innominata* sonnet cycle, there is nothing innovative nor subversive about Rossetti's biblical citations. The sixteen-line commentary, 'Good Friday Morning' (*Poems*, II, 227), written in 1893, a year before Rossetti's death, is typical of the approach manifested in the later pious work. Its scriptural epigram is simply 'Bearing His Cross':

> Up Thy Hill of Sorrows
> Thou all alone,
> Jesus, man's Redeemer,
> Climbing to a Throne:
> Thro' the world triumphant,
> Thro' the Church in pain,
> Which think to look upon Thee,
> No more again.

> Upon my hill of sorrows
> I, Lord, with Thee,
> Cheered, upheld, yea, carried
> If a need should be:
> Cheered, upheld, yea, carried,
> Never left alone,
> Carried in Thy heart of hearts
> To a throne.

The most striking aspect of this unchallenging exposition of Christian belief is the speaker's relinquishment of an active subjectivity in the second stanza, to place the point of origin of the poem (literally) from within the divine manifestation: 'I, Lord, with Thee ... in Thy heart'. The overwhelming tone of the poem, even in the face of Christ's suffering, is one of positive affirmation, with the speaker's repeated assertion of comfort, 'Cheered, upheld, yea, carried...', removing any sense of strain or doubt from the piece. Unlike Rossetti's earlier theological monologues, 'Good Friday Morning' is neither a quest poem — the speaker is 'Carried... / To a throne' she is certain of reaching — nor an articulation of separation since the subject rejoices in being 'Never left alone'. The bipartite structure of the piece, employed in those former lyrics to juxtapose faith and scepticism, is now utilised as a consolidatory measure; the second stanza is used merely to repeat, in an unimaginative and rather self-satisfied manner, the patterning of the first, sitting the speaker's contented embrace of the holy route to salvation atop the symbolic structure established in the opening octave. As the speaker is passively 'Carried' along, supported by the divine presence, so the poem proceeds passively, and without question, from the perspective of blissful certitude.

'Ascension Eve' (*Poems*, II, 231-2), from the same period, forms an even more open celebration of the newfound ability to live one's existence through the channels of divinely inspired order. The speaker of 'Good Friday Morning' rejoiced in being 'Cheered, upheld, yea, carried', sentiments directly echoed by the 'beautified, replenished, comforted' state described in 'Ascension Eve':

> Lord, Thou art Love, fill us with charity.
> O Thou the Life of living and of dead,
> Who givest more the more Thyself hast given,
> Suffice us as Thy saints Thou hast sufficed;
> That beautified, replenished, comforted,
>
> Still gazing off from earth and up at heaven
> We may pursue Thy steps, Lord Jesus Christ.

Again, the desire is to 'pursue' the path of Christian discipline to a stable, centred position that is never held to be in doubt. Saturated with biblical register, the speaker's suppliant, reverential tone throughout emphasises the prayer-like quality of this piece; its tone is a great deal removed from the interrogative examination of pious platitudes performed in the poet's earlier religious work. 'We know the way', insists another poem of the 'Feasts and Fasts' series ('Easter Tuesday',

Poems, II, 231)), 'thanks God Who hath showed us the way!', and the poetry of this period brims with a self-satisfied confidence in the authority of the biblical dogma it invokes in a plethora of colourless, archaic diction. The 'beautiful Paradise', so eagerly questioned as an ideal in previous writings, is now gratefully accepted as an absolute truth.

The Christian deity repeatedly appears as an unshakeable principle of intelligibility, now neither deconstructed nor tested by context, granting enduring stability to the logos thereby generated. 'Lord, Save Us, We Perish' published in the 1893 *Verses* collection, plainly emphasises the all-pervasive nature of this newly accepted, unchallengeable centring principle:

> O Lord, seek us, O Lord, find us
> In Thy patient care;
> Be Thy Love before, behind us,
> Round us, everywhere:
> Lest the god of this world blind us,
> Lest he speak us fair,
> Lest he forge a chain to bind us,
> Lest he bait a snare.
> Turn not from us, call to mind us,
> Find, embrace us, bear;
> Be Thy Love before, behind us,
> Round us, everywhere. (*Poems*, II, 261)

Once more in rhythms and diction incantatory and prayer-like, the speaker celebrates her newfound sense of order and harmony in terms which, by repetition, emphasise its pervasive stability, the guarantee of salvation that is 'before, behind us, / Round us, everywhere', in contrast to the unstable orders articulated in the secular poetry, with their incoherence and inherent inconsistencies. Beneath the auspices of the divinely ordered system Rossetti now gladly inhabits, ideological notions which, before, would have been open to objection (or at least would have had their inconsistencies highlighted) are allowed to pass unchallenged. A striking example may be witnessed in 'A Helpmeet For Him' (*Poems*, II, 169), a short poem of 1888, where the 'women is a helpmeet for man' maxim, knowingly recontextualised to some effect in the fifth sonnet of *Monna Innominata*, is now offered without a hint of irony:

> Woman was made for man's delight;
> Charm, O woman, be not afraid!
> His shadow by day, his moon by night,
> Woman was made.

The once subverted patriarchal code is now accepted, since the ordination is one born of a greater patriarchy, that of God's writ. It can be seen from instances such as this that the singular, orthodox Christian ideology expounded in the later devotional verses of Christina Rossetti is oppositional to the collision of perspectives, pious and profane, effected in her earlier work as interpreted in previous chapters of this study.

Christina Rossetti's devotional poetry of the 1880s and 1890s openly assumes the thematic uniformity and complacent assimilation of dogma that her earlier writing had so stringently resisted. The tone (and often the content) is interchangeable from poem to poem and the examples analysed above are by no means the most suppliant in manner, nor the most purely exegetical in approach. For a systematically expressed, final glimpse of the ideological position ultimately adopted by Christina Rossetti, it is essential to consider the last original work the authoress published in her lifetime, *The Face of the Deep: A Devotional Commentary on the Apocalypse* (1892). (*Verses: Reprinted from Called to Be Saints, Time Flies, The Face of the Deep* (London & Brighton: Society for Promoting Christian Knowledge, 1893) was, as its title implies, a collection of previously available devotional poems.) This prose volume, containing a large selection of short religious poems previously unpublished, is a close, textual study of the Book of Revelation upon which Rossetti had been at work for six years, the period leading up to the ominous diagnosis of cancer in her chest and shoulder. Like all her prose productions, *The Face of the Deep*, published again by the Society for Promoting Christian Knowledge, is solidly written and not without moments of engagingly perceptive insight, and yet the very solidity of its generally sombre prose reminds us once more that it is in the area of lyric verse that Rossetti's real talent as a writer always existed. What is more notable in this last authorial statement is the unswerving adherence to the principles set forth by the orthodox Christian ideology upon which Rossetti sets out to comment. A tone of over-acted, self-satisfied sincerity pervades the work's languid illustration of biblical dogma, as the fragmented, painfully unstable world view Christina Rossetti had continually met in her earlier intellectual quest for unity and certitude is neatly reconciled within the terms of her newly embraced religious vision.

> Multitude no less than Unity characterises various types of God the Holy Spirit. Water indefinitely divisible, and every portion equivalent in completeness to the whole. Fire kindling unlimited flames, each in like manner complete in itself. Dew made up of innumerable drops: so also rain, and if we may make the distinction, showers. A cloud as a cloud is one, while as raindrops it is a multitude. And as in division each portion is a complete whole devoid of parts, so equally in reunion all portions together form one complete whole similarly devoid of parts: let drops or let flames run together, and there exists no distinction of parts in their uniform volume.[7]

How far removed from the subtle deconstructions of stability performed in Rossetti's earlier writings, both secular and devotional, is this laboured, almost risibly stilted attempt at justification of fragmentation within? Gone, lost forever, are the challenging tensions of *Monna Innominata* in favour of this rather naive, pantheistic prosody, more suited to a Sunday School sermon for infants than a mature ontological reflection. It is disappointing, again and again, to witness the smug assimilation of dogma unquestioned in the work of a writer capable, as we have seen, of such remarkably incisive interrogation of absolutist complacency. The notion of immutability, so painfully recontextualised in previous works, is finally embraced here as Rossetti contentedly echoes the import of Revelation 22. 13:

> 13. I am Alpha and Omega, the Beginning and the End, the First and the Last. Thus is it at the beginning… and still thus at the end; thus at the first, and still thus at the last. We change, He changes not. Yet even in ourselves constitutional changeableness cannot annul a certain inherent unchangeableness, which in so far corresponds with His in whom we live and move and have our being: for we are His offspring. His immutability is reflected in our identity: as He cannot deny Himself, so neither can we deny ourselves. Rocks may fall on us, mountains cover us; but under mountain and rock remains the inextinguishable I.[8]

The 'inextinguishable I' marks the achievement, before inconceivable, of a position of ultimate stability within the self from which the Rossetti subjectivity, as expressed in literature, may now proceed. 'His immutability is reflected in our identity': there exists no firm precedent for this manner of statement, framed in affirmatory tones, in the earlier poetry, devotional or otherwise, of Christina Rossetti. That sense of strain, the tense impact of doubt so valuable to the generation of varying perspectives in Rossetti's earlier work, is now no longer a threat to a certitude which, whatever counter-arguments come along, 'remains… inextinguishable'.

Orthodox Christian dictates are now accepted without reservation. When commenting upon her own poetry, symbolically from within the text or in prefatory pieces such as that introducing *Monna Innominata*, Rossetti was formerly keen to pull ideologies apart and illustrate ironies and contradictions. To do so in this biblical commentary would now constitute blasphemy and so Rossetti's critique (or, rather, exposition) of God's law becomes mere regurgitation of platitudes, repetitive and unquestioning, wholly at odds with the strategy of all her best work. *The Face of the Deep* exudes an atmosphere of humble passivity, directly antithetical to the position that the speaker of *Monna Innominata* struggled to occupy: 'Only should I have readers, let me remind them that what I write professes to be a *surface* study of an unfathomable depth: if it incites any to dive deeper than I attain to, it will so far have accomplished a worthy work'.[9] By the time of this lengthy study, Rossetti's poetry and prose is little more than a mouthpiece reciting pious platitudes in a way that makes for monotonous reading indeed. In the course of her rote illustrations of biblical doctrine, Rossetti's speaker boldly states what 'must be understood literally' and what 'seems figurative' with a confidence born of outright acceptance of one, consummate reading of a text which goes against the explicit advocacy of pluralism recommended by her own earlier poetry. Absolutely no doubt remains; the speaker openly admits herself to be 'convinced':

> What then do I think? God helping me, I will think this. The Divine Call has been addressed to me, has reached me, has urged my will, convinced my understanding, moved my heart ... I observe moreover that my call being a practical one, demanding not intellect on my side but obedience, enjoins practice rather than subtil theory, and is responded to by simplest obedience. My understanding breaks down: so be it. Please God, my will shall not break down, nor my faith make me shipwreck. O Love of Christ, constrain me, constrain all.[10]

'My understanding breaks down: so be it', confesses the speaker as
'practice' of 'obedience' is now preferred to the 'intellect' and 'subtil
theory' which characterises Christina Rossetti's finest writings.
Repeatedly turning to archaic, liturgical diction — 'O Love of Christ...'
— the text consistently invokes a position of utter subordination to
the Christian cause. As the speaker looks to the last judgement, we
witness the resigned attempt to rationalise her own relinquishment of
intellectual inquisitiveness; by repetition, typically, Rossetti convinces
herself of the righteousness of the place at which she has arrived:

> Some can meditate and interpret. All can meditate
> and pray. To interpret should do good. To pray will do
> good. Interpretation may err and darken knowledge.
> Prayer fetches down wisdom from the Father of Lights.
> Prayer is the safeguard of interpretation, and without
> interpretation is still profitable... Interpretation is safe
> and seemly for some. Prayer is safe and seemly for all.[11]

With these unreservedly suppliant, pious sentiments, Christina
Rossetti chooses to close her literary career, as she did her actual life,
in a state of unquestioning prayer.[12] There is an oddly tragic irony in all
of this. Not only does Christina Rossetti's submissive acceptance of an
orthodox faith remove those invigorating, restless tensions that make
her finest poetry so compelling and forward-looking; her religion,
according to her brother William Michael, 'weighed her down at the
last... Not that she died despairing — very far from that: but she died
with a more imminent sense of unworthiness and apprehension than
of acceptance and unshakeable confiding hope'.[13]

Through unquestioning, finally blinkered 'acceptance' of one
ideology above all others, Christina Rossetti endeavoured, self-
consciously, to construct in art that 'unshakeable' stability which
her most rewarding poetry had identified as an unattainable goal.
Superficially, and unremittingly, the later devotional texts, both
poetry and prose, convey the blissful achievement of a settled, unified

position; as to just how much actual doubt these seemingly watertight and affirmed works concealed, we may only guess.

Christina Rossetti's greatest poetry is that which strives to adopt the conventional Christian position but finds that pose, once tried out, an awkward fit, uncomfortable in its suggestion of intellectual inertia and implicit resolution of alternatives. Poems such as *Goblin Market* and *The Prince's Progress* show her capable of sustaining an acutely managed lexical artistry, present in even her shortest lyrics, and turning that artistry toward a definite purpose, the redirection of literary tradition. But it is when that peculiarly inventive linguistic vision is directed towards matters of belief and faith that Rossetti's writing exudes a passionate self-awareness that is at once inspiring and, ultimately, painful. The turning towards God at the close of *Monna Innominata* tells us about the poet's own pious declarations at the end of her career not because scriptural doctrine is warmly embraced, but because it results from a compromised state and has a hollow ring to it when set beside the clamorous questioning of absolutes that has gone before. Thematically, *Monna Innominata* attempted to follow the set pattern established in many of Christina Rossetti's lyrics: construction of a perspective, gentle interrogation of that position, stability disturbed to the point of irresolution, and finally a kind of relocated resolve coloured in the devotional works by orthodox Christian hope of redemption in the afterlife. But, through reason of her gender, her place in society, her poetic vocation, Christina Rossetti's hope is (to use a favourite biblical phrase of her own, originating in Proverbs 13. 7) forever 'hope deferred', hope removed one step, conveying an air of unquiet at taking the pledge, at accepting redemption (or any ideological position) without being allowed the grace to question that hope.

Had Christina Rossetti never adopted the stance of unfailing pious humility effected in her late writing, she may conceivably have produced even finer work in her mature years than that which she composed earlier in her career. We will never know. But, certainly, it is the fine interplay between faith and doubt that motivates Christina Rossetti's most affecting writing. The two interact to create a fascinating, compelling tension marvellously suited to expression through the delicately poised lexical style she had developed in her 'secular' work. Through being forced (by her own conscience) to justify and come to terms with a self-imposed pious viewpoint, Rossetti's earlier devotional writing shows a mind unafraid to question ideas of 'truth' and a poetic artistry consistently capable of maintaining that sharp, engaging sense of tension that underlies all her strongest work. Harrison has remarked upon 'how the earnest repressiveness of the Victorians could ultimately explode into the sensual extravagance of the decadents'.[14] With Rossetti herself there was no explosion; in fact, quite the opposite. The tensions in her early poems build up to a spectacular and sudden (but silenced) implosion of passion and emotion, simultaneously marking the relinquishment of worldly extravagance (poetry being the aesthetic representation of this) and the oppositional adoption of an ascetic, conventionally pious, ordered existence.

Only in *Goblin Market* had Rossetti's verbal manner been unfettered and luxuriant (and only then, half-vicariously so, via the mouthpiece of the 'goblin men'): elsewhere it is controlled and free from ornament, capable of great moments of insight but never ostentatious about it. With the late devotional writing, the reserved lexical style no longer stretches a tense surface over a welling intellectual vision beneath, but mirrors a flat, unvarying and ascetically pious content. From her earliest lyrics to the last prose exegetical pieces, we witness Christina Rossetti's aesthetic vision gradually being checked and brought into line with the orthodox Christian outlook that always governed her outward, physical existence. The religion that had always underpinned her poetic vision was eventually to stifle it, but, throughout this progression, poetry for Rossetti was essentially cathartic. Through her writing, female identity and the place of women is scrutinised, re-addressed and ultimately, on a personal level, offered up to God for redemption in an eternal afterlife. The intellectually provocative subtext of Christina Rossetti's best poems, the refusal complacently to accept what might just as easily be questioned, hints at the sense of strain which must have occupied her mind in its ultimate, self-imposed embrace of orthodox piety, and all that such piety entailed for her art.

NOTES

Preface

1. These extracts are taken from, respectively, Seed, Rev. T. A., 'Review of Goblin Market and Other Poems' in *Great Thoughts* (1862) and an anonymous reviewer in *The Daily News*. Both are included in 'Extracts from Reviews' in *The Poetical Works of Christina Georgina Rossetti. With Memoir and Notes, &c.* edited by William Michael Rossetti (London & New York: Macmillan, 1904) (referred to hereafter in the main text as *Works*), xv-xix.

2. Ford (pseud. Hueffer), Ford Madox, 'Modern Poetry' in *The Critical Attitude* (London: Duckworth, 1911) 173-90, quotation 179.

3. Packer, Lona Mosk, *Christina Rossetti* (Cambridge: Cambridge University Press, 1963).

4. see Battiscombe, Georgina, *Christina Rossetti: A Divided Life* (London: Constable, 1981); Jones, Katherine, *Learning Not to Be First: the Life of Christina Rossetti* (Oxford: Oxford University Press, 1992), a socio-religious biographical study; Marsh, Jan, *Christina Rossetti: a Literary Biography* London: Jonathan Cape, 1994), a psychoanalytic appraisal of the poet's life and Thomas, Frances, *Christina Rossetti: a Biography* (London: Virago, 1994), a feminist biography.

5. see Hunt, Violet, *The Wife of Rossetti* (London: John Lane, Bodley Head, 1932) and Rossetti, William Michael, ed., *The Family Letters of Christina Georgina Rossetti* (London: Brown, Langham and Co., 1908).

Chapter 1 – *Beginnings*

1. All references to Christina Rossetti's poems in this study are to Crump, Rebecca W. ed, *The Complete Poems of Christina Rossetti* (Baton Rouge; Louisiana State U. P., 1979-90) 3 vols. These are cited in the main text as *Poems* and by volume and page number(s). In similar fashion, all references in this study to *The Poetical Works of Christina Georgina Rossetti. With Memoir and Notes, &c.* edited by William Michael Rossetti (London & New York: Macmillan, 1904) are cited in the main text as *Works* and by page number(s).
2. Rossetti, W. M., *Family Letters*, 220.
3. Carlyle, Thomas, *Past and Present*, (London: Centenary Edition, 1897) 267.
4. see note 1, above.
5. see Kent, David A., ed., *The Achievement of Christina Rossetti* (Ithaca: Cornell, 1987), and Harrison, Antony H., *Christina Rossetti in Context* (Sussex; Harvester, 1988).
6. see Packer, *Christina Rossetti*, and Fredeman, Willliam E., 'Review' in *Victorian Studies*, VIII, (Sept. 1964) (Indiana: Indiana University Press, 1964) 71-77. The demolition of Packer's flawed hypothesis is described in some detail in Chapter 6 of this study.
7. Flowers, Betty S., 'The Kingly Self' in Kent, *The Achievement of Christina Rossetti* 159-74, quotation 160.
8. Harrison, *Christina Rossetti in Context* 10.
9. Ibid. 3.
10. Eliot, T. S., 'Tradition and the Individual Talent' in *The Sacred Wood* (London: Methuen, 1920) 42-53, quotation 48.
11. Letter quoted in Sandars, Mary F., *The Life of Christina Rossetti* (London: Hutchinson, 1930) 85-6.
12. Milton, John, *The Poems of John Milton* ed. Carey J. and Fowler, A. (London: Longmans, 1966) 146-8
13. Wordsworth, William, *Poetical Works* (London: Edward Moxon, 1869) 441-3.

14. Coleridge, Samuel T., *Complete Poetical Works* ed. Coleridge, E. H. (Oxford: Clarendon, 1912) 362-8, quotation 364-5.
15. Shakespeare, William, *Shakespeare's Sonnets* ed. A. L. Rowse, Third Edition (London: Macmillan, 1984) Sonnet 73, 148.
16. see Dobbs, Brian and Judy, *Dante Gabriel Rossetti: An Alien Victorian* (London: Macdonald, 1977) 34, 145.
17. Blake, William, *Poems*, ed. Stevenson, Warren H., (London: Longman, 1971) 146.

Chapter 2 – *Romanticism and Christina*

1. No proof exists as to whether or not Rossetti read Newman, though she did own a hand-annotated copy of Keble's *Christian Year* and she admired the poetry of Isaac Williams. Her most 'significant and influential' exposure to Tractarian values, however, came from the sermons of the Reverend William Dodsworth, Perpetual Curate of Christ's Church, 1837-50. See Mayberry, Katherine J., *Christina Rossetti and the Poetry of Discovery* (Baton Rouge: Louisiana State University Press, 1989) 111; and Harrison, *Christina Rossetti in Context* 69.
2. Chapman, Raymond, 'Uphill all the Way' in *Faith and Revolt: Studies in the Literary Influence of the Oxford Movement* (London: Weidenfeld and Nicholson, 1970) 170-97.
3. Mayberry, *Christina Rossetti and The Poetry of Discovery* 111.
4. Tennyson, George B., *Victorian Devotional Poetry* (Cambridge, Mass.: Harvard University Press, 1981) 202.
5. Ibid. 203.
6. Keble, John, 'Tract 89' in *Tracts for the Times* (London: Rivingtons, 1840) vol. V, 143.
7. Tennyson, 202.
8. Ibid. 203.
9. See Harrison, *Christina Rossetti in Context* 73, 77.
10. Keble, John, *Lectures on Poetry*, translated by E. K. Francis (Oxford: Clarendon, 1912) vol. II, 481.

11. Cantalupo, Catherine M., 'Christina Rossetti the Devotional Poet and the Rejection of Romantic Nature' in Kent, *The Achievement of Christina Rossetti* 279.

12. Quotations from *Later Life* are given by the number of the sonnet in the sequence and the line numbers of that sonnet. *Later Life* was published in *A Pageant, and Other Poems* (London: Macmillan, 1881), but the sonnets' dates of composition, thought to range from 1860 to 1879, were not recorded by the author.

13. Shelley, Percy B., 'A Defence of Poetry' in *Complete Works* ed. Ingpen, R., and Peck, W. E., (London: Ernest Benn, 1965) vol. VII, 116.

14. Ibid. 112.

15. Wordsworth, William, *The Prelude*, ed. De Selincourt, E., (Oxford: Oxford University Press, 1970) 100.

16. Belsey, Catherine, 'The Romantic Construction of the Unconscious' in *Literature, Politics and Theory: Papers from the Essex Conference 1976-84* ed. F. Barker, (London: Methuen, 1986, 58-9.

17. Rossetti, Christina G., *Letter and Spirit: Notes on the Commandments* (London & Brighton: Society for Promoting Christian Knowledge, 1883) 10.

18. Ibid. 13.

19. Cantalupo, in Kent ed., *The Achievement of Christina Rossetti* 282-3.

20. see Blake, Kathleen, *Love and the Woman Question in Victorian Literature* (Sussex: Harvester, 1983) 3-25.

21. Armstrong, Isobel, *Language as Living Form in Nineteenth Century Poetry* (Sussex: Harvester, 1982) xiii.

Chapter 3 – *Dreams and Dreaming*

1. Stoppard, Tom, *Rosencrantz and Guildenstern are Dead* (London: Faber, 1967) 44. This piece is discussed in Hume, Kathryn, *Fantasy and Mimesis: Responses to Reality in Western Literature* (London: Methuen, 1984). 126.

2. Hume, *Fantasy and Mimesis*, 127-31.
3. Rycroft, Charles, *The Innocence of Dreams* (London: Hogarth, 1979) 4.
4. Shakespeare, William, *A Midsummer Night's Dream* (Harmondsworth: Penguin, 1980 rpt.) IV, i, 105.
5. Ibid. V, i, 107.
6. Ibid. IV, i, 104.
7. Ibid. V, i, 107.
8. Ibid. 'Introduction' by Stanley Wells, 34.
9. Ibid. V, i, 107.
10. Eysenck Hans J., *Sense and Nonsense in Psychology* (Harmondsworth: Penguin, 1963) 159.
11. Welsh, Andrew, *Roots of Lyric* (Princeton: Princeton University Press, 1978) 15.
12. cited in Prescott, Frederick C., *The Poetic Mind* (New York: Cornell University Press, 1959) 44.
13. Coleridge, Samuel T., *Notebooks* ed., K. Coburn, Vol. II, (1804-8) (London: Routledge, 1962) 2086, 15.52, ff, 40-40v.
14. Bald, R. C., 'Coleridge and The Ancient Mariner' in *Nineteenth Century Studies* (Ithaca, 1940) 39-40.
15. cited in Coleridge, *Complete Poetical Works* 186-209, epigram 186.
16. Ibid. 295-8.
17. Adair, Patricia M., *The Waking Dream: A Study of Coleridge's Poetry* (London: Edward Arnold, 1967) 7.
18. Poulet, Georges, 'Timelessness and Romanticism' in *Journal of the History of Ideas* (15.1) (January 1954) 7.
19. Beguin, Andre, *L'Ame Romantique et le Reve* (1937), passage translated in Thorlby, Anthony, ed., *The Romantic Movement* (London: Longmans, 1966) 45.
20. Hartman, Geoffrey, *The Unmediated Vision* (New Haven: Yale U. P., 1954) 34.
21. Ibid. 39.
22. Rycroft, *The Innocence of Dreams* 4.

23. Freud, Sigmund, *An Outline of Psychoanalysis* (London: Hogarth, 1967) 177.

24. Coleridge, Samuel T., 'Lecture XII' in *The Literary Remains in Prose and Verse of Samuel Taylor Coleridge,* 4 volumes, edited by Henry Nelson Coleridge (London: Pickering, 1836-1839) Vol. 1, 202.

25. Keats, John, *The Poems of John Keats* ed. Allott, Miriam, (London: Longman, 1920) 523-32.

26. Shakespeare, *A Midsummer Night's Dream* IV, i, 102-4.

27. Breton, Andre, *Manifestoes of Surrealism* (Michigan: University Press, 1972) esp. 'Manifesto of Surrealism (1924)' 1-49.

28. Bowra, Sir Maurice, *The Romantic Imagination* (London: O. U. P., 1961 rpt.) 246.

29. Ibid. 250.

30. Rycoft, *The Innocence of Dreams* 148.

31. see Shakespeare, W., *Hamlet* (New York: American Library, 1963) III, i, 93-4 and Keats, *Poems*, 510-2.

32. McGann, Jerome J., 'The Religious Poetry of Christina Rossetti' in *Critical Inquiry* 10 (1983) 135.

33. Ibid. 135.

34. Shakespeare, *Hamlet* (Harmondsworth: Penguin, 1980 rpt.) I, v, 64.

35. see Edwards, Paul, 'Ambiguous Seductions: "La Belle Dame Sans Merci", *The Faerie Queene* and *Thomas the Rhymer*' in *Durham University Journal* (July 1990) 199-203.

36. Darwin, Charles, *The Descent of Man* (London: Murray, 1871) 74.

37. Eyesenk, *Sense and Nonsense in Psychology* 159.

38. Keats, *Poems,* 655 85.

39. Packer, *Christina Rossetti* 90-1.

40. Hartman, G. H., ed. *The Selected Poetry and Prose of Wordsworth* (London: Meridian, 1970) 423.

41. Coleridge, *Notebooks* 6, 1.8.

42. Packer, *Christina Rossetti* 93-8.

43. Rossetti, W. M. ed., *Rossetti Papers* 1862-70 (London: Sands, 1903) 67.

44. Shakespeare William., *Antony and Cleopatra* (New York: New American Library, 1963) II, vii, 94-5.
45. James, Henry, *The Turn of the Screw* (Harmondsworth: Penguin, 1984) 147.

Chapter 4 – *Modes of Temptation in Goblin Market*

1. *Goblin Market*, Christina Rossetti's most famous poem, was written between 1859 and 1861 and first published in *Goblin Market and Other Poems* (London: Macmillan, 1862). For Christina's declaration that the poem was not aimed at children, see Kooistra, Lorraine J., *Christina Rossetti and Illustration: A Publishing History* (Ohio: Ohio University Press, 2002) 266, note 16. For description of the work as a 'fairy tale' see Elton, O., *A Survey of English Literature (1830-80)* (London: Arnold, 1920) vol. II, 23.
2. Von Franz, Marie L., *Problems of the Feminine in Fairytales* (Texas: Spring, 1972) 1.
3. Mulford, W., 'Notes on Writing' in Wandor, M. ed., *On Gender and Writing* (London: Pandora, 1983) 34.
4. Prickett, Stephen, *Victorian Fantasy* (Sussex: Harvester, 1979) 103.
5. Chetwynd, Tom, *A Dictionary of Symbols* (London: Paladin, 1982) 147.
6. Prickett, *Victorian Fantasy* 105.
7. see McGillis, Roderick, 'Simple Surfaces: Christina Rossetti's Work for Children' in Kent, D. A. ed., *The Achievement of Christina Rossetti* (London: Cornell, 1987) 209, footnote ii.
8. Watson, Jeanie, '"Men sell not such in any town": Christina Rossetti's Goblin Fruit of Fairy Tale' in *Children's Literature* 12 (1984) 73.
9. Prickett, *Victorian Fantasy* 106.
10. Jackson, Rosemary, *Fantasy: The Literature of Subversion* (London: Methuen, 1981) 103.
11. McGillis, 'Simple Surfaces' 209.

12. Ibid. 217.

13. Rossetti, Christina G., *The Prince's Progress and Other Poems* (London: Macmillan, 1866).

Chapter 5 – *The Prince's Progress*

1.   Jones, Kathleen, *Learning Not to Be First: The Life of Christina Rossetti* (Oxford: Oxford University Press, 1992) 131.
2.   Rossetti, William M., ed., *Rossetti Papers, 1862-70: A Compilation* (London: Sands, 1903) 68.
3.   Ibid. 69.
4.   Ibid. 72.
5.   Ibid. 72.
6.   Ibid. 74.
7.   Ibid. 78.
8.   Packer, Lona M., ed., *The Rossetti-Macmillan Letters* (Berkeley: University of California Press, 1963) 10-12.
9.   Harrison, Antony H., ed., *The Letters of Christina Rossetti* (London: University of Virginia Press, 1997) Volume 1, 1843-1873, 226.
10. Quoted in Sandars, Mary F., *The Life of Christina Rossetti* (London: Hutchinson, 1930) 85-6.
11. Packer, *The Rossetti-Macmillan Letters* VI, 10-12.
12. Rossetti, W. M., *Rossetti Papers* 74.
13. Ibid. 88.
14. Hill Jnr., Robert W., ed., *Tennyson's Poetry: Norton Critical Edition* (New York: Norton, 1971) 408.
15. *The Holy Bible* (King James Version), Matthew 25. 5-6.
16. Rossetti, W. M., *Rossetti Papers* 81.
17. Ibid. 81.
18. Dombrowski, Theodore, 'Dualism in the Poetry of Christina Rossetti' in *Victorian Poetry* 14 (1976) 70-6, quotation 70.
19. Bettelheim, Bruno, *The Uses of Enchantment* (Harmondsworth: Penguin, 1978) 5.
20. Ibid. 5.

21. Bloom, Harold, *The Ringers in the Tower: Studies in Romantic Tradition* (London: Chicago University Press, 1971) 15.

22. Hartman, Geoffrey, H., 'Romanticism and Anti-Self Consciousness' in Bloom, Harold, ed., *Romanticism and Consciousness* (New York: Norton, 1970) 46-56, quotation 54.

23. Hill, *Tennyson's Poetry* 16.

24. Harrison, *The Letters of Christina Rossetti* 226.

25. Roberts, Maureen B. '"Ethereal Chemicals": Alchemy and the Romantic Imagination' in *Romanticism On the Net* 5 (February 1997) retrieved from < https://www.erudit.org/revue/ron/1997/v/n5/005734ar.html>.

26. Ibid. 1.

27. Ibid. 1.

28. Harrison, *The Letters of Christina Rossetti* 226.

29. Allott, Miriam, ed., *Keats: The Complete Poems* (London: Longman, 1972) 500-506.

30. D'Amico, Diane, *Christina Rossetti: Faith, Gender, and Time* (Baton Rouge: Louisiana State University Press, 1999) 87.

31. Stuart, Dorothy M., *Christina Rossetti* (London: Macmillan, 1930) 74.

32. Gettings, Fred, *Visions of the Occult* (London: Hutchinson, 1987) 140-1.

33. see Rossetti, W. M., 'Obituary' in *Spectator* 6 May 1854.

34. Chetwynd, *A Dictionary of Symbols* 9.

35. Eliot, Thomas S., 'Ulysses, Order, and Myth' in *Selected Prose of T. S. Eliot* ed. Kermode, F. (London: Faber and Faber, 1975) 175-8, quotation 177.

36. Lynda Palazzo, *Christina Rossetti's Feminist Theology* (New York: Palgrave, 2002) 40.

Chapter 6 – *Approaching Monna Innominata*

1. Waldman, Suzanne M., *The Demon and the Damozel: Dynamics of Desire in the Works of Christina Rossetti and Dante Gabriel Rossetti* (Ohio: Ohio University Press, 2008) 27.

2. References to the *Monna Innominata* sequence (*Poems*, II, 86-93) are given in the main text after quotations by the number of the sonnet in the cycle and the line numbers taken from that particular sonnet.

3. Rossetti, W. M. ed., *Family Letters* 93.

4. Ibid. 94.

5. Packer, *Christina Rossetti* 309.

6. "'No, Thank You, John'" was rightly referred to by the poet James Fenton in the *Independent on Sunday* newspaper (23 June 1991, 34) as an 'excellent poem … which stands as a landmark in lyric, a woman's answer to centuries of pained outpourings from chaps'. This indicates that some people, at least, are capable of shifting mentally from the particular to the general.

7. Packer, *Christina Rossetti* 422.

8. Ibid. viii.

9. Fredeman, Willliam E., 'Review' in *Victorian Studies*, VIII, (Sept. 1964) (Indiana: Indiana University Press, 1964) 71-77.

10. Rossetti, Christina G., *The Face of the Deep: A Devotional Commentary on the Apocalypse* (London & Brighton: Society for Promoting Christian Knowledge, 1892) 396.

11. Oppenheimer, Paul, *The Birth of The Modern Mind: Self, Consciousness and the Invention of the Sonnet* (London: Oxford University Press, 1989) 3.

12. Crump, Rebecca W., 'Eighteen Moments' Monuments' in Fraser, Robert S. ed., *Essays on the Rossettis* (Princeton: Princeton University Library, 1972) 210-29, quotation 210.

13. Caine, T. Hall, *Recollections of Dante Gabriel Rossetti* (London: Elliot Stock, 1882) 244.

14. Going, William T., *Scanty Plot of Ground: Studies in the Victorian Sonnet* (The Hague: Mouton & Co., 1976) 36.

15. Wordsworth, William, *Letters of William and Dorothy Wordsworth* 6 vols. Second Edition, ed., De Selincourt, E., Revised by Shaver, C. L., (Oxford: Clarendon, 1967) Vol. I (Early Years 1787-1805) 234.

16. Lind, Levi R., *Lyric Poetry of the Italian Renaissance* (New Haven: Yale University Press, 1954) 89.
17. Holmes, George, *Dante* (London: Oxford University Press, 1980) 6.
18. Hassett, Constance W. *Christina Rossetti: the Patience of Style* (Virginia: University of Virginia Press, 2005) 167.
19. Rossetti, Dante G., *Poems and Translations 1850-1870* (London: Oxford University Press, 1913) 365
20. Petrarca, Francesco, *Selections from the Canzoniere and Other Works* (Oxford: Oxford University Press, 1985) 59.
21. Lind, *Lyric Poetry of the Italian Renaissance* 11-13.
22. Ibid. 35.
23. Ibid. 39.
24. Petrarca, *Selections* 56.
25. Lind, *Lyric Poetry of the Italian Renaissance* 35.
26. Spenser, Edmunde, *Amoretti and Epithalamion Facsimile Edition*, Sonnet XXIIII (New York: De Capo, 1969) Pages unnumbered.
27. Ibid. Sonnet LIIII.
28. Drayton, Michael, *Poems of Michael Drayton* ed., Buxton, J., (London: Routledge and Kegan Paul, 1953) vol. I, 2.
29. Ibid. 14.
30. Ibid. 14.
31. Ibid. 14.
32. Ibid. 4.
33. Ibid. 17.
34. Shakespeare, *Shakespeare's Sonnets*, Sonnet 21. 44.
35. Ibid.
36. Ibid. Sonnet 130. 262.
37. Ibid. Sonnet 141. 284.
38. Ibid. Sonnet 23, 48.
39. Ibid. Sonnet 145. 292.
40. Alighieri, Dante, *Purgatorio: A Verse Translation* by A. Mandelbaum (Berkeley: University of California Press, 1982) 212.
41. Holmes, *Dante* 8.

42. Lind, Lyric *Poetry of the Italian Renaissance* 87.

43. cited in Holmes, *Dante* 10.

44. Petrarca, *Selections* 23.

45. Roe, Dinah, *Christina Rossetti's Faithful Imagination* (New York: Palgrave Macmillan, 2006) 95.

46. Rossetti, W. M., *Family Letters* 98.

47. see Doughty, Oswald, *A Victorian Romantic: Dante Gabriel Rossetti* (London: Frederick Muller Ltd., 1949) 108.

48. Rossetti, Dante G., *The Early Italian Poets together with Dante's Vita Nuova* (London: Smith, Elder and Co., 1861).

49. Rossetti, D. G., *Poems and Translations 1850-1870* 300 n.

50. Rossetti, W. M., *Family Letters* 184, and Mackenzie Bell, Henry T., *Christina Rossetti: A Biographical and Critical Study* (London: Thomas Burleigh, 1898) 58, 319.

51. Weintraub, Stanley, *Four Rossettis: A Victorian Biography* (London: W. H. Allen, 1978) 2.

52. Rossetti, William M., 'Obituary' in *Spectator* 6 May 1854.

53. Rossetti, Gabriele, *La Beatrica di Dante* (London: Privatera, 1842) and Rossetti, Maria F., *A Shadow of Dante* (London: Rivingtons, 1871).

54. Sawtell, Margaret, *Christina Rossetti* (Oxford: Mowbray & Co., 1955) 87. Maria Francesca Rossetti's *A Shadow of Dante* was actually published by Rivingtons of London in November 1871 (see n. 49 above). No sources are given for the quotations attributed to Christina Rossetti in this extract.

55. Rossetti, D. G., *Poems and Translations 1850-1870* 297.

56. Ibid. 325.

57. Ibid. 326.

58. Ibid. 325.

59. Ibid. 343.

60. Ibid. 339.

61. Ibid. 339.

62. Ibid. 328.

63. Ibid. 329.

64. Ibid. 346.
65. Ibid. 329.
66. Ibid. 372.
67. Ibid. 379.
68. Ibid. 336 n. 1 and n. 2.
69. Derrida, Jacques, *Writing and Difference* (London: Routledge, 1978) 279. I cite this particular passage simply because it neatly and succinctly expresses what this study proposes to be a notion central to the *Monna Innominata* cycle and an idea crucial to an understanding of the processes of intertextuality and recontextualisation which advance Rossetti's sequence. The citation of Derrida is not offered as any form of commendation of the broader theoretical position advocated in Derrida's philosophical works.
70. Dunlop, Alexander, 'Introduction to Amoretti and Epithalamion' in William A. Oram et al., eds., *The Shorter Poems of Edmunde Spenser: Yale Edition* (London: Yale University Press, 1989) 586.
71. Petrarca, *Selections* 1.
72. Ibid. 21.
73. Ibid. 24.
74. Mommsen, Theodor E., 'Petrarch's Conception of the Dark Ages' in *Mediaeval and Renaissance Studies* ed. E. F. Rice Jnr. (New York: Cornell University Press, 1959) 106-29.
75. This elevation of Rome was nevertheless supported by a kind of sub-Platonism based upon Roman Unities of Architecture, Theatrical Form, etc. Rome became the type of the Secular Holy City - later Blake's 'Jerusalem', Yeats' visionary 'Byzantium' - always potentially presented in 'real' terms, cf. Dickens' London in *Bleak House*, Thompson's *City of Dreadful Night*, the opposition of Wordsworth's two sonnets of 1802 on views of London.
76. Petrarca, *Selections* 24.

Chapter 7 – *Reading Monna Innominata*

1.   Harrison, Antony H., *Victorian Poets and Romantic Poems: Intertextuality and Ideology* (Charlottesville: Virginia University Press, 1990) 112.

2.   Mackenzie Bell, *Christina Rossetti* (London: Thos. Burleigh, 1898) 90-91.

3.   Barrett Browning, Elizabeth, *Poetical Works* (Edinburgh: Nimmo, Hay & Mitchell, 1912) 443.

4.   Ibid. 447-8.

5.   Mermin, Dorothy, 'The Female Poet and the Embarrassed Reader: Elizabeth Barrett Browning's *Sonnets from the Portuguese*' in *English Literature and History* 48 (1981) 351-67.

6.   Harrison, *Christina Rossetti in Context* 153.

7.   In fact, the sestet that concludes this sonnet is a recontextualised repetition of the closing lines of a sonnet of 1870, 'By Way of Remembrance' ['I love you and you know it - this at least'] (*Poems*, III, 314).

8.   Derrida, *Writing and Difference*, 279.

9.   William M. Rossetti's translations of the *Monna Innominata* epigrams (*Works*, 462-3) are used in this study.

10. Montefiore, Jan, *Feminism and Poetry* (London: Pandora, 1987) 128.

11. Keats, *Poems*, 650-5.

12. Petrarca, *Selections* 35.

13. Packer, *Rossetti-Macmillan Letters* 154.

14. Ibid. 155, n. 3.

15. Rossetti, Gabriele, *A Versified Autobiography* translated and supplemented by W. M. Rossetti (London: Sands, 1901) 137-9.

16. see Fowler, Alastair, *Triumphal Forms: Structural Patterns in Elizabethan Poetry* (Cambridge: Cambridge University Press, 1970), particularly Chapter 9, 'Sonnet Sequences' 174-97.

17. Fuller, John, *The Sonnet* (London: Methuen, 1972) 40.

18. Burlinson, Kathryn, *Christina Rossetti* (Plymouth: Northcote House, 1998) 45.

19. Bateson, Frederick W., 'The Quickest Way out of Manchester' in *English Poetry: A Critical Introduction* (London: Longmans, 1950) 200-6.

20. Scheinberg, Cynthia, *Women's Poetry and Religion in Victorian England* (Cambridge: Cambridge University Press, 2002) 136. Scheinberg refers specifically to Antony Harrison, who calls the Esther sonnet 'perplexing' twice: see Harrison, *Christina Rossetti in Context* 154, 180.

21. Arnold, Matthew, 'Preface' to the 'Poems of 1853', in *Poetical Works of Matthew Arnold* ed. C. B. Tinker and H. F. Lowry (London: Oxford University Press, 1950) xviii.

22. D'Amico, Diane, *Christina Rossetti: Faith, Gender, and Time* 154.

23. Harrison, *Christina Rossetti in Context* 110.

Chapter 8 – *The Earlier Devotional Poetry*

1. Rossetti, Christina G., *Time Flies: A Reading Diary* (London & Brighton: Society for Promoting Christian Knowledge, 1885) 210.

2. Packer, *The Rossetti-Macmillan Letters*, 99.

3. Rossetti, W. M., *Family Letters* 31.

4. McGann, Jerome J., 'The Religious Poetry of Christina Rossetti' in *Critical Inquiry* 10 (1983), 127-44, quotation 127.

5. Kohl, James A., 'A Medical Comment on Christina Rossetti' in *Notes and Queries* CCXIII (November 1968), 423-4.

6. In 1873, when her sister Maria became a nun, Christina herself showed interest in the conventual vocation, associating herself with the Park Village Sisterhood, Albany Street (Maria joined the Anglican Sisterhood of Saints, Margaret Street). Christina did some work for the linked Park Village organisation, the Young Woman's Friendly Society, which sought to aid poor women of the parish, but preferred to explore the conventual pathway in

her verse rather than in her life. 'I might have been a hermit, but not a nun', Christina is reported to have told her niece, Olive Rossetti. See Packer, *Christina Rossetti* 55, 304.

7. Wheeler, Michael, *Death and the Future Life in Victorian Literature and Theology* (Cambridge: Cambridge University Press, 1990) 163.

8. Rossetti, W. M., *Family Letters* 103.

9. The profane and pious divide is reflected in the arrangement of Christina Rossetti's published poems, up until 1893, into specifically 'Pre-Raphaelite' and 'Devotional' sections in each Macmillan volume. As its title implies, *Verses: Reprinted from Called to Be Saints, Time Flies, The Face of the Deep* (London & Brighton: Society for Promoting Christian Knowledge, 1893) collected some hitherto available 'devotional' pieces into a single volume. As of 1879, with the publication of *Seek and Find*, Christina's collections of exegetical poetry and biblical prose commentary were all published in Britain by the Society for Promoting Christian Knowledge; *Annus Domini* (1874) had been published by James Parker and Co. (see 'Bibliography').

10. Evans, B. Ifor, *English Poetry in the Later Nineteenth Century* (London: Methuen, 1933) 67.

11. Waller, Richard D., *The Rossetti Family 1824-54* (Manchester: Manchester University Press, 1932) 219.

12. Rossetti, Christina G., *Maude: A Story For Girls* (London: J. Bowden, 1897)

13. Ibid. 6-8.

14. Ibid. vii-ix.

15. Ibid. 4.

16. Ibid. 29.

17. Ibid. 36.

18. see Brontë, Charlotte, *Jane Eyre* (Harmondsworth: Penguin Classics, 2006) Chapter 13.

19. Ibid. 5-6. Also see *Poems*, III, 299.

20. Hill Jnr., *Tennyson's Poetry* 52.

21. Packer, *Christina Rossetti* 72.

Chapter 9 – *The Later Devotional Poetry*

1. Packer unsurprisingly, but altogether rather quaintly, proposes that the shrieking, fire-footed 'kingly' one represents the artist William Bell Scott, offering as evidence the fact that 'his ermine cloak was woven from a synthetic fabric of Christina's invention, and … it was she who bestowed it upon him'. See Packer, *Christina Rossetti* 129.

2. Rossetti, Christina, *Maude* 54.

3. Jiminez, Nilda, *The Bible and the Poetry of Christina Rossetti: A Concordance* (London: Greenwood Press, 1979) i.

4. Rossetti, W. M., 'Preface' to *Poetical Works* xii.

5. Ibid. ix.

6. Rossetti, Christina G., *Called to be Saints: The Minor Festivals Devotionally Studied* (London & Brighton: Society for Promoting Christian Knowledge, 1881) xvii.

7. Rossetti, Christina G., *The Face of the Deep* (London & Brighton: Society for Promoting Christian Knowledge, 1892) 15.

8. Ibid. 156.

9. Ibid. 365.

10. Ibid. 547.

11. Ibid. 548-9.

12. Rossetti, W. M., *Some Reminiscences* (London: Brown, Langham and Co., 1906), 2 vols. II, 533.

13. Ibid. 534.

14. Harrison, *Christina Rossetti in Context* 187.

APPENDIX

Poems by Christina Rossetti that meaningfully refer to dreams and/ or dreaming. Volume and page references are to *Poems*. The poems are listed here in chronological order by date of composition, where this is known. Where a poem consists of separate stages, the date of completion of the last stage to be written is taken. Thereafter, those poems which are undated (marked with an asterisk) are listed in alphabetical order by title.

'Sappho' 11 September 1846 (III, 81-2)
'Will these Hands ne'er be Clean' 16 September 1846 (I, 93)
'The Last Words of Sir Eustace Grey' 14 October 1846 (I, 55)
'The Dead City' 9 April 1847 (III, 63-71)
'Wishes' 22 July 1847 (III, 135-6)
'Eleanor' 30 July 1847 (III, 136-7)
'Heart's Chill Between' 22 September 1847 (III, 16-7)
'The Lotus-Eaters' 7 October 1847 (III, 144-5)
'Lady Montrevor' 18 February 1848 (III, 153)
'A Hopeless Case' 24 April 1848 (III, 157-8)
'Zara' ["The pale sad face of her I wronged..."] 18 June 1848 (III, 159-62)
'Song' ["She sat and sang alway..."] 26 November 1848 (I, 58)
'What Sappho Would Have Said Had Her Leap Cured Instead of Killing Her' 7 December 1848 (III, 166-8)
'Ruin' 1848 (III, 162-5)
'Two Pursuits' 12 April 1849 (III, 176)
'Dream-Land' April 1849 (I, 27)
'Looking Forward' 8 June 1849 (III, 176-7)

'Life Hidden' 23 July 1849 (III, 177-8)
'Sound Sleep' 13 August 1849 (I, 57)
'Three Nuns' 10 May 1850 (III, 187-93)
'A Dream' 14 May 1851 (III, 197-8)
'Song' ["It is not for her even brow …"] 1951 (III, 197)
'To what Purpose is this Waste' 22 January 1853 (III, 208-12)
'What?' May 1853 (III, 214-5)
'There Remaineth therefore a Rest for the People of God'
                                        12 July 1853 (III, 216-7)
'Sleep at Sea' 17 October 1853 (I, 79-82)
'Paradise' 28 February 1854 (I, 221-2)
'Dream-Love' 19 May 1854 (I, 123-4)
'From the Antique' 28 June 1854 (III, 231)
'Three Stages' 25 July 1854 (III, 232-4)
'Echo' 18 December 1854 (I, 46)
'Zara' ["I dreamed that loving me he would love on…"]
                                        8 January 1855 (III, 236)
'My Dream' 9 March 1855 (I, 39-40)
'Now they Desire' 13 August 1856 (III, 259-60)
'The Hour and the Ghost' 11 September 1856 (I, 40-2)
'The Lowest Room' 30 September 1856 (I, 200-7)
'Light Love' 28 October 1856 (I, 136-8)
'In an Artist's Studio' 24 December 1856 (III, 264)
'Fata Morgana' 18 April 1857 (I, 49-50)
'The Heart Knoweth its Own Bitterness' 27 August 1857 (III, 207-8)
'Reflection' 8 September 1857 (III, 266-8)
'A Ghost Nightmare' 12 September 1857 (III, 268-9)
'For One Sake' 25 October 1957 (III, 269-7)
'Autumn' 14 April 1858 (I, 143-5)
'The Convent Threshold' 9 July 1858 (I, 61-5)
'My Old Friends' 16 July 1858 (III, 270-2)
'Yet a Little While' 6 August 1858 (III, 272-4)
'From House to Home' 19 November 1858 (I, 82-8)
Goblin Market 27 April 1859 (I, 11-26)

'Mirage' 12 June 1860 (I, 55-6)
'On the Wing' 17 December 1862 (I, 138-9)
'Life and Death' 24 April 1863 (I, 155)
'A Farm Walk' 11 July 1864 (I, 159-61)
The Prince's Progress December 1864 (I, 95-110)
'The Iniquity of the Fathers upon the Children' March 1865 (I, 164-78)
'A Daughter of Eve' 30 October 1865 (I, 208-9)
'Of my Life' 15 May 1866 (III, 298-9)
* 'A Balled of Boding' (II, 79-85)
* 'Days of Vanity' (I, 192-3)
* "The Dream" (III, 104-5)
* 'I Dreamt I Caught a Little Owl' (II, 45)
* Later Life (II, 138-50)
* 'Maiden May' (II, 98-101)
* *Monna Innominata* (II, 86-93)
* 'Now they Desire a Better Country' (II, 313-4)
* 'An Old-World Thicket' (II, 123-8)
* 'Sleeping at Last' (III, 339-40)
* 'Till Tomorrow' (II, 101)
* 'Today's Burden' (II, 171)
* 'Two Parted' (III, 222)
* 'What's in a Name?' (II, 110-1)

SELECTED BIBLIOGRAPHY

POETRY by Christina Rossetti

Verses (London: Privately printed by G. Polidori, 1847).

Goblin Market and Other Poems (Cambridge & London: Macmillan, 1862).

The Prince's Progress and Other Poems (London: Macmillan, 1866).

Poems (Boston: Roberts, 1866).

Commonplace and Other Short Stories (London: Ellis, 1870; Boston: Roberts, 1870).

Sing-Song: A Nursery Rhyme Book (London: Routledge, 1872; revised and enlarged edition, London: Macmillan, 1893).

Annus Domini: A Prayer for Each Day of the Year, Founded on a Text of Holy Scripture (Oxford & London: James Parker and Co., 1874).

Speaking Likenesses, with Pictures thereof by Arthur Hughes (London: Macmillan, 1874).

Goblin Market, The Prince's Progress, and Other Poems (London & New York: Macmillan, 1875).

Seek and Find: A Double Series of Short Studies of the Benedicite (London & Brighton: Society for Promoting Christian Knowledge, 1879).

A Pageant and Other Poems (London: Macmillan, 1880).

Called to Be Saints: The Minor Festivals Devotionally Studied (London & Brighton: Society for Promoting Christian Knowledge, 1881).

Poems (Boston: Roberts, 1882; enlarged edition, London & New York: Macmillan, 1890).

Letter and Spirit: Notes on the Commandments (London & Brighton: Society for Promoting Christian Knowledge, 1883).

Time Flies: A Reading Diary (London & Brighton: Society for Promoting Christian Knowledge, 1885).

The Face of the Deep: A Devotional Commentary on the Apocalypse (London & Brighton: Society for Promoting Christian Knowledge, 1892).

Verses: Reprinted from Called to Be Saints, Time Flies, The Face of the Deep (London & Brighton: Society for Promoting Christian Knowledge, 1893).

New Poems, Hitherto Unpublished or Uncollected edited by William Michael Rossetti (London & New York: Macmillan, 1896).

Maude: A Story for Girls (London: J. Bowden, 1897).

The Poetical Works of Christina Georgina Rossetti. With Memoir and Notes, &c. edited by William Michael Rossetti (London & New York: Macmillan, 1904).

The Complete Poems of Christina Rossetti: A Variorum Edition 3 volumes, edited by Rebecca W. Crump (Baton Rouge & London: Louisiana State University Press, 1979-1990).

SELECTED PERIODICAL PUBLICATIONS & UNCOLLECTED POETRY

'Versi' and 'L'Incognita' in *Bouquet from Marylebone Gardens* (June 1851-January 1852) 175, 216.

FICTION

'Corrispondenza Famigliare' in *Bouquet from Marylebone Gardens* (January-July 1852) 120-121, 218-219; (July-December 1852) 14-15, 55-57.

'True in the Main: Two Sketches' in *Dawn of Day* (1 May 1882) 57-59, (1 June 1882) 69-70.

NONFICTION

'Dante, an English Classic' in *Churchman's Shilling Magazine and Family Treasury* 2 (1867) 200-205.

'A Harmony on First Corinthians XIII' in *New and Old* 7 (January 1879) 34-39.

'Dante: The Poet Illustrated out of the Poem' in *Century* 27 (1884) 566-573.

LETTERS

Rossetti Papers, 1862 to 1870: A Compilation edited by William Michael Rossetti (London: Sands, 1903).

The Family Letters of Christina Georgina Rossetti edited by William Michael Rossetti (London: Brown, Langham and Co., 1908).

Three Rossettis: Unpublished Letters to and from Dante Gabriel, Christina, William edited by Janet Camp Troxell (Cambridge, Mass.: Harvard University Press, 1937).

The Rossetti-Macmillan Letters edited by Lona Mosk Packer (Berkeley: University of California Press, 1963).

The Owl and the Rossettis: Letters of Charles A. Howell and Dante Gabriel, Christina, and William Michael Rossetti edited by Clarence L. Cline (University Park: Pennsylvania State University Press, 1978).

Christina Rossetti in the Maser Collection edited by Frederick E. Maser and Mary Louise Jarden Maser (Bryn Mawr, Pa.: Bryn Mawr College Library, 1991).

The Letters of Christina Rossetti edited by Antony H. Harrison, 4 volumes (Charlottesville & London: University of Virginia Press, 1997-2004).

OTHER

John Francis Waller ed., *The Imperial Dictionary of Universal Biography* includes contributions by Christina G. Rossetti, 3 volumes (London: Mackenzie, 1863).

NOTEBOOKS & MANUSCRIPTS

Christina Rossetti's notebooks are severally held by the British Library, the Oxford Bodleian Library, and the Canterbury King's School. Contents of the collections are listed by Rebecca W. Crump in Appendix A, volume 3, of *The Complete Poems of Christina Rossetti: A Variorum Edition* (1990). Significant manuscript collections are also at Princeton University, the University of British Columbia, and Bryn Mawr College. Holograph poems are scattered among various public and private collections, also listed by Crump. Antony H. Harrison notes in his edition of *The Letters of Christina Rossetti* (1997-2004) that more than 2,100 autograph letters are dispersed in over one hundred public and private collections. The most substantial collections of letters are at the University of British Columbia, Princeton University, the British Library, the Harry Ransom Research Center of the University of Texas at Austin, the University of Kansas, the New York Public Library, the Wellesley College Library, the Beinecke Library at Yale University, and the Bryn Mawr College Library.

BIBLIOGRAPHIES

William E. Fredeman, *Pre Raphaelitism: A Bibliocritical Study* (Cambridge, Mass.: Harvard University Press, 1965) 176-182.

Fredeman, 'Christina Rossetti' in *The Victorian Poets: A Guide to Research* edited by Frederic E. Faverty (Cambridge, Mass.: Harvard University Press, 1968) 284-293.

Rebecca W. Crump, *Christina Rossetti: A Reference Guide* (Boston: G. K. Hall, 1976).

Jane Addison, 'Christina Rossetti Studies, 1974-1991: A Checklist and Synthesis' *Bulletin of Bibliography* 52 (March 1995) 73-93.

BIOGRAPHIES

Ellen A. Proctor, *A Brief Memoir of Christina G. Rossetti* (London & Brighton: Society for Promoting Christian Knowledge, 1895).

Mackenzie Bell, *Christina Rossetti: A Biographical and Critical Study* (London: Thos. Burleigh, 1898).

William M., Rossetti, *Some Reminiscences* 2 vols. (London: Brown, Langham and Co., 1906).

Mary F. Sandars, *The Life of Christina Rossetti* (London: Hutchinson, 1930).

Dorothy M. Stuart, *Christina Rossetti* (London: Macmillan, 1930).

Eleanor Walter Thomas, *Christina Georgina Rossetti* (New York: Columbia University Press, 1931).

Marya Zaturenska, *Christina Rossetti: A Portrait with a Background* (New York: Macmillan, 1949).

Margaret Sawtell, *Christina Rossetti: Her Life and Religion* (London: Mowbray, 1955).

Lona Mosk Packer, *Christina Rossetti* (Berkeley: University of California Press, 1963).

Ralph Bellas, *Christina Rossetti* (Boston: Twayne, 1977)

Georgina Battiscombe, *Christina Rossetti: A Divided Life* (London: Constable, 1981).

Kathleen Jones, *Learning Not to Be First: The Life of Christina Rossetti* (Oxford: Oxford University Press, 1992).

Frances Thomas, *Christina Rossetti: A Biography* (London: Virago, 1994).

Jan Marsh, *Christina Rossetti: A Literary Biography* (London: Jonathan Cape, 1994).

REFERENCES & FURTHER READING

Meyer H. Abrams, *The Mirror and the Lamp: Romantic Theory and the Critical Tradition* (London: Oxford University Press, 1963).

Patricia M. Adair, *The Waking Dream: A Study of Coleridge's Poetry* (London: Edward Arnold, 1967).

Dante Alighieri, *Purgatorio: A Verse Translation* by A. Mandelbaum (Berkeley: University of California Press, 1982).

Isobel Armstrong, *Language as Living Form in Nineteenth Century Poetry* (Sussex: Harvester, 1982).

Isobel Armstrong, *Victorian Poetry: Poetry, Poetics and Politics* (London & New York: Routledge, 1993) 344-367.

Mary Arseneau, 'Incarnation and Interpretation: Christina Rossetti, the Oxford Movement, and *Goblin Market*' in *Victorian Poetry* 31 (1993) 79-93.

Mary Arseneau, Antony H. Harrison, and Lorraine Janzen Kooistra eds., *The Culture of Christina Rossetti: Female Poetics and Victorian Contexts* (Athens: Ohio University Press, 1999).

Jean A. Barrick, *The Authority of Childhood: Three Components of the Childlike Spirit in Poems by Robert Louis Stevenson, Kate Greenaway, and Christina Rossetti* (Michigan: Ann Arbor, 1971).

Frederick W. Bateson, *English Poetry: A Critical Introduction* (London: Longmans, 1950).

Andrew Belsey and Catherine Belsey, 'Christina Rossetti: Sister to the Brotherhood' in *Textual Practice*, 2 (1900) 30-50.

Catherine Belsey, 'The Romantic Construction of the Unconscious' in Barker, F. ed., *Literature, Politics, and Theory: Papers from the Essex Conference 1976-84* (London: Methuen, 1986).

Bruno Bettelheim, *The Uses of Enchantment* (Harmondsworth: Penguin, 1978).

Kathleen Blake, *Love and the Woman Question in Victorian Literature: The Art of Self-Postponement* (Sussex: Harvester, 1983).

William Blake, *Poems*, ed. W. H. Stevenson (London: Longman, 1971).

Harold Bloom, *The Visionary Company: A Reading of English Romantic Poetry* (New York: Doubleday, 1961).

Harold Bloom ed., *Romanticism and Consciousness: Essays in Criticism* (New York: Norton, 1970).

Harold Bloom, *The Ringers in the Tower: Studies in Romantic Tradition* (London: University of Chicago Press, 1971).

Harold Bloom, *Ruin the Sacred Truths: Poetry and Belief from the Bible to the Present* (London: Harvard University Press, 1989).

Sir Maurice Bowra, *The Romantic Imagination* (London: Oxford University Press, 1961 rpt.)

Andre Breton, *Manifestoes of Surrealism* (Michigan: University Press, 1972).

Joseph Bristow ed., *Victorian Women Poets: Emily Brontë, Elizabeth Barrett Browning, Christina Rossetti* (London: Macmillan / New York: St. Martin's Press, 1995).

James A. C. Brown, *Freud and the Post-Freudians* (Harmondsworth: Penguin, 1964).

Ernst J. Brzenk, '"Up-Hill" and "Down-"' in *Victorian Poetry* 10 (1972) 367.

Jerome Bump, 'Hopkins, Christina Rossetti, and Pre-Raphaelitism' in *Victorian Newsletter,* 57 (1980) 1-6.

Kathryn Burlinson, '"All Mouth and Trousers": Christina Rossetti's Grotesque and Abjected Bodies' in *Women's Poetry, Late Romantic to Late Victorian: Gender and Genre, 1830-1900* ed. I. Armstrong and V. Blain (Houndsmills: Macmillan, 1999) 292-312.

Kathryn Burlinson, *Christina Rossetti* (Plymouth: Northcote House in association with the British Council, 1998).

T. Hall Caine, *Recollections of Dante Gabriel Rossetti* (London: Elliot Stock, 1882).

Elizabeth Campbell, 'Of Mothers and Merchants: Female Economics in Christina Rossetti's *Goblin Market*' in *Victorian Studies* 33 (1990) 393-410.

Mary Wilson Carpenter, '"Eat me, drink me, love me": The Consumable Female Body in Christina Rossetti's *Goblin Market*' in *Victorian Poetry* 29 (1991) 415-434.

Alice Chandler, *A Dream of Order: The Mediaeval Idea in Nineteenth Century English Literature* (Lincoln: Nebraska University Press, 1970).

Alison Chapman, *The Afterlife of Christina Rossetti* (Houndsmills: Macmillan, 2000; New York: St. Martin's Press, 2000).

Raymond Chapman, *Faith and Revolt: Studies in the Literary Influence of the Oxford Movement* (London: Weidenfeld and Nicholson, 1970).

Tom Chetwynd, *A Dictionary of Symbols* (London: Paladin, 1982).

Samuel T Coleridge, *Complete Poetical Works* ed. E. H. Coleridge (Oxford: Clarendon, 1912).

Samuel T Coleridge, *Notebooks* ed. K. Coburn, 3 vols. (London: Routledge, 1962).

Steven Connor, '"Speaking Likenesses": Language and Repetition in Christina Rossetti's *Goblin Market*' in *Victorian Poetry* 22 (1984) 439-448.

Stuart Curran, 'The Lyric Voice of Christina Rossetti' in *Victorian Poetry* 9 (1971) 287-299.

Diane D'Amico, *Christina Rossetti: Faith, Gender, and Time* (Baton Rouge: Louisiana State University Press, 1999).

Diane D'Amico and David A. Kent, 'Rossetti and the Tractarians' in *Victorian Poetry* 44 (2006) 93-104.

Charles Darwin, *The Descent of Man* (London: Murray, 1871)

Brian and Judy Dobbs, *Dante Gabriel Rossetti: An Alien Victorian* (London: Macdonald, 1977).

Jacques Derrida, *Writing and Difference* (London: Routledge, 1978).

Theo Dombrowski, 'Dualism in the Poetry of Christina Rossetti' in *Victorian Poetry* 14 (1976) 70-76.

Oswald Doughty, *A Victorian Romantic: Dante Gabriel Rossetti* (London: Frederick Muller Ltd., 1949).

Oswald Doughty and John Robert Wahl eds., *Letters of Dante Gabriel Rossetti* 4 vols. (New York: Oxford University Press, 1965).

Michael Drayton, *Poems* 2 vols. ed. Buxton, J., (London: Routledge and Kegan Paul, 1953).

Maureen Duffy, *The Erotic World of Faery* (St. Albans: Panther, 1974).

Paul Edwards, 'Ambiguous Seductions: "La Belle Dame Sans Merci", *The Faerie Queene*, and *Thomas the Rhymer*' in *Durham University Journal* (July 1990) 199-203.

Thomas S. Eliot, *The Sacred Wood* (London: Methuen, 1920).

Thomas S. Eliot, *Selected Prose* ed. F. Kermode (London: Faber, 1975).

Oliver Elton, *A Survey of English Literature (1830-80)* 2 vols. (London: Arnold, 1920)

Ifor B. Evans, *English Poetry in the Later Nineteenth Century* (London: Methuen, 1933).

Hans J. Eysenck *Sense and Nonsense in Psychology* (Harmondsworth: Penguin, 1963).

Hoxie Neale Fairchild, *Religious Trends in English Poetry IV: 1830-1880* (New York: Columbia University Press, 1957) 302-316.

Barbara Fass, 'Christina Rossetti and St. Agnes' Eve' in *Victorian Poetry* 14 (1976) 33-46.

Mary E. Finn, *Writing the Incommensurable: Kierkegaard, Rossetti, and Hopkins* (University Park: Pennsylvania State University Press, 1992).

Ford Madox Ford, *The Critical Attitude* (London: Duckworth, 1911).

Alastair Fowler, *Triumphal Forms: Structural Patterns in Elizabethan Poetry* (Cambridge: Cambridge University Press, 1970).

Robert S. Fraser ed., *Essays on the Rossettis* (Princeton: Princeton University Library, 1972).

Sigmund Freud, *An Outline of Psychoanalysis* (London: Hogarth, 1967).

Northrop Frye ed., *Romanticism Reconsidered* (London: Columbia Unversity Press, 1973).

John Fuller, *The Sonnet* (London: Methuen, 1972).

Barbara Garlick, 'Christina Rossetti and the Gender Politics of Fantasy' in *The Victorian Fantasists* ed. K. Filmer (Basingstoke: Macmillan, 1991) 133-152.

Fred Gettings, *Visions of the Occult* (London: Hutchinson, 1987).

Pamela K. Gilbert, '"A Horrid Game": Woman as Social Entity in Christina Rossetti's Prose' *English* 41 (Spring 1992) 1-23.

Sandra Gilbert and Susan Gubar, *The Madwoman in the Attic: The Woman Writer and the Nineteenth-Century Literary Imagination* (New Haven: Yale University Press, 1979).

William T. Going, *Scanty Plot of Ground: Studies in the Victorian Sonnet* (The Hague: Mouton & Co., 1976).

William T. Going, '*Goblin Market* and the Pre-Raphaelite Brotherhood' in *Pre-Raphaelite Review* III (1980) 54-62.

Gail Lynn Goldberg, 'Dante Gabriel's "Revising Hand": His Illustrations for Christina Rossetti's Poems' in *Victorian Poetry* 20 (1982) 145-59.

Edmund Gosse, 'Christina Rossetti' in *Century Magazine* 46 (June 1893) 211-17.

Eric Griffiths, 'The Disappointment of Christina G. Rossetti' in *Essays in Criticism* 47 (April 1997) 107- 142.

Lila Hanft, 'The Politics of Maternal Ambivalence in Christina Rossetti's *Sing-Song*' in *Victorian Literature and Culture* 19 (1991) 213-232.

Antony H. Harrison, *Christina Rossetti in Context* (Chapel Hill: University of North Carolina Press, 1988).

Antony H. Harrison, *Victorian Poets and Romantic Poems: Intertextuality and Ideology* (Charlottesville: Virginia University Press., 1990)

Antony H. Harrison, 'Christina Rossetti and the Sage Discourse of Feminist High Anglicanism' in *Victorian Sages and Cultural Discourse: Renegotiating Gender and Power* ed. T. E. Morgan (New Brunswick, N.J.: Rutgers University Press, 1990) 87-104.

Antony H. Harrison and Beverly Taylor eds., *Gender and Discourse in Victorian Literature and Art* (De Kalb: Northern Illinois University Press, 1992).

Antony H. Harrison, 'Christina Rossetti and the Romantics: Influence and Ideology' in *Influence and Resistance in Nineteenth-Century English Poetry* ed. G. K. Blank and M. K. Louis (London & Basingstoke: Macmillan, 1993) 131-149.

Antony H. Harrison ed., 'Centennial of Christina Rossetti: 1830-1894' in *Victorian Poetry* 32, nos. 3-4 (1994) 201-428.

Antony H. Harrison, 'Christina Rossetti: Illness and Ideology' in *Victorian Poetry* 45 (2007) 415-28.

Geoffrey H. Hartman, *The Unmediated Vision* (New Haven: Yale University Press, 1954).

Geoffrey H. Hartman ed., *The Selected Poetry and Prose of Wordsworth* (London: Meridian, 1970).

Constance W. Hassett, 'Christina Rossetti and the Poetry of Reticence' in *Philological Quarterly* 65 (1986) 495-514.

Constance W. Hassett, *Christina Rossetti: the Patience of Style* (Virginia: University of Virginia Press, 2005).

John Heath-Stubbs, *The Darkling Plain: A Study of the Later Fortunes of Romanticism in English Poetry* (London: Eyre and Spottiswoode, 1950).

Elizabeth K. Helsinger, 'Consumer Power and the Utopia of Desire: Christina Rossetti's *Goblin Market*' in *English Literary History* 58 (1991) 903-933.

Dawn Henwood, 'Christian Allegory and Subversive Poetics: Christina Rossetti's *Prince's Progress* Reexamined' in *Victorian Poetry* 35 (1997) 83-94.

Kathleen Hickok, *Representations of Women: Nineteenth-Century British Women's Poetry* (London: Greenwood Press, 1984).

Robert W. Hill Jnr. ed., *Tennyson's Poetry: Norton Critical Edition* (New York: Norton, 1971).

James Hillman, *Re-Visioning Psychology* (London: Harper Colophon Books, 1977).

Colleen Hobbs, 'A View from "The Lowest Place": Christina Rossetti's Devotional Prose' in *Victorian Poetry* 32 (1994) 409-28.

George Holmes, *Dante* (London: Oxford University Press, 1980).

Terrence Holt, '"Men sell not such in any town": Exchange in *Goblin Market*' in *Victorian Poetry* 28 (1990) 51-67.

Margaret Homans, 'Syllables of Velvet: Dickinson, Rossetti, and the Rhetorics of Sexuality' in *Feminist Studies* 11 (1985) 569-593.

Giselda Honnighausen, *Christina Rossetti als viktorianische Dichterin* (Bonn: Bonn University Press, 1972).

Giselda Honnighausen, 'Emblematic Tendencies in the Works of Christina Rossetti' in *Victorian Poetry* 10 (1972) 1-15.

Graham Hough, *The Last Romantics* (London: Methuen, 1947).

Walter E. Houghton, *The Victorian Frame of Mind* (New Haven: Yale University Press, 1957).

Kathryn Hume, *Fantasy and Mimesis: Responses to Reality in Western Literature* (London: Methuen, 1984).

Rosemary Jackson, *Fantasy: The Literature of Subversion* (London: Methuen, 1981).

Nilda Jiminez, *The Bible and the Poetry of Christina Rossetti: A Concordance* (London: Greenwood Press, 1979).

Carl G. Jung, *Selected Writings* (London Fontana, 1983).

John Keats, *Poems* ed. M. Allott (London: Longmans, 1920).

John Keble, *Tracts for the Times* 6 vols. (London: Rivingtons, 1839-41).

John Keble, *Lectures on Poetry* 2 vols. (Oxford: Clarendon Press, 1912).

Thomas Keightley, *The Fairy Mythology: Illustrative of the Romance and Superstition of Various Countries* 2 vols. (London: W. H. Ainsworth, 1828).

David A. Kent, 'W. M. Rossetti and the Editing of Christina Rossetti's Religious Poetry' in *Pre-Raphaelite Review* 1 (1978) 18-26.

David A. Kent, 'Sequence and Meaning in Christina Rossetti's Poems' in *Victorian Poetry* 17 (1979) 259-64.

David A. Kent ed., *The Achievement of Christina Rossetti* (Ithaca, N.Y.: Cornell University Press, 1987).

Ulrich C. Knoepflmacher, 'Avenging Alice: Christina Rossetti and Lewis Carroll' in *Nineteenth-Century Literature* 41 (1986) 299-328.

James A. Kohl, 'A Medical Comment on Christina Rossetti' in *Notes and Queries* CCXIII (November 1968) 423-4.

Lorraine Janzen Kooistra 'The Jael Who Led the Hosts to Victory: Christina Rossetti and Pre-Raphaelite Book-Making' in *Journal of Pre-Raphaelite Studies* new series 8 (Spring 1999) 50-68.

Karl Kroeber, *Romantic Narrative Art* (Madison: Wisconson University Press, 1960).

Sharon Leder and Andrea Abbott, *The Language of Exclusion: The Poetry of Emily Dickinson and Christina Rossetti* (New York: Greenwood Press, 1987).

Angela Leighton, '"Because men made the laws": The Fallen Woman and the Woman Poet' in *Victorian Poetry* 27 (1989) 109-127.

Angela Leighton, *Victorian Women Poets: Writing Against the Heart* (London & New York: Harvester, 1992) 118- 163.

Angela Leighton ed., *Victorian Women Poets: A Critical Reader* (London: Blackwell, 1996).

Levi R. Lind, *Lyric Poetry of the Italian Renaissance* (New Haven: Yale University Press, 1954).

George A. Macmillan ed., *Letters of Alexander Macmillan* (London: Macmillan, 1908).

Linda E. Marshall, 'Mysteries beyond Angels in Christina Rossetti's 'From House to Home' in *Women's Poetry, Late Romantic to Late Victorian: Gender and Genre, 1830-1900* ed. I. Armstrong and V. Blain (Houndsmills: Macmillan, 1999) 313-324.

Linda E. Marshall, '"Transfigured to His Likeness": Sensible Transcendentalism in Christina Rossetti's *Goblin Market*' in *University of Toronto Quarterly* 63 (1994) 429-450.

Linda E. Marshall, 'What the Dead are Doing Underground: Hades and Heaven in the Writings of Christina Rossetti' in *Victorian Newsletter* 72 (1987) 55-60.

Leila Silvana May, *Disorderly Sisters: Sibling Relations and Sororal Resistance in Nineteenth Century Literature* (London: Associated University Presses, 2001).

Katherine J. Mayberry, *Christina Rossetti and the Poetry of Discovery* (Baton Rouge: Louisiana State University Press, 1989).

Jerome J. McGann, 'Christina Rossetti's Poems: A New Edition and a Revaluation' in *Victorian Studies* 23 (1980) 237-254.

Jerome J. McGann, 'The Religious Poetry of Christina Rossetti' in *Critical Inquiry* 10 (1983) 127-144.

Jerome J. McGann, *The Beauty of Inflections: Literary Investigations in Historical Method and Theory* (Oxford: Clarendon, 1985).

Dorothy Mermin, 'The Female Poet and the Embarrassed Reader: Elizabeth Barrett Browning's *Sonnets from the Portuguese*' in *English Literature and History* 48 (1981) 351-67.

Dorothy Mermin, 'Heroic Sisterhood in *Goblin Market*' in *Victorian Poetry* 21 (1983) 107-118.

Dorothy Mermin, 'The Damsel, the Knight, and the Victorian Woman Poet' in *Critical Inquiry*, 13 (1986) 64-80.

Helena Michie, '"There is no friend like a sister": Sisterhood as Sexual Difference' in *English Literary History*, 52 (1989) 401-421.

Nan Miller, 'Christina Rossetti and Sarah Woodruff: Two Remedies for a Divided Self' in *Journal of Pre-Raphaelite Studies* III (November 1982) 68-77.

John Milton, *Poems* ed. J. Carey and A. Fowler (London: Longman, 1966).

Ellen Moers, *Literary Women* (New York.: Doubleday, 1976).

Theodor E Mommsen, 'Petrarch's Conception of the Dark Ages' in *Mediaeval and Renaissance Studies* ed. E. F. Rice Jnr. (New York: Cornell University Press, 1959) 106-29.

Jan Montefiore, *Feminism and Poetry* (London: Pandora, 1987).

David F. Morrill, '"Twilight is Not Good for Maidens": Uncle Polidori and the Psychodynamics of Vampirism in *Goblin Market*' in *Victorian Poetry* 28 (1990) 1-16.

Michelene Wandor ed., *On Gender and Writing* (London: Pandora, 1983).

Paul Oppenheimer, *The Birth of The Modern Mind: Self, Consciousness and the Invention of the Sonnet* (London: Oxford University Press, 1989).

Lona Mosk Packer, 'Symbol and Reality in Christina Rossetti's *Goblin Market*' in *Publications of the Modern Language Association* LXXIII (1958) 375-85.

Lynda Palazzo, *Christina Rossetti's Feminist Theology* (New York: Palgrave, 2002).

Francesco Petrarca, *Selections from the Canzoniere and Other Works* (Oxford: Oxford University Press, 1985).

Georges Poulet, 'Timelessness and Romanticism' in *Journal of the History of Ideas* (15.1) (January 1954) 3-22.

Frederick C. Prescott, *The Poetic Mind* (New York: Cornell University Press, 1959).

Stephen Prickett, *Victorian Fantasy* (Sussex: Harvester, 1979).

Kathy Alexis Psomiades, 'Feminine and Poetic Privacy in Christina Rossetti's "Autumn" and "A Royal Princess"' in *Victorian Poetry* 31 (1993) 187-202.

Kathy Alexis Psomiades, 'Whose Body? Christina Rossetti and Aestheticist Femininity' in *Women and British Aestheticism,* ed. T. Schaffer and K. Psomiades (Charlottesville: University Press of Virginia, 1999) 101-118.

Tilottama Rajan, *Dark Interpreter: The Discourse of Romanticism* (London: Cornell University Press, 1980).

David G. Reide, *Dante Gabriel Rossetti and the Limits of Victorian Vision* (London: Cornell University Press, 1983).

Joan Rees, 'Christina Rossetti. Poet' in *Critical Quarterly*, 26 (Autumn 1984) 59-72.

Eugene F. Rice Jnr. ed., *Mediaeval and Renaissance Studies* (New York: Cornell University Press, 1959).

Nesca Adeline Robb, 'Christina Rossetti' in *Four in Exile* (London: Hutchinson, 1948) 82-119.

Wallace W. Robson, *Critical Essays* (London: Routledge and Kegan Paul, 1966).

Dinah Roe, *Christina Rossetti's Faithful Imagination* (New York: Palgrave Macmillan, 2006).

Dolores Rosenblum, *Christina Rossetti: The Poetry of Endurance* (Carbondale: Southern Illinois University Press, 1986).

Dolores Rosenblum, 'Christina Rossetti's Religious Poetry: Watching, Looking, Keeping Vigil' in *Victorian Poetry*, 20 (1982) 33-49.

Dante Gabriel Rossetti, *The Early Italian Poets together with Dante's Vita Nuova* (London: Smith, Elder and Co., 1861).

Dante Gabriel Rossetti, *Poems and Translations 1850-70* (London: Oxford University Press, 1913).

Gabriele Rossetti, *La Beatrica di Dante* (London: Privatera, 1842).

Gabriele Rossetti, *A Versified Autobiography* translated and supplemented by W. M. Rossetti (London: Sands, 1901).

Maria Francesca Rossetti, *A Shadow of Dante* (London: Rivingtons, 1871).

William Michael Rossetti ed., *Ruskin; Rossetti; Pre-Raphaelitism* (London: George Allen, 1899).

William Michael Rossetti, *The Diary of W. M. Rossetti* ed. O. Bornand (Oxford: Clarendon, 1977).

Frederick A. Rudd, 'Christina G. Rossetti' in *Catholic World* IV (1867) 839-46.

Charles Rycroft, *The Innocence of Dreams* (London: Hogarth, 1979).

Miriam Sagan, 'Christina Rossetti's *Goblin Market* and Feminist Literary Criticism' in *Pre-Raphaelite Review* III (1980) 66-76.

Cynthia Scheinberg, *Women's Poetry and Religion in Victorian England* (Cambridge: Cambridge University Press, 2002).

Linda Schofield, 'Displaced and Absent Texts as Contexts for Christina Rossetti's *Monna Innominata' Journal of Pre-Raphaelite Studies,* new series 6 (Spring 1997) 38-52.

Shakespeare, William, *Antony and Cleopatra* (New York: American Library, 1963).

Shakespeare, William, *Hamlet* (New York: American Library, 1963).

Shakespeare, William, *A Midsummer Night's Dream* (Harmondsworth: Penguin, 1980 rpt.).

Shakespeare, William, *Shakespeare's Sonnets* ed. A. L. Rowse, Third Edition (London: Macmillan, 1984).

William Sharp, 'Some Reminiscences of Christina Rossetti' *Atlantic Monthly,* 75 (June 1895) 736-749.

David W. Shaw, *The Lucid Veil: Poetic Truth in the Victorian Age* (London: Athlone, 1987).

Percy B. Shelley, Complete Works 10 vols. ed. R. Ingpen and W. E. Peck (London: Ernest Benn, 1965).

Fredegond Shove, *Christina Rossetti: A Study* (Cambridge: Cambridge University Press, 1931).

Elaine Showalter, *A Literature of Their Own: British Women Novelists from Brontë to Lessing* (Princeton: Princeton University Press, 1977).

Virginia Sickbert, 'Christina Rossetti and Victorian Children's Poetry: A Maternal Challenge to the Patriarchal Family' in *Victorian Poetry,* 31 (1993) 385-410.

Edith Sitwell, 'Christina Rossetti' in *English Women* (London: William Collins, 1942) 41-3.

Sharon Smulders, *Christina Rossetti Revisited,* Twayne English Authors Series (New York: Twayne, 1996).

Sharon Smulders, '"A Form that Differences": Vocational Metaphors in the Poetry of Christina Rossetti and Gerard Manley Hopkins' in *Victorian Poetry,* 29 (1991) 161-173.

Sharon Smulders, 'Woman's Enfranchisement in Christina Rossetti's Poetry' *Texas Studies in Literature and Language,* 34 (1992) 568-588.

Edmunde Spenser, *Amoretti and Epithalamion Facsimile Edition* (New York: De Capo, 1969).

Edmunde Spenser, *The Shorter Poems of Edmunde Spenser: Yale Edition* ed. William A. Oram et al., (London: Yale University Press, 1989).

Lionel Stevenson, *The Pre-Raphaelite Poets* (Chapel Hill: University of North Carolina Press, 1972) 78-122.

Tom Stoppard, *Rosencrantz and Guidenstern are Dead* (London: Faber, 1967).

Algernon C. Swinburne, 'A New Year's Eve, Christina Rossetti Died December 29, 1894' in *The Nineteenth Century* (February, 1895) 367-8.

George B. Tennyson, *Victorian Devotional Poetry* (Cambridge, Mass.: Harvard University Press, 1981).

Deborah Ann Thompson, 'Anorexia as a Lived Trope: Christina Rossetti's *Goblin Market' Mosaic,* 24 (1991) 89-106.

Anthony Thorlby ed., *The Romantic Movement* (London: Longmans, 1966).

Martha Vicinus, *Suffer and Be Still: Women in the Victorian Age* (London: Indiana University Press, 1972).

Marie L. Von Franz, *Problems of the Feminine in Fairytales* (Texas: Spring, 1972).

Suzanne M. Waldman, *The Demon and the Damozel: Dynamics of Desire in the Works of Christina Rossetti and Dante Gabriel Rossetti* (Ohio: Ohio University Press, 2008).

Richard D. Waller, *The Rossetti Family 1824-54* (Manchester: Manchester University Press, 1932).

Jeanie Watson, '"Men sell not such in any town": Christina Rossetti's Goblin Fruit of Fairy Tale' in *Children's Literature* 12 (1984) 61-77.

Winston Weathers, 'Christina Rossetti: The Sisterhood of Self' in *Victorian Poetry,* 3 (1965) 81-89.

Stanley Weintraub, *Four Rossettis: A Victorian Biography* (London: W. H. Allen, 1978).

Andrew Welsh, *Roots of Lyric* (Princeton: Princeton University Press, 1978).

Helen Wenger, 'The Influence of the Bible in Christina Rossetti's *Monna Innominata*' in *Christian Scholar Review* 3 (1973) 15-24.

Joel Westerholm, '"I Magnify Mine Office": Christina Rossetti's Authoritative Voice in Her Devotional Prose' in *Victorian Newsletter,* 84 (Fall 1993) 11-17.

Michael Wheeler, *Death and the Future Life in Victorian Literature and Theology* (Cambridge: Cambridge University Press, 1990).

Virginia Woolf, '"I am Christina Rossetti"' in *The Common Reader: Second Series* (London: Hogarth, 1932) 237-44.

William Wordsworth, *Poetical Works* (London: Edward Moxon, 1869).

William Wordsworth, *The Prelude*, ed. E. de Selincourt, (Oxford: Oxford University Press, 1970).

William and Dorothy Wordsworth, *Letters of William and Dorothy Wordsworth* 6 vols. Second Edition, ed. E. De Selincourt, Revised by C. L. Shaver (Oxford: Clarendon, 1967).

David Wright ed., *Seven Victorian Poets* (London: Heinemann, 1964).

ABOUT THE AUTHOR

A veteran of the British music and poetry scenes — described by *Sounds* magazine as a 'silver-tongued devil — journalist, academic, and all-round lush', while one of his many unsuccessful bands, Teenage Dog Orgy, was termed 'legendary' by the *NME* — Paul Hullah (MA Hons, PhD) is currently tenured Associate Professor of British Poetry and Culture at Meiji Gakuin University, Tokyo. Co-founder of *Liberlit*, an international conference forum for 'Discussion and Defence of the Role of Literary Texts in the English Curriculum' <www.liberlit.com>, he has published, presented, and performed internationally in literary studies, EFL, and multimedia poetics. His previous publications include the only officially authorised edition of *Poems by Iris Murdoch* (University Education Press, 1997), *Romanticism and Wild Places* (Quadriga Press, 1998), 14 textbooks for university-level English learners in Japan, most featuring 'literary' texts, most often poetry, at their core, and *Rock UK: A Sociocultural History of British Popular Music* (Cengage Learning, 2013). In 2013 he was a recipient of the Asia Pacific Brand Laureate International Personality Award, an honour endorsed by the 4th Prime Minister of Malaysia as well as the country's 13th King. The award citation stated that he was chosen for 'paramount contribution to the cultivation of literature [that has] exceptionally restored the appreciation of poetry and contributed to the literary education of students in Asia.' He has also published seven collections of his own poetry, including *Homing* (illustrated by Susan Mowatt: Word Power Books, 2011), *Scenes: Words, Pictures, Music* (with Martin Metcalfe: Word Power Books, 2014), and *Climbable* (Partridge Books, 2016) all of which are still available.

<www.facebook.com/hullah>

Who knows? We know not. Afar, if the dead be far,
Alive, if the dead be alive as the soul's works are,
The soul whose breath was among us a heavenward song
Sings, loves, and shines as it shines for us here a star.

Algernon C. Swinburne,
'A New Year's Eve, Christina Rossetti Died December 29, 1894'

I was lost inside the darkness,
So I built myself a house there,
And I found myself at home there;
Now I live inside the darkness.

But I dream about the daylight,
As a captive dreams of freedom;
In the darkness of my dwelling
I go dreaming of the daylight.

Paul Hullah,
'Hikari (Age Before Beauty)' from *Climbable* (2016)

Lightning Source UK Ltd.
Milton Keynes UK
UKOW06f1804240616

277017UK00022B/331/P

9 781482 865783